A PARLIAMENT OF MINDS

A PARLIAMENT OF MINDS

Philosophy for a New Millennium

Edited by

Michael Tobias
J. Patrick Fitzgerald
David Rothenberg

State University of New York Press

Cover photo by Robert Radin.

Published by
State University of New York Press, Albany

© 2000 State University of New York

For information, address State University of New York Press,
State University Plaza, Albany, N.Y., 12246

Production by Marilyn P. Semerad
Marketing by Dana E. Yanulavich

Library of Congress Cataloging-in-Publication Data

A parliament of minds : philosophy for a new millennium / edited by
    Michael Tobias, Patrick Fitzgerald, David Rothenberg.
            p.   cm.
        Includes bibliographical references and index.
        ISBN 0 –7914–4483 –x (hardcover : alk. paper). — ISBN 0 –7914–4484 – 8
    (pbk. : alk. paper)
        1. Philosophy. 2. Philosophers Interviews. I. Tobias, Michael.
    II. Fitzgerald, Patrick, 1950 –   . III. Rothenberg, David, 1962–   .
    IV. World Congress of Philosophy (20th : 1998 : Boston, Mass.)
    B72.P33   2000
    100—dc21   99 – 43557
                                                              CIP

10 9 8 7 6 5 4 3 2 1

For Jane Gray Morrison, whose thoughts, dreams,
and actions forever inspire me.
M.T.

For Beverly R. Fitzgerald, my wife, my love, my
first and last thought each day for over thirty
years. And for my children, Shane and Molly,
who exemplify pure potentiality.
J.P.F.

To Jaan Umru Rothenberg, born 1999
a philosopher before language
D.B.R.

Contents

Contents

Acknowledgments

The television series, *A Parliament of Minds,* was developed in association with KTEH-TV, the PBS affiliate in San Jose, California, and JMT Productions of Los Angeles, in association with the Wisdom Network. It was produced by J. Patrick Fitzgerald, directed by Michael Tobias, co-produced by David Rothenberg and Bettina Gray, and executive produced by Danny McGuire.

We would like to express our appreciation to the television production team from KTEH, the PBS affiliate in San Jose, California, for their dedication and professionalism in producing this series: Executive Producer Danny McGuire, Co-Producer Bettina Gray, Associate Producer Linda Dennis, Camera Operators Marty Collins and Paul Stapleton-Smith, Audio Engineer Richard Medrano, Make-up Deborah Cross, On-line Editor Bridget Louie, Production Assistants Laura Abeyta and Mark Johnson.

Among the many people who contributed to this project, we want to single out our host, Michael Malone, who more than met the challenge of conducting twenty-one interviews in six days with a diverse group of renowned intellectuals.

We wish to express our thanks to Boston University and the America Organizing Committee for the Twentieth World Congress of Philosophy: Executive Director Dr. Alan Olson, Co-Chairmen Dr. Robert C. Neville and Dr. Jaakko Hintikka, Assistants Kevin Stoehr and Mark Gedney.

We extend special thanks to Beverly Fitzgerald for her editorial assistance and careful attention to incorporating the participants' corrections and revisions.

We greatly appreciate Robert Radin for his photographic skills; he also served as the soul and conscience for our production team.

We also want to thank Seminole Community College for providing support services to this project, in particular: Dr. E. Ann McGee, Dr. Stephen C. Wright, Dr. Elaine Greenwood, Angela Kersenbrock, Richard Loper, William Schmidt.

Introduction

MICHAEL TOBIAS,   J. PATRICK FITZGERALD,   DAVID ROTHENBERG

Three Thousand Philosophers in One Room

In August 1998, thousands of thinkers—philosophers by any other name—assembled in Boston for the Twentieth World Congress of Philosophy. In many respects it was a momentous occasion in American intellectual history and provided a rare opportunity to demonstrate to the general public, through this book and the accompanying television series, the relevance of philosophy to everyday life. More important, this was an opportunity for the profession of philosophy, at the end of the century and the beginning of a new millennium, to take stock of itself, to ask what philosophy has done to contribute to the betterment of humanity and what philosophy should contribute toward the future of life on earth and life in human communities—political, emotional, spiritual, and contemplative life.

These questions have not substantially differed in thousands of years. Only the contexts have. And those ever changing, absorbing, paradoxical, depressing, infuriating, inspiring, and ultimately mysterious trends are at the core of what the many philosophers gathered in Boston sought to address. *A Parliament of Minds* spins off these many themes like sparks; personal obsessions; choral notes in a diverse series of investigations propagated by diverse minds—philosophers from many countries whose own lives, and those of their many students, have been greatly enriched by the orientation and pursuit of philosophy. In that respect, this book is a celebration of philosophy at the end of a millennium.

The interviews were conducted by Michael Malone of the long-running PBS interview program *Malone* and newly appointed editor of the Forbes *ASAP* magazine. Conducted in a relaxed and conversational style with open-ended questions, the interviews promoted a creative dialogue exploring a vast array of topics. The list of philosophers was compiled to represent a medley of voices with respect to gender, nationality, topics, and age—from the accomplished senior philosophers to younger faculty members from several universities. This groundbreaking series of interviews on philosophy was created with a dual purpose: First, to present a diverse cross section of contemporary philosophers attending the Twentieth World Congress of Philosophy and in such manner as to demystify and humanize the formal discipline of philosophy; second, to help make philosophy accessible and relevant to a general audience; and, ultimately, to lend lyricism and urgency to the perennial concerns of philosophic traditions. The result: a series of articulate, provocative, dynamic, outspoken thinkers willing to make philosophy germane to everyday life. These men and women were not presented as academics but as modern citizens with wisdom and insights whom readers from any number of diverse backgrounds might find pleasure drawing upon. At the same time, the academic world would be equally intrigued by the candor and passion of their colleagues' addressing the cutting-edge, real-life issues.

More important, however, this book will serve as an invitation to the reader to consider questions that are at once core to philosophical tradition—the life of the world as viewed through the lenses of dialogue and contemplation. Put another way, this book should encourage the reader to become a philosopher—a very real possibility, according to all those interviewed herein, for each thinker, in her and his own words, seems to be arguing that philosophy is by no means confined to ivory towers. It lives, breathes, and dreams in the workplace, in our most private moments, in despair and exaltation, in the child as in the adult. Philosophy, says Japanese thinker Yoko Arisaka, combats rigidity and can liberate us from the "trauma" of having to "pour tea correctly." It can make for a "magnificent life," says famed Finnish philosopher Esa Saarinen. It can bring us into wild consciousness, argues David Rothenberg, and initiate us into a world of pure consciousness, according to Ashok Gangadean. It can shed light on gender tyranny, global oppression, issues of race, sexuality, political turmoil, national struggle, scandal, and pride. Philosophy offers insight into the nature of social continuity and discontinuity, slavery, the Holocaust, war, passion, and democracy. Ethics, beauty, spirituality, music (particularly jazz), and farming are all explored in this roving, candid look at just what philosophy is and is not; and how, in particular, those individuals represented in this book found their own way into the world of philosophy and where they expect it to go with it—as a discipline and a reality—in the coming century.

This group of distinguished and accomplished individuals discuss everyday issues in a style of deliberate informality and leisure that is intended to bring philosophical traditions down to earth. In large measure, that goal has been realized and the reader should find here a wealth of handholds and nuggets that enable all of us to better appreciate the essence of philosophical desire, the contagiousness of reflection, the available refuge that is every human being's access to deeper thought, deeper meaning, and a more joyous connection to the life of the mind.

There are startling revelations here that have to do with "eurekas" visited on the individual contributors as well as Michael Malone's own penetrating and delightful reactions and repartee. Trained as philosopher in his undergraduate work, and thrust into the public limelight as a television journalist and writer for well over a decade, Malone has interviewed a vast array of cultural figures. But in this project, he was particularly challenged by the task of interviewing nearly two dozen great philosophers in one week. The result is, at times, amusing, for Malone says what's on his mind and the philosophers have no choice but to say what's on their own. This makes for a text that deliberately eschews the safer confines of circumabulatory abstraction and studied circumspection. What might read with conventional academic safety and aplomb is here sacrificed for the more immediate and unusual glimpses into the vital, active, moment-by-moment germination of philosophers under pressure to respond. The reader should also keep in mind that there were three studio cameras focused on each one of these individuals and a large film team behind the scenes watching and listening. None of this material arose in the quiet isolation of a solitary study, but under the hot lights of public television.

A Call to Action

Following the "call to action," which echoed throughout the World Congress of Philosophy, this series put special emphasis on the social significance of philosophy. With philosophy seemingly standing on the sidelines for most of the twentieth century, which has seen two world wars and the Holocaust, each philosopher was encouraged to speak to the role of philosophy in helping humanity confront the pressing issues we currently face. The philosophers are seen questioning the nature of being, of will power, questions of the mind, the soul, the emotions, of logic and intuition, of self-awareness and transcendence, the nature of love and forgiveness, environmental ethics and animal rights, cognition, and the power of dreams. Here in flesh and blood are matters pertaining to the relationship of politics to philosophy (can philosophers be kings?) and the bridges between thought, ideals, and action; the eternal relationships between utopia and reality; the nature of goodness, the various theories of knowledge (epistemology); and the underlying search of all philosophy for absolutes. Each of these enormous subject matters is brought down in scope to the scale of one person at a time, struggling to understand, to be rendered more whole as a human being. Each intellectual passion comes in the shape, desire, and cornerstone of a human being, with a particular story and set of anecdotes. And it is these personal touches that provide a level of insight rare in philosophical tradition.

We see Lewis Gordon growing up in the Bronx and Anthony Appiah leaving a life of royalty in Ghana to journey to the United States. We learn of Robert Muller's impassioned years at the United Nations and Marjorie Grene's incredible time as a farmer. We see David Rothenberg achieving the ineffable as a jazz musician and deep ecologist and Tu Wei-ming reflecting deeply on the crisis of Tibet and Chinese culture. In every essay we come to know something about the philosopher, which helps us to understand their philosophy.

In the end, we see a collective affirmation that is both rare and appropriate for our times. Amplified by fine photographs by Robert Radin, the book sheds intrinsic light on the whole purpose of philosophical traditions. As Robert Muller declares in the final chapter—a forum comprising four philosophers debating the great issues of our time—"I'm a seventy-five-year old optimist. I'm absolutely sure that we can have a beautiful, preserved planet with a harmonious population. . . . We can do this. We have to dream it." From Plato to African existentialism, *A Parliament of Minds* takes us into the living traditions of a diverse and exhilarating school of thought that may be the oldest and most gratifying school known to the human animal, namely, the world of philosophy.

The Value of Philosophy

Listening to all these diverse philosophers telling their stories and speaking their minds, one is struck immediately with at least one common theme. They all believe philosophy is tremendously important, but all are dissatisfied with what's happened to the field in recent years and believe its place in the world at large has got to change.

Philosophy is valuable because it encourages us to think for ourselves; to question our everyday reality as well as our pasts and futures; and to take responsibility for what happens to us and what we have faith in, rather than turning these tasks over to some other authority. It wants us to work through our own problems, to never be satisfied with easy answers, to accept an inherent ambiguity in the way the world works and what it is made of. Philosophy wants us to work through our own ideas and trust the power of ideas more than anything else.

But don't we all want to relax? Isn't it so much easier if someone else tells us what to feel and what to think? An unexamined life may not be worth living according to Socrates, but that negation is not enough: An explored life, a feeling life, an inhabited life, a deciding life—these are the kinds that are worth living. Philosophy gets us there not by telling us what to do, but by continuing to ask questions so important that they outlast the veracity of any possible answers. What is the good? How can we tell when something is true? How should we distinguish between the individual and the community? The natural and the human? The right and the wrong? The historical or the eternal?

Such questions are not solved by more information, but by deeply living inside their uncertainties for many years. Philosophy is tackling the same kinds of questions it did thousands of years ago. Can it be that no progress has been made? To some this suggests that such questions are hopeless to ponder, while to others they become the only things worth considering across the years and decades. These latter individuals are likely to become philosophical, whether in profession or by inclination, to be patient enough to inhabit the question rather than quickly seeking its solution.

Philosophy is repetitive, frustrating, cold at times, beholden to logic but dreaming it can encompass passion. It wants to explain, but lacks the specialized tools of science; it wants to be beautiful, yet lacks the elegant techniques of art. Stuck in the middle, it distances itself from all the specialties of expression. It wants to get to the heart of things, but mistrusts all images that show us the path down to there. Described thus, philosophy, perhaps, sounds too personal, devout, and—alas—impractical. One can engage in it anywhere, anytime one's mind has the space to be clear. Why, then, do so many of our philosophers here, from the seasoned to those just starting out, all have so much to complain about? Like much in this society, philosophy has become professionalized, compartmentalized, turned into a career rather than a passion, something to specialize in rather than be part of the life that any educated person ought to aspire to lead. We have analytic philosophers fighting against continental philosophers, empiricists battling phenomenologists, and pragmatists arguing with ontologists. Like art critics, they have only their wits and range of references to aid them in the war of ideas. It all depends on how one chooses to view the world.

The best thing about philosophy might just be the fact that no one can win. Nearly all our interlocutors here believe that internal skirmishes between different intellectual positions within the field have got to be set aside for our society at large to decide that philosophy is an approach worth turning to in times of crisis. Philosophy is surely at once one of the finest places to train us all to think for ourselves and to question authority and faith. Philosophy helps us to become honest masters of our own destiny. It teaches us how to trust the workings of our own minds, beyond the incessant but superficial stimulation our busy world thrusts upon us.

This is not to say that philosophy must cast a dark outlook on our world thus far. There are many progressive developments of the twentieth century that would be impossible without philosophy. Research into the theory of logic in the first decades of the century demonstrated that it would be possible to divide all complicated step-by-step problems into binary operations, making possible the development of the digital computer, which is the most philosophical machine ever constructed. It reduces the world to logic, and its successes and failures show us just what can be encompassed by logic and what continues to elude it.

The extremes of cruelty unleashed in the Second World War, from the Holocaust in Europe to the use of nuclear weapons in Japan, cast a pallor on the forward march of the Enlightenment and the whole notion that a war is something that can be won. Philosophy failed to stop these horrors as much as it was amply applied in attempts to justify their necessity. Neither pessimistic nor optimistic in essence, philosophy is fundamentally uncertain. It wants us to question everything we have been told, everything we imagine we need to believe that the world stands on some kind of firm ground, physically, spiritually, or culturally. Philosophy turns us loose, eradicates our comforts, promises nothing but doubt.

Despite these uncertainties, most of the thinkers represented here reflect an inherently positive outlook. They all want to change things, first of all by trusting in the ability of their students and the people at large to think for themselves. The philosophy teacher is often the first to ask the audience members what they think, rather than giving them answers predigested as right or wrong. Philosophers prefer to seed not doubt but speculation, and to inspire in those who listen a sense of wonder and possibility, with so much to do and so much to change.

Philosophy is not religion, nor psychology, though it certainly engages each. It cannot alleviate your headache or guarantee deliverance in some heaven of moral resolutions. But it is its own science of wake-up calls, poised by definition to stir people out of complacency into a place where we believe that we are able to change the parts of our world that we would otherwise just complain about.

"People one by one should have better lives. . . . I hope my words might make even one person's life just a tiny bit better," says Martha Nussbaum, who also stressed that attending to the nuances of ancient Greek political philosophy would show us how to make democracy more real and more deliberate, rather than something whose inadequacies we simply take for granted. The results of ancient ideas are with us in the real world around us, and we ought to have the history clear in our minds so we can have access to it when we have important decisions to make.

"Hobbes! Locke! No one should be out there not knowing what these people have to offer us," says John McDermott in a fast-talking Bronx accent. "These ideas should be available to everyone." They are not dead and gray. They need not be obscure. The ideas fall out of our grasp only when they are turned into private themes for only the profession to debate within itself. John Dewey made the point early in the century when he said that philosophy starts to lose ground when it concentrates on "the problems of philosophers, not the problems of human beings." Robert Neville echoed this famous sentiment when he explained how much of contemporary philosophy has moved toward debating issues of interest only to a narrow intellectual community, while the man-in-the-street still wonders about the meaning of life: "Plato showed how we could re-understand our tradition so as to be able to have real norms for life. We're in exactly the same situation today. We've had world wars among some of the most enlightened nations in this century. Clearly something has gone wrong. We need to look at how the encounter of world cultures can respond to this moral dilemma and I think that philosophers are doing that. Not many other people are raising these questions."

The Ultimate Challenge of Philosophy

Philosophy will give no easy answer, but it should be the discipline that tells you the question is valid and worth asking. Dare to ask the kind of question that will remain unanswered for thousands of years. Join in the search, welcome others in, and do not restrict the journey to those handy with specialized and turgid terminology. Why has philosophy failed its public? Like so much else in our society, it tried to become a specialty, a discourse only for the experts. Yet it began life as the pursuit for the arch-generalist, the license to speculate in the most open and most free manner. The dark narrowness of insistent explanation proved to be its downfall. Eighty-nine-year-old Marjorie Grene said it crisply: "The philosopher's room is a chamber that's sealed. All the doors are shut firmly against reality. It's this self-contained game. And an awful lot of it has no connection with anything. I don't understand how young people get interested in this whirligig, though some of them are terribly clever. And some of them I like listening to because they're just so damn smart, but they aren't talking about anything at all."

Grene herself spent twenty years as a farmer, and many of our other guests had other ways of sneaking out of that sealed room. Most of them want to pull philosophy up from the musty corridors and out into an unknown future. "We must educate our children for indeterminacy," suggests John Stuhr. "America is committed to pragmatism, practicality, and above all, pluralism." There is no right way ahead. We must teach openness, possibility, awareness, and that great encompassing way to enjoy it all: wonder. The Confucianist Tu Wei-ming points out that this is no modern invention: "Greek philosophers such as Aristotle put a great emphasis on practice. The contemplative mode is not at all separate from engagement in the world here and now." The real philosopher progresses only through direct involvement with the world. "There's a beautiful term, chi, which means the body. But, that word, chi, can also be used as a verb." The body is also the embodied. We inhabit the real qualities of the world as much as we use them and analyze the way they are spoken about: phenomenology, pragmatism, analysis. All deserve to be part of philosophy in the new millennium, not one tradition triumphed above the others.

Introduction

The Book, the Series

The philosophers we spoke with were generally pessimistic about the present indulgences of philosophy, but optimistic about its future, hoping for some kind of conciliation between the warring factions of the field. An agreement not just to disagree but to recognize that different methods of philosophizing reveal different aspects of the world of thought, both within the field and without. They all consider themselves part of the campaign to change the ineffectual aspects of the field into something that could engage a greater populace. While recognizing that television has never been thought of as a medium that does well with serious thought, they all were game to try. The format of a half-hour conversation is no substitute for years of research and argument laboring deep into a serious book, but philosophy has a long history of dialogue, and the essence of many great ideas comes out in the informality and directness of such discussion.

With Joseph Margolis, we hear philosophy at a very abstract level coming out fluidly, with a kind of glittering lucidity that is hard to turn away from: "It isn't that the world either had a structure which we have not discovered or that it had no structure. It's just that it's meaningless to put the question forward except in terms of the history of trying to make sense of the world. Do you see what I mean? What we call the intelligible world is cooperatively, you might say, built out of the constraints that the world imposes on our thinking so that we don't go haywire." Margolis makes the abstract engaging simply with the light you see in his eyes as he fixes on a thought. Here is a very special kind of passion. A passion for practicality, perhaps, motivates David Crocker to assert that philosophy has a firm role to play in the assessment of international political and economic conflicts. Global conflicts are ethical conflicts, battles not only of different ways of living but different ways of seeing the world. It is a serious job for the philosopher to use argument to justify "a world society that's trying to gradually evolve in a decent direction rather than an atrocious direction."

The dark side of ineffectual explanation must depart from philosophy, while the honest sense of magnificent living, unassailable wonder, and profound ambiguity should remain. It is neither poetry nor science, law nor faith, art nor organization. This strange discipline that used to contain everything is now lost in between the confused cracks of modern life. We did not embark on this project to mourn its failure, and of course any reports of the death of the discipline are greatly exaggerated. What we want to show is how the men and women who do philosophy sparkle with intelligence and wit and those who succeed do so while helping us to better think for ourselves.

We can all be philosophers at some point in the course of our lives, and it's hard but rewarding work. First we need to be inspired, and the many voices contained in this book are testament to the great diversity of possible inspiration that's out there, available right now, poised to change the world with new ideas; respectfully based on the long history of the old, yet, at the same time, reaching into the next millennium, with all those changes that are impossible to predict.

One fairly certain point resonates throughout the pages of *A Parliament of Minds:* if humanity endures, philosophy will endure, and the ancients in this endeavor will still sound as contemporary as they have for all ages. We are the questions while the questions last; and they are here to stay.

A PARLIAMENT OF MINDS

ROBERT CUMMINGS NEVILLE
Philosophy at the Beginning
of a New Millennium

Robert Cummings Neville, Dean, Boston University School of Theology, and Co-Chairman of the Twentieth World Congress of Philosophy. *Reconstruction of Thinking* is a penetrating discussion of the state of philosophy at the end of the twentieth century with bona-fide solutions for bringing philosophy to the forefront in dealing with the pressing problems facing humanity in the next century. He previously appeared on the *MacNeil-Lehrer News Hour* regarding ethics and values in education.

MM: Michael Malone   **RN:** Robert Cummings Neville

MM: Listen, Robert, here we are at the Twentieth World Congress of Philosophy, finishing out the century, finishing out the millennium, 2,400 years into modern philosophy. What have we learned? What's the message of this conference?

RN: I think the chief message of this conference is that there are at least three great literate traditions of philosophy, not just the Greek and European, but the Indian and the Chinese, which have ramified themselves in many ways. And then, also, there are other traditions of philosophy that don't have the literature, African and Native American and other traditional kinds of philosophy. And I think that for the first time in a gathering that has, what, 3,000 philosophers from all over the world together, those traditions are engaged with one another. And, at the least, people insular in one tradition suddenly have discovered that there are other ways of thinking about many of the same topics they have thought about. Before this conference, you have to go back hundreds of years. I suspect in Paris in the thirteenth century when Thomas Aquinas was trying to figure out how to respond to Muslim philosophy, there was a real engagement.

MM: So philosophy, just like every other part of modern life, is beginning to reflect globalism.

RN: Yes, it's done that at times in the past, but this includes the whole globe and it's very difficult to have serious philosophic conversation in that context because the first thing a philosopher has to do is to be able to appropriate and come to terms with the basic ideas in his or her own tradition. That's hard. But, to have a public discourse with people from other traditions, you have to go back into their background, their basic ideas, the fundamental metaphors that set their philosophies going in order to . . .

MM: Conferences like this are a time for taking stock. So, let's take some stock right now. What has philosophy accomplished in this century?

3

RN: I think there are philosophies in different senses that are coming together here. In Western philosophy, particularly in American and European philosophy, there has been a great adventure in making philosophy a profession, like business or law. And I think that we have learned that's a failure. It has achieved very great sophistication in narrow ways and developed a kind of internal language.

MM: So, philosophy got tenure-tracked? It stopped paying attention to the real world.

RN: It paid attention, but from a very narrow perspective. And I think perhaps, in the long run, in some kinds of modernist philosophy, it became a self-generating discipline as opposed to a discipline that looks at the problems of human beings. John Dewey, in the first half of this century, said again and again that philosophy cannot be the study of the problems of philosophers. It has to be the study of the problems of, of life, of human beings. And, in Western philosophy, his tradition has always been an important part, but the Academy has been dominated by other kinds of philosophy. And I think that we have learned in the twentieth century that's of very limited value.

MM: Well, this was sort of the century we needed the help of philosophy, wasn't it? I mean, did philosophy fail in its duty in the twentieth century?

RN: I don't know that philosophy failed more than any of the other Western cultural enterprises that went through a phase of modernism. Where they wanted to be grounded in their own substance and have their own internal development as opposed to being related. So, abstraction in art, for instance, is art for the sake of the art movement. Music also has gone through modernist internal movements. And I think that . . .

MM: And we all lost the average man.

RN: They did and I think that what we've learned at the end of the century is, in all of these fields is that these cultural enterprises need to look outward. In the East Asian situation and the South Asian situation there are very different dynamics with regard to what's happened in philosophy.

MM: At this conference did you see any indication that Western philosophy is now prepared, is desperate enough, is in sufficient crisis to begin to change, to begin to move back? I mean, you know what I'm saying. You can go out there on the street and ask people about philosophy and they're going to say it really doesn't help. I don't understand it, it's too arcane, they talk in a language I don't understand anymore, it doesn't say anything to me. Or, their notion of philosophy is pop psychology—you know, guides to better living, astrology, everything but philosophy.

RN: Yes. But, most of the people on the street would still have questions about the meaning of life. And that might not be expressed in those terms, but if someone close to you dies, then you ask what's the meaning of life and philosophy needs to be able to address those kinds of issues. And it does.

MM: It used to. Is it prepared to go back to taking on that job again?

RN: Probably not analytic philosophy, but certainly existentialism and its heirs. And those are the main issues in Confucianism and Taoism and most forms of Indian philosophy which are heavily represented at this Congress. And there are many Western-trained philosophers who are now interacting with that. Learning how to develop the concepts that allow for dialogue so as to be able to address the fundamental issues of politics, of the issues of ecology. I think that for the first time, because of the modernist development of science, we know enough about global economics to be able to raise crucial questions about distributive justice. That is, how can we have worldwide distributive justice? There's no philosophic tradition that has thought about that in great detail. The western philosophers have thought about justice in Europe without ever having to cope with being just to cultures that are radically different, even those like the Islamic culture which for 1,400 years Europe has interacted with. So now we have to be able to ask questions about how to recognize cultures that are very different from our own and engage them in the dialogue that allows us to ask the questions such as what would justice be?

MM: As a reporter, one of the things I've noticed is that business, commerce, seems to be farther down this path. Of learning about other cultures, by necessity. New markets opening up divisions in Southeast Asia, that sort of thing. The business executives I talk to have a better sense of other cultures than most college professors I know.

RN: Well, you've got your friends and I've got my friends. So, it depends on what kinds of connections there are. I think, surely, international business has effected a social interaction. And the social interaction ought to be guided by a cultural interaction. It would be great if the cultural interactions were sophisticated, which is one of the contributions that philosophy can make. And also the study of religious cultures; it's difficult in some context to distinguish philosophy from religion. Well, to make the social interactions culturally sophisticated requires a civilization that's global, that allows for the separate integrities of different cultures. And that's a hard thing to pull off. You think it's difficult to have a pluralistic culture in America—think about the globalistic dimension of that problem. And the business people, of course, interact, but I don't know that they're any farther ahead than the philosophers and religious studies people in creating the imagination to think about bridging the cultures.

MM: I want to talk to you about traditions. Let's go back to that for a moment. Now, in the course of my conversations here, I've talked to analytic logical philosophers, I've talked to people from the continental tradition, from the American pragmatists tradition, but you're a fourth wing of Western philosophy. A process philosophy. What is that all about? I know the name Whitehead. But, that's about all I know about. Tell me about it.

RN: Most forms of the philosophy that you mentioned are modernist philosophies. They were very much concerned to get to a nonhistorical, absolute foundation. There are two forms of philosophy that were not modernist. Process philosophy and pragmatism. And I identify with both of those. Process philosophy was started by Whitehead who had the idea that a large speculative system of nature could be hypothesized and then tested in science, in the social sciences, in the humanities, in the issues of ethics and civilization. And he was brilliant. He was able to think ideas that brought together things other ideas were unable to bring together. I think he was mistaken in some ways, but I fundamentally appreciate his attempt to redefine the basic ideas of philosophy in terms of events and processes rather than in terms of substances. Because, when you think of things as processes, then you can talk about their interactions and connections much better than if they're substances where they get stuck together.

MM: Well, it's certainly a notion that's confirmed in physics, too, isn't it? Ultimately, everything is process.

RN: Yes, and Whitehead was one of the first philosophers to not do philosophy of science. He wasn't talking about science in a technical sense. He was getting ideas from science so that his metaphysical system was developed in ways that were friendly to the latest developments in science up to the mid part of the century, when he died.

MM: So what is process, what has it contributed to twentieth-century philosophy? What's been its role?

RN: First of all, it has provided a serious alternative to analytic philosophy, which deals with very small problems and segregated from one another. Process philosophy integrates all the problems. It provides an alternative to continental philosophy by stressing the importance of nature and the human place in nature rather than the reduction of nature through its implications for human beings, which is the existentialist and phenomenological line. And by virtue of being so concerned with nature, it is able to provide a wonderful language for translating some of the other philosophic traditions of the world, such as the East Asian and the Indian, which also have understood human beings to live within nature as opposed to being the central focus where nature comes in on the side.

MM: I'm curious of your choice of adherence to this school of philosophy, given your regular life. I mean, you're out there in the world. You run the divinity school, Boston University, so, you know, you give speeches, you talk to business people, you're a fund-raiser, you're also a minister. This sort of real-life stuff and then here you are, when you go back to your office, you're doing metaphysics. How do you bridge that gap?

RN: Well, there are lots of levels of connection, metaphysical ideas, the ones that are the most practical in the long run, because metaphysical ideas have to do with everything that you do. So, if you understand your meetings with faculty or fund-raising or interviewing people as processes set within larger processes, set within larger processes, where there are ways by which these come apart and come together, that's a much better way of understanding things, it seems to me, much more practical than lots of alternative philosophies.

MM: So, you're sitting at one of those Kiwanis luncheons about to give a speech, do you really think about metaphysics?

RN: Probably not in those terms, no, no. But then there are different times of the day. And making the connections back and forth is very important. So, what one of the ideas that I think is most important that I have put together myself out of a lot of different influences but have developed in some large number of books over my career—and this not a metaphysical idea—is that to be a thing is to be a harmony of features that are essential to yourself and that are conditional upon what you're related to. That's a very abstract idea and it applies to everything. To be a thing is to be harmony with connections and also some things that allow you to put together those connections. Well, that applies in a lot of different areas. So many people are philosophical atomists and they think that everybody's by themselves. And, the connections are only advantageous. They're not advantageous. A lot of connections are internal to the two of us. And to be aware of your body is to be aware of sitting on this sofa and to be many floors up in a building, that kind of awareness, requires that you understand how things have their own hearts and are also connected. That's an idea that has enormous ethical ramifications, spiritual ramifications, bodily ramifications.

MM: Let's deal for a moment with matters of the spirit. Isn't it a contradiction to be a philosophy professor and a theology professor? I mean, isn't theology dealing with at least some certainties? And philosophy is just the opposite of that. It's challenging all the certainties. How do you combine these two points of view?

RN: Well, the demand for certainty that you ascribe to theology is really a kind of a . . . that's the modernist man for certainty in philosophy. I'm not a modernist philosopher. So the pragmatists and the process philosophers say that all knowledge is hypothetical. But we're living with our hypotheses. We rarely question most of our hypotheses. We don't question how to sit here. But that question could be raised. Now, if everything is hypothetical and yet we're in the middle of life living with it, we look to life to test and correct our views. Most of the traditions of the world don't distinguish philosophy from the intellectual side of religious life and I don't either, but that's because I'm not a modernist in philosophy and, in theology, I'm not a modernist either.

MM: Well, I find it very interesting when I talk to Confucian philosophers, when I talk to Islamic philosophers, that the matters of the spirit are highly integrated into thoughts of philosophy. But, when I talk to Western philosophers, it's as if that stuff isn't important.

RN: There is a way of reading the Western tradition that starts off with Socrates, that represents philosophy as being essentially skeptical because Socrates asked, what do you mean, how can you define such and so? And that reading of the Western tradition became very important during the Enlightenment which was, by and large, very skeptical. An alternative reading is that philosophy is a way of correcting the mode of life that is at hand, where the mode of life may need correcting because it comes up against the other traditions, other ways of life. So Plato himself, who wrote about Socrates, created the literary character of Socrates, whoever Socrates really was. He put forward his philosophy as a way of life, more like a religion than an analytic philosophy department. And that was in the context of him being . . . of his culture suddenly encountering the Persian culture and the Egyptian culture, which raised the question of relativism. The Sophists were the relativists. And Plato said how can we re-understand our tradition so as to be able to have real norms for life. I think that we're in exactly the same situation today that there's an engagement of different world cultures. There's a sudden recognition of the dangers in science if it's not taken seriously in its moral dimension. We've had world wars among the most enlightened nations of the world in this century. So, something has gone wrong. We need to look to see how this encounter of world cultures can respond to that moral dilemma and I think that philosophers are doing that. Not many other people are raising those questions . . .

MM: But, first, doesn't philosophy have to correct philosophy? I mean, you talk about a gulf in imagery between the different schools. Now what does that mean?

RN: The gulf in imagery means that we have not yet established a language for being able to communicate in depth from one culture to another. But that's a creative project. That's a project for the imagination of philosophy in the next decade or two.

MM: Is that within the . . . between the various schools of philosophy, too? Because, as an outsider looking in, you think, well, if they can't even agree on fundamentals in philosophy, how are they ever going to come out with . . .

RN: Well, you know, you're a serious modernist now. You want to make sure we've got things established at the beginning.

MM: I would like you guys to get along and come up with a sort of common point of view.

RN: But that's to be achieved. That's what we're working toward. What we're anxious to develop is a public discourse in which we can raise the questions and bring the resources of the various different traditions to that, but then engage the real issues. It's not that we know the answers to issues of ecology or distributive justice or how to have privacy in the Internet. Those are all issues that are new, that no tradition has the answer to. But we've got to find those by virtue of being able to marshal our forces.

MM: So, how long does this process take?

RN: Oh, I think it will take forever. Because at any point there are going to be new issues. So, we are in the middle. We need to correct ourselves, but we correct ourselves . . .

MM: But when do you close the gulf in imagery?

RN: Well, you don't. You don't close the gulf in imagery by reflecting always back on what you have done. We have to reappropriate our past, but we don't answer the questions by first agreeing about what philosophy is. We'll after the fact say, oh, this is what philosophy turned out to be when we have engaged that. I think two conditions are necessary for closing the gap or at least bridging what gaps there are now. One of those conditions is a lot of study of one another's past traditions, so that each can internalize the natural metaphors, the ones that seem almost intuitive in the different traditions; and the other is that, together, the philosophers have to engage the contemporary issues. That is, think about what authority in government ought to be for a world government and so forth.

MM: Isn't there a third one, which is to speak in a language that other people can understand? Because philosophy seems to be becoming more and more obtuse. The major texts in the twentieth century are not things that regular folks can penetrate, much less digest.

RN: I think most people could read Whitehead's *Function of Reason* or *The Adventure of Ideas*.

MM: They could read Whitehead; sure he wrote at the beginning years of this century, but not now. Not the writing being done now. I mean, you write about being concrete. What does concrete mean?

RN: Concrete is, fundamentally, being engaged, and I don't think philosophy is a commodity that we need to sell to make it popular. I guess I shouldn't say that since I need to raise money for philosophy sometimes. But philosophy will sell itself when it's doing creative things. It's a work of imagination, like the arts in many respects, or like good politics.

MM: But there's a duty, too, to talk to the world, with the world? That means you have to have the experiences and you have to have the language, even the patois of everyday life.

RN: Right. Well, you have to engage the people in everyday life to create a language. If the language of everyday life were enough, you wouldn't need philosophers. But then, people in everyday life would know the meaning of life, they would know the nature of political authority, they would know how things are unified and how they're diverse, and they don't. And, so, the question is to create a culture in which there is an interaction between the different patois that people speak and the creative imagination of philosophy.

MM: How do you get engaged? Is there a proper way for philosophers to be engaged in things like policy discussions and politics? I mean, you are out there, I mean, you're getting interviewed all the time and being quoted in the newspaper. You have a sense of how that works. What are the rules of engagement?

RN: First of all, you've got to have something to say. And it's easy for philosophers who don't have much to say to be able to express some canned view. If you do have something to say, you probably are not in control of your own language very well. You only understand after the fact what it is that you've been saying. So, the most important thing is to be engaged with people, not talking to them as if you're presenting something, but engaged so that what you are learning can be connected up with what they're learning. I work in the academic world and I can talk with other academics, who probably would make your point rather than mine. And I work in the religious world. I do a lot of preaching. I know how to give sermons that address people who would not have the fancy theological vocabulary but express that, and I've learned that by doing it a lot. I've worked in medical ethics where the patois is narrow anatomy . . .

MM: Yes, and that's true engagement, being out there. Ethics seem to me to be the trenches.

RN: That's, right. But you have to be careful of the metaphors that you use. It might seem as if everyday life were the concrete stuff and the academic world were abstract. I don't think that's quite the right metaphor. Because what, not the academic world so much, as the people in creative disciplines, many of whom are in the academy, what they do most and best is work with imagination. And life is not . . .

MM: So life is the concrete?

RN: Absolutely. It's the most concrete thing because that is what allows us to have the possibilities to make connections and to sever connections where they ought to be. Imagination is much more concrete than dull repetition. That's process philosophy.

MM: Let's talk about you for a moment—the role of faith in your life. How does that interact with your work in philosophy? Do they ever collide?

RN: Well, there are and have been for thirty-five, forty years, very interesting questions that, and interesting is the wrong word, penetrating, often anguishing existential questions about the nature of God, freedom, and immortality, to use Kant's great three issues. I'm a person who has always been in process, in the middle. So I always had some faith, pretty silly, childish faith when I was a little kid, but the corrections to that, although sometimes wrenching, have never been foundational. It's not that I ever looked for a foundation that was certain, only to improve the understanding and the faith and the practice that I had.

There are lots of things that come together. I was raised in an entirely Western Christian, midwestern culture.

MM: Can you derive sustenance from a faith that is in process, that's not concrete, that's not a solid foundation?

RN: Oh, absolutely. Every major religious tradition I know has something like the Christian doctrine of the Holy Spirit, which is that, when you engage life, reality, and God in your current problems, you're continually learning, you're getting new stuff, grace in the Christian language. When Tu Wei-ming talks about becoming a sage, the access of the sage to principal or heavenly principal in the heart is always opening up something new. So, it's not that the past is irrelevant, we are historical beings, but we live in the present and often toward the future. It's dangerous to live toward the distant future because you get pretty foolish about that, but I've never found that to be a requirement that you have to have a certain starting part.

MM: But your faith and your philosophy never collide?

RN: Well, they certainly ask hard questions of one another. I'm an imaginative fellow, though, and I recognize that where two things seem to be true, I need to find some way of recognizing the truth in each and then identify what there is in each side that makes it seem as if the other cannot be true. Whitehead said that philosophers are usually right in what they affirm and wrong in what they deny. And, the structure of your ideas is what makes you affirm these things, but then also causes you to deny other things. So, an atomist is somebody who says, well, we have an inner core. Everything has its own inner core but, by virtue of being an atomist, cannot acknowledge that there are interconnections with other things that affect that inner core.

MM: As well as a connection with something greater? Something supreme?

RN: That's right. That's right. Yes. You see, the concrete runs from the subtlest and most imaginative ways of being in touch with the vastness of reality or the depths of God or the height of Confucian heavenly principle or the emptiness of Zen Buddhists' conception of what's most real. And that is integrated with the little concrete things about whether you're hungry.

MM: Is there anything in philosophy, in the process of philosophy and philosophical refection, equivalent to grace in matters of the spirit?

RN: Oh, certainly, for pragmatists, yes, but if you have an idea about the way things ought to be, for instance, in establishing a political authority for a town or to try to figure out what responsibility a wealthy, powerful country such as the United States has for the breakdown of government in a place like Rwanda, develop hypotheses about that, and see how those hypotheses work out. Experience teaches. Reality teaches us. It usually teaches us that our hypotheses are wrong, but not wholly wrong, a little bit wrong. So you have to modify your positions. I think that unless philosophy takes as its topic philosophy, it's going to be dealing with reality and reality will correct it. Maybe not fast enough, but that's pretty much like grace.

MM: Philosophy has long dealt with the question of what is a good life. Religion deals with the question of what is a good life in God, what is the proper life in God? Do we need both philosophy and faith to live a proper life?

RN: Oh, I think both of those are crucial questions, yes. Now, there are lots of religions that don't believe in God where you would present yourself to God. But, that's a good metaphor for all religions and I could find ways in Confucianism of saying that your life needs to add up to something, it has a certain worth, you're human identity, not just moral identity, but your aesthetic and familial identity is something that, in a sense, is absolute. And, that's what you present for judgment, to use the Christian language. You present that for judgment. Now, your own life is lived in the context of a whole society. The issue of a good life is not one that applies to you alone, but to the contribution you can make to your community, to your culture, to your civilization. And it could be that none of us is in a position to enjoy the good life, but we can all make a contribution to what a good life means in a civilization, in a culture. And that's a crucial contribution to make.

MM: Robert, thank you.

RN: Oh, thank you.

DAVID A. CROCKER
Democracy, Ethics, and the
Relevancy of Philosophy

David A. Crocker, Senior Research Scholar at the Institute for Philosophy and Public Policy School of Public Affairs at the University of Maryland. Professor Crocker addresses ethical issues in international development surrounding his recent work on *The Ethics of Consumption: The Good Life, Justice, and Global Stewardship.* He discusses the ethics and politics of transitional justice: How should emerging democracies address human rights violations in prior civil conflicts or repressive regimes?

MM: Michael Malone   **DC:** David Crocker

MM: You've edited a book called *The Ethics of Consumption.* What do ethics and consumption have to do with one another?

DC: Well, Goldilocks put the question very well: How much is enough, and how much is too much, and how much is not enough? And she had a way of figuring out what bed to sleep in. But we don't have a sure sense of standards to evaluate lives, so we get carried away with the latest consumerist fad. And there's some need to kind of sit back and say, okay, what's the right way to answer the question of how much is enough. Do we have an idea of how much is enough? No. That's why we need to think about it.

MM: Do we have a systematic way to determine how much is enough?

DC: No, we've got a whole bunch of fragments from the past and ideas from different cultures and different traditions and we need to sit back and say what makes sense now. You visited Walden a few days ago and Thoreau had one approach to it that makes sense for a lot of people.

MM: Yeah. But every time I see a place like Walden, I think, you know, that's lovely for Thoreau to be out there on the side of that pond. But if worse came to worse, he would go back into Concord, right? And if everybody did a Thoreau, nobody would be developing fetal heart monitors. Nobody would be pushing forward the scientific method or developing new technologies or creating products that, you know, extend one's life span or antibiotics.

DC: And it turned out, when he got tired of what he was doing—even while he was there, he would go and visit Emerson and some other folks, and have a good conversation and have a little good wine maybe.

MM: And he would also sit there every day and wait for that train to show up, right, 'cause he thought trains were great. Now that's not quite our image of Thoreau.

DC: Part of what we need to do is to avoid these extremes of "All consumption is bad," on the one hand, which you get into as an extreme Thoreauian standpoint, and "All consumption is good," on the other hand, and try to work out some notions of, "It's not a matter of too much or too little, but too much of some things, not enough of others"—a matter of quality and not quantity.

MM: But then you get into questions, even if you've decided that, how do you enforce that right? Do you, do people internalize that principle? And so it then becomes a manifestation of their own desires.

DC: Right.

MM: Or do you, the czar who determines on the consumption, "Listen to me, I'm the consumption czar. This is how much you're going to . . ."

DC: A bulletin from the front: "This is what you're supposed to buy this week."

MM: That's right.

DC: Well, I think one of our problems is that we go from the individual immediately to the state, which we see as the solution to everything. Indeed the government, on different levels, has a lot of roles to play—you don't want to buy food that's contaminated. You want some regulation. You want some inspection. You want cars that are safe.

MM: But government, the governments don't even know, though, I mean in the sense that they will actually subsidize contradictory activities.

DC: And some parts of the government work against other parts, so you need to clean up the government's act, too. But I think, to answer your question more directly, a lot of institutions in civil society have a very important role to play: families, churches, community groups, raising this question for themselves and not just seeing it as a purely private individual choice. I mean, we say, to ourselves and to our friends, "You know, what you're buying and eating or using is not good for you." In that sense, a lot of things that we buy are not good for us. Other things are very good for us. And so we need to kind of get some balance, and my own thinking on this is . . .

MM: So, I'm a philosopher and I believe in human freedom and free will. And

I decided I want to eat Big Macs the rest of my life. And I want them in Styrofoam containers 'cause it keeps 'em warm. And you reply?

DC: And I reply, well, let's prize the human freedom and human liberty to make that choice. But let's kind of step back and see what the longer-term consequences might be, and not necessarily bring in the government. I mean, if you make the same point, though: "I like my freedom to stick knives in people's chests for the hell of it," then we need to rethink that because of the harm that you do to other people. I think it's when the harm is done to yourself—that's where the government doesn't have a role to play. When it's harm done to other people and/or the impact on the environment . . .

MM: So it's like a first step of some sort of empirical measure of what the harm is.

DC: Sure, sure. And this is one thing I think that philosophers need—to really be very sensitive to the best empirical work about the impact of this decision.

MM: I'm intrigued by what you do in the sense that, unlike a lot of philosophers we're talking to, you're not sitting somewhere pondering, you know, the great thoughts.

DC: No, I'm eating Big Macs, right.

MM: Well, yes. In Yugoslavia, I mean you're out there in the world, in the trenches. Trying to apply philosophy to everyday life. Now, philosophy has not been real interested in real-life applications for a while now, so where do you go for your sources?

DC: Yes, yes. Well, there is a tradition that philosophy should grow out of everyday life and return to it. And it's often replaced by another tradition which views it as in some sense disconnected from everyday life, and better than everyday life when it's in the ivory towers or removed from life.

MM: So who do you use? Who are your reference points?

DC: Well, I think there are several. I think Socrates continues to be a model—although we all interpret him in different ways to get to what we want out of him—but I think the idea of raising tough questions about his own life and the lives of people around him. And not just raising questions, but having some at least tentative answers—and that he was willing to try to change his culture. I think Gandhi in some ways represents the kind of searcher after truth, no holds barred. Got himself into a lot of trouble. Also made a big difference in the world.

MM: But they are both nontextual philosophers. They weren't writing much down.

DC: Well, Gandhi did do some writing. Another example would be a Nelson Mandela, who wrote a very big book while he was in Robben Island in prison.

MM: Also a man of action now.

DC: Exactly. And I think the balance between thought and action has got to be different for different people, so it's not as if there's a "one size fits all" formula for the way philosophical reflection can relate to action.

MM: So you're out there in the developing world, you're out there in Central America, you're out there in Yugoslavia. Do you ever sense that what you're seeing in front of you doesn't fit in your philosophy books?

DC: Yes, yes, yes. And it needs to be rethought, although sometimes the philosophy books can help you see that what you see in front of you should be changed and shouldn't be the way it is. So you have that back-and-forth between the two, changing your ideas to fit the reality and changing the reality to make it come closer to ideals that you think are important.

MM: We've had a lot of talk about globalism. But, if anything, it would seem to me you're seeing a lot of nonglobalism out there, a lot of sectarianism. And who's going to win?

DC: Well, that's a hard one to call at this point, just like it was hard to call France versus Brazil the night before the Soccer World Cup. Everybody thought it was going in one way and it went another way.

MM: Yes, I see the same thing as a business writer. We treat globalism as a fait accompli. And I think philosophers are doing exactly the same thing, talking about global consciousness and this sort of thing. And yet, when you're sitting at a roadblock in Bosnia, you may not agree with that, the globalism and global consciousness is just around the corner.

DC: Right. Well, I think you've got to be very sensitive to the forces that separate the ethnic identity, the way in which cultures are dividing. At the same time, you've got a lot of different kinds of globalization, not just markets and Big Macs, Golden Arches East, but also the globalization of human rights, the globalization of notions that there's some kind of acts that shouldn't be tolerated by any society, and so you've got that kind of balance between the two.

MM: So from that can I assume you believe that there is such a thing—to have a global ethics?

DC: You bet. And human rights should be very much a part of that, a right not to be tortured, a right not to . . .

MM: And that brings us into the ethics of consumption.

DC: Yes. And a right to have an opportunity at least, to live a life of well-being, of decency. And maybe not just your government but other governments and institutions have some obligation to be sure that you've got the tools to get up to a certain kind of level. No matter what society you're living in.

MM: Okay, now, you'll run into people, political scientists, who will tell you that the best way to do that is democratic capitalism. But democratic capitalism, as we know in the United States, oftentimes leads to runaway consumption. So how do you fix, how do you find that middle ground?

DC: How do you fix that little dilemma?

MM: Right.

DC: Well, there are different kinds of capitalism and different kinds of democracy and different kinds of democratic capitalism. I think you need to be working for a kind of government that involves not only full and free elections, but also a citizenry that is concerned about public issues and acts—not only in relation to the government but in their own lives and their civil social organizations—to raise some of these questions and to get change. We talked before about the program started in Honduras. One of the problems in Honduras has been for years and years a kind of culture of impunity, which I would suspect exists in many communities in the United States, too. Where I do something I know is wrong, but I know that you know it's wrong, but you're not going to do anything about it because you're doing the same thing and we wink at each other and things go on the way they do. And that takes us away from the consumption theme to corruption and other kinds of issues. But these are issues that are worldwide kinds of issues. And they often have a different tone or hue in a particular culture, but we need, I think, to forge together some international standards that can enable us to evaluate any society.

MM: So do we have a declaration of the ethics of any kind?

DC: Well, we have the Declaration of Human Rights in the charter of the United Nations. I think the best work on this kind of thing being done right now is by the United Nations Development Program, one which tries to get an index of what it means for a society to be developed—which is basically that human beings have the opportunity to be developed, at least in the minimal sense, of adequate buying power, being able to live without disease and to have a reasonably long life, and to be well educated—and that is used then to evaluate how societies are doing. Now that's not a perfect measure. For example, it leaves out political freedom, which they tried to bring in and did it in kind of a rough way and left it out in their next *Human Development Report*. But every year they publish a *Human Development Report* that, I think, is an example of the kind of thing we're evolving, which is a globalization of standards—of moral success, we might say.

MM: Can we enforce those?

DC: Well, enforcement takes lots of different forms. I would say often we shouldn't enforce because of the human freedom that we talked about earlier. But between absolute free choice of the individual and a heavy-handed state getting in our pockets and getting on our backs, there are a lot of other options of moral suasion from different kinds of communities. States that encourage, that give tax breaks, that regulate, that don't say what to buy, but make sure that certain kinds of products are not on the market—so there are a lot of ways in which governments can intervene. But on some things, they should intervene and say, "You know, torture is wrong and it's not to be permitted in our society." And the issue I'm most exercised about right now with respect to new democracies, talking about democracy, is what to do in relation to atrocities and human rights violations.

MM: What do you do about that past? South Africa and seeing Argentina.

DC: Yes, what do you do about the past? Argentina, Chile, now Guatemala and South Africa have truth commissions.

MM: Well, yes. Professional ethicists. So what should they do?

DC: Well, first they should engage in a public debate and wrestle with this issue rather than just sweep it under the rug and forget and move on or forgive and forget. Also, they should argue against private vengeance—this is also an option that many people have seized. If you don't deal with the past in some sense publicly, it's going to get dealt with one way or another.

MM: There's like, France, still dealing with Napoleonic government.

DC: Yes, and after Turkey did so many horrible things to the Armenians and nothing was done, there was the idea "Let's not deal with that, let's move on to the future." The Pasha and all his henchmen ended up getting assassinated by Armenians in the streets of various capitals in Europe in the next fifteen years.

MM: So, public debate, some light, exposed what happened.

DC: Right. And then there's a whole raft of other things that can be done, you know, there are obviously writers who can deal with it. Ariel Dorfman's *Death of the Maiden* is an attempt, a Chilean novelist. Other tools are public commemoration, public apology, compensation to the victims, giving the victims a chance to find out what happened.

MM: How about public revenge?

DC: I think trials and punishments are a real important part of the whole thing, especially for those who are most responsible, the big fish, not the medium-size fish and the little fish.

MM: Obviously one of the problems is at some point, if it lasts long enough, the despotism—everybody becomes an accessory to one degree or another.

DC: And in some societies more than others. You've got fifty years of Stasi spying in East Germany, and in some sense half the population has been involved and compliant with the earlier regime. While in Chile the numbers were much smaller. I think there's a different solution for each society, but each society has got to come up with this. And my own view is that an international war crimes tribunal is something that we should have, and it should have more power than it was given in the agreement that came on July 17.

MM: But certainly behind all that, then, your argument, there is some sort of universal set of ethical principles.

DC: Yes, yes. And I don't think those are something that we kind of get from somebody coming down from the mountain and saying, "Here they are." It's something that the international community has to kind of forge together. And I think a huge step in that direction was the Declaration of Human Rights. But now that's evolving. It's not just civil and political liberties and rights; it's also social and economic ones. And the human story is one of making some progress, taking into account horrible things that happened, trying to learn from them and trying to go forward. But you've called attention already to so many negative things that are happening in the world.

MM: Well, let's talk about the developing world a minute. Because that's a great interest of yours and I'm sort of haunted by the image of the poor farmer who finally sees magazines and television programs about the world, about the United States, and says, "I want that." And is told, "No you can't have that, because those people are living way beyond their means. And so you're not going to get all that stuff." And the person says, "Wait a minute, I want that, you know, I've been dreaming about this my whole life, why can't I have that?" "Because it's not good for you." I mean, isn't that kind of what we're beginning to tell people in the developing world?

DC: It's not just we as rich, affluent, North Americans who are telling people, it's that people within the cultures themselves are saying, "Wait a minute. Here we've got the image of a good life that is emerging on North American television, which we're all getting through cable or whatever in our own countries. Is this what we want? And then, "Who should do anything about it if we don't want it?" And you had asked what sources am I drawing on? Each of these countries has alternative sources. When I was in India about a year and a half ago, a woman in her sixties said, "I was a militant Gandhian." Someone said, "Those are nice gold bracelets, gold necklace, and earrings you have." And she said, "Yes, I like 'em too. We went too far." But there is something in the Gandhian tradition that is very important today as we get this new image that to live a fully satisfactory life, you've got to imitate the Americans. So then what about your farmer now? "Well, I want to imitate the Americans."

MM: It looks good to me.

DC: It looks good and is in many ways. But here's where the kind of full information is important, for there are some downsides to that picture as well, as well as some upsides to some of the traditional ways of living and what you need.

MM: Okay, do you see your work as disseminating that information?

DC: Not disseminating so much as providing a kind of cross-cultural dialogue about the strengths and weaknesses of various cultural traditions and what we can learn from each other.

MM: Okay, but now the dark side of this native traditionalism is that it can be a smoke screen for continuing to do the bad things you're doing. "Well, yes, but, feet binding is part of our native tradition. And so is slavery, too, by the way. And branding and lopping off arms and legs for minor crimes, but that's part of our tradition." Now how do you deal with that?

DC: Now there's where the critical reflection on the tradition, primarily but not exclusively by people in the tradition, is very important. But, by the way—talking of camouflage—the human rights vision can be camouflaged to do horrible things to other people, too. So we've got to recognize that the outside universalist view can also, unless it's promoted in the right way, be subterfuge for . . .

MM: . . . other hidden agendas.

DC: Other kinds of agendas, right. But I think, one of the reasons that it's important to forge a kind of a global ethic is in order to subject local traditions, primarily by the people living in them themselves, to critical examination. And you've got indigenous human rights groups in all these countries that are concerned that this culture of impunity that we were talking about earlier is subjected to examination and modification and, sometimes, rejection.

MM: It would seem that would sometimes collide with these fundamental principles of ethics unless you take them down so far that they're meaningless—they're mainly just a description of being a human being.

DC: Yes, yes. Another temptation here is to just have a global ethic as a bunch of banalities and clichés that everybody can agree to, but it doesn't really cut any ice as to making important changes.

MM: Now we still have this paradoxical situation that the rest of the world wants to be, understandably, more prosperous. They want to have a better quality of life. And yet there's this growing fear that if everybody's dreams came true, well, they would never come true, because it can't be done. We can't raise the prosperity of the entire world to a sufficiently high level that everybody would be happy without just destroying the planet. So, at some point, do we have to say to countries, "This is as far as you're going to get to go," or does the unseen hand take care of that?

DC: No, there's no unseen hand, unfortunately—no invisible hand that's guiding us here. Well, I think we come back to that Goldilocks question of how much is enough. And there, when you said prosperity, you know, what do you mean by prosperity at this point? Do you mean being wealthy in a monetary sense?

MM: Well, what if my idea of prosperity is, you know, Mercedes, and somebody in Somalia's idea of prosperity is not to lose any kids this year.

DC: Right, and I think that what we've got to try to forge is the ideal of a kind of basic minimum, a moral minimum, being able to live a reasonably long life free of debilitating disease, to be able to have access to the cultural symbols or meanings of the community, which involves formal education, usually. To be able to have enough purchasing power to get the basic necessities of food and clothing and shelter, to be able to participate politically, and that will take different forms in different cultures. But I think that's something that most people will agree to. And a doctrine of human rights that we've been talking about comes in to say, "We call these things rights, or we have a right to these things. All people have a right to these things because they mark very, very valuable, important dimensions of our life." And commodities that we buy or gain access to can play a role. Books can contribute to that, and that's something that's part of the consumption world, too.

MM: Is this the job of the United Nations?

DC: It's certainly one of the jobs of the United Nations, yes.

MM: What about the argument—and you hear this a lot in the United Nations—that the developed world owes the developing world? And that the developed world's reaction, response seems to be, "Okay, you know, we stripped your landscape of coal, but we also got rid of smallpox, so doesn't it all balance out?" And the developing world says, "No, because look at us and look at you."

DC: Well, you've got a backward-looking approach and a forward-looking approach. Apart from what happened in the past, people that are better off seem to be obliged to help at least some of those who are most at risk, especially if they are children and kids who aren't responsible for where they are.

MM: So what's the ethics of that? Is there an ethical principle?

DC: Oh, I think there is an ethical principle of helping, when you've got more than you need, someone who is so at risk that they're in danger of death and/or of other kinds of deprivations that are equivalent to a kind of moral death. But that doesn't even deal with the past issues which, as you say, are very complex. But I think you need to recognize that while rich nations have done a lot of good in bringing medicine and opportunity to a lot of people around the world, they've also done a lot of harm, and that has to be kind of figured in some compensation for the past. I feel responsible, to some extent, for what went on in Chile during the Pinochet years, because my government colluded with the Pinochet government to first ensure that it got into power and then stayed in power. So I have a special kind of obligation as an American citizen to do what I can to help the Chileans deal with that terrible seventeen years of terror and death and to work toward a future that doesn't encourage that same kind of thing being repeated. While I don't have that extra obligation, perhaps, in another country in which the United States hasn't been nearly as involved. But you can't quantify and say, "There's this amount of obligation, and now it stops, and now you can go on and do what you want." We also have obligations to our own American citizens and to our own families. And many of them are not doing so well, either. But it's not an either/or, *first* we kind of take care of all our problems.

MM: Is there a hierarchy of responsibilities? I mean, Chile first, you know, family first, what's the order?

DC: Well, I don't think you can work out any hierarchy ahead of time and then use it as a kind of blueprint.

MM: You know in your heart what I mean.

DC: Well, I think there's where you need to practice this kind of deliberation and judgment at the time, not just yourself, but talking to other people and then talking to people in other cultures because you may be biased.

MM: When's the time for deliberation? I mean, at this point, whatever is on CNN as the most heart-wrenching image is what gets our attention.

DC: Well, we need to know what's going on in Sudan and whether there's anything that can be done that won't make things worse. And a lot of our intervention, whether it's military or humanitarian, has been well intentioned and then resulted in disaster. And part of what ethics does is to try to say, "You know, the road to hell is paved with good intentions, but you can get to hell even faster with bad intentions, and let's try to learn from these cases."

MM: But if a despot chooses to kill a million people, slowly and quietly without any cameras around, he is not going to receive the same ethical notice and attention as an event that is very public and happens in front of cameras, right?

DC: That's why groups like Amnesty International and Human Rights Watch, with international organizations and local chapters throughout the world, monitor these things—and this is, by the way, not government but civil society, international civil society, if you will. Church groups watching what's going on, monitoring, are extremely important so that the quiet terror, the quiet dictator, in the long run, is not able to continue. However, some kinds of interventions can make the problem even worse, and you've got to be aware of that.

MM: Now, let's go to the ultimate test case, because you've been there recently. This is an area of great interest to you: Yugoslavia. Now, Yugoslavia seems to be the great challenge, every once in a while we get great counterarguments to just about everything we believe in about civilization, about dialogue, about the end of ethnic strife. And then we get a place like Yugoslavia, which is sort of barbarism incarnate right now. What does an ethicist do when he encounters Yugoslavia?

DC: Are you thinking of Yugoslavia and Kosovo or are you thinking about Bosnia?

MM: Yes, I'm thinking about the whole morass.

DC: The Balkan problem, the former Yugoslavia, yes, because we have to take these separately, but let's take Kosovo, Yugoslavia. Here we have the Yugoslavia that still exists: Serbia, Montenegro, and here we have Kosovo, which is 90 percent Albanian (Muslim) and 10 percent Serbian. On the other hand, it is

David A. Crocker

an area that has all these cultural shrines of the Serbs. And just two weeks ago, I visited some right on the border of Kosovo that are part of the Serbian Orthodox tradition—very important back to the Middle Ages. It would be like Americans cavalierly saying, "Oh, the Washington Monument, Valley Forge, Mount Vernon, Monticello, those we can give away. Let somebody else have them." Well, here's independence for Kosovo; we have this principle of the right of self-determination. But there are other principles involved. The right of self-determination—what does that mean in Kosovo, when 10 percent are opposed to that independence?

MM: What happens to the minority?

DC: The minority of the minority of the minority—and you've got a kind of domino effect here—and I think the Serbians, my Serbian friends, are saying to me, "Look, these kinds of abrupt separations often happen in a nonethical way, just like some divorces. People try to just split with no entanglements, no consideration of impact on other people, third parties, as well as on themselves and institutions. What about the children? Those things have to be worked out. So if Kosovo would become independent, what about the impact on those Muslims who live in Bosnia, then, who would want their independence? And then Bosnia falls apart and then we have the risk of ethnic strife and atrocities coming again there." And . . .

MM: Does not sound like an easy job for an ethicist.

DC: No, it isn't. And what it shows, I think—and it's a fine question—is how important it is for an ethicist to know the facts and know the policy options and know what's feasible. But the problem, in a lot of public . . .

MM: And you have to know magnitude, too, right? I mean there are solutions and there are solutions.

DC: Right. And there's short term and middle term and long term, and the further we get away from the present, the less we have a crystal ball that can tell us what's really going to happen. And yet we're under the pressure of making a decision. So should we Americans, we world citizens, we whatever, be backing the Kosovo Liberation Army or the political leader, Ibrahim Rugova, who apparently has lost all power in Kosovo?

MM: It seems to me it's this very paradoxical situation as Americans, because on the one hand we like independence movements because we harken back to the Revolutionary War and we understand civil wars when they say, "Stay out, we're working this out amongst ourselves." But we didn't want other foreign powers coming in during the Civil War, we worked it out ourselves. Yet, at the same time, we're the most powerful country in the world. We've been to Sarajevo once in this century, we don't want to go back, we don't want, you know, eastern Europe to explode all over again. These are real contradictory desires on our part, we don't know what to do. You feel that way as an ethicist. I mean, this must haunt you, this is the ultimate ethical question.

DC: We've got several principles involved here that have emerged in our discussion. One is this importance of self-determination, the right of self-determination of a country. But also within that you've got groups, some of which are minorities facing majorities. And we are concerned about individuals, too—the human rights movement grew up concerned not just about the rights of states, but the rights of individuals. And our own American experience is one in which you left out slavery, right? That was part of the whole reason for the Civil War.

MM: And we can walk two blocks to a graveyard where people were willing to kill and die for.

DC: Right, and some things are worth fighting and dying for, too. So what I'm urging is to be aware of all these facts that we've been talking about, but also aware of the ethical principles, some of which we've talked about here, and recognize that what we've got to do in our own particular societies, but also as part of a global society, is face the particular situations that we confront—and we talked about several of them: overconsumption, underconsumption. Human rights violations in the past and what do you do about them. Rights of people to live their own lives, on one hand; and yet that may involve doing horrible things to other people. All of these have to be part of what the philosopher, as a part of public debate and public discussion, deals with, as we get clear on the best ethical principles and then, in the particular situation, help to decide which are the most important, which weigh most heavily on us as individuals, on our communities and on something called a world society that's trying to gradually evolve in a decent direction rather than an atrocious direction.

MM: And somehow, in the midst of all of that, not forget the individual person.

DC: And this farmer that you talked about. Because one of the ethical values that we both agree to is the right to decide how to live one's own life, but

28

within limits. And what those limits are, and what that right entails, is something that philosophers have a tradition to draw on. But they can also facilitate ordinary citizens in being philosophical, in the sense of deliberating in public, arguing, give-and-take—like we've tried to do here—as a part of what it means, not just to be human, but to be a good national patriot and global citizen.

MM: Great, thank you.

MARTHA NUSSBAUM
Aristotle in the Workplace

Martha Nussbaum, Ernst Freund Distinguished Service Professor of Law and Ethics at the University of Chicago, with appointments in the Philosophy Department, Law School, Divinity School, and the College, an Associate Appointment in the Classics Department, and an affiliate membership in the Committee on Southern Asian Studies. A participant in a previous Bill Moyers series for PBS, Martha Nussbaum explores the need and benefits of a liberal arts education—the application of classical thought to modern day issues in education. She provides an informative and insightful discussion of the need for educational reform in America with concrete examples.

MM: Michael Malone   **MN:** Martha Nussbaum

MM: I'm curious—central to a lot of your writing is the notion that the insights of ancient Greece can help us solve contemporary problems. Do you still believe that? I mean in the age of the Internet and the microprocessor, is that still true?

MN: Yes, I do think that, because I think, first of all, that it's very good philosophical work. A lot of the ideas that the Greeks had are still alive just because they are good. The other thing is that the Greeks cared about the practical side of life in a way that a lot of modern philosophers don't, and so they wrote all the time about issues like the fear of death, the destructive social consequences of anger, the need to think about love—and then, my current greatest interest, the need that people in the political community have for basic resources in order to be capable of flourishing. So I think there's a whole range of their ideas that are still very alive, partly because they were really thinking about how philosophy should sell itself to human beings as offering help in their lives; and they were not academics, they were out there competing with astrologers, magicians, and they had to tell people why you should care about philosophy.

MM: In the marketplace of ideas, they have to sell their product.

MN: In the marketplace of ideas, they were selling their product, and they were saying that philosophy can do more to make you live well than other forms of consolation and insight that you might turn to.

MM: I am certain that they talked about two things that I wonder if they are still applicable today. One of them is the role of reflection in a 24–7 world where we're surfing the net and working sixteen hours a day, when is there time for reflection?

MN: Well, I don't think reflection has to take very long, I think it just has to be there and, in fact, once it is there, I think it doesn't take formal exercise. But I think, to begin with, you really do need to give young people classes in philosophy in order to get them to be good citizens, as I have argued in my book on liberal education. I argued that every undergraduate in America should have two semesters of philosophy. The reason for that is I think we're all too much caught up in a sound-bite culture. Kids are listening to talk radio and they get the idea that you don't have an argument with an opponent, you just make a claim and somebody makes a counterclaim. But what democracy really needs is more deliberation. We need to pool our resources and think about the common good and what philosophy courses can contribute. I have seen a lot of very good teaching in this subject. What teachers give students is the idea that there is such a thing as arguing for your position and there's such a thing as the other person's arguing for that person's position, and you listen to that and you learn from that. So I followed, in the book, the career of one undergraduate at Bentley, a college in Massachusetts that specializes in business.

MM: You toured the whole country, didn't you?

MN: I've been in my time to many more schools than I wrote about in the book, but in the book I focused on fifteen and they were selected to be different, from big and small, rural and urban, business oriented and more academically oriented, religious and secular. What I wanted to say is that in all those different schools, philosophy has something to contribute to good citizenship and it is this element of reflecting, listening to what the other person is saying, listening to the structure of the argument, learning how to read a political speech and find that it's a bad argument, all those things. People find they can do and they do them extremely well, students of all kinds and they need those abilities if they're going to sit on a jury or they're even going to vote in a complex election.

MM: So it should go beyond colleges then? Should we be teaching philosophy in third grade?

MN: I do think we should, and there's wonderful work done on the philosophical ability of children. I think children have a lot of natural curiosity about arguments and how they work, and if you catch that at the right time, it's great. But I don't know enough about primary education and secondary education so I only write about higher education because that's what I know best.

MM: Could you draw any general conclusions or were these all distinct cases? Could you say that business-oriented colleges do a better job or a worse job of teaching philosophy than humanities-oriented schools or religious schools do a better job than secular schools?

Martha Nussbaum

MN: Well, I was not just looking at philosophy, I was looking at the humanities in general and looking at how new studies—let's say of non-Western cultures, of women's studies—how those contribute to the production of citizens. But just to stick with philosophy, I think that what I concluded was that schools that do have a philosophy requirement do better at producing citizens than schools that don't. Now the schools that have it are widely varied. Of course, all the major Catholic colleges and universities have a strong philosophy requirement and they really get a lot out of that. I mean people really learn how to think about their own tradition and to take charge of their own participation in that tradition. But also, you know, schools of very different kinds have philosophy requirements. The University of Pittsburgh, which is a state school, is one that I looked at. Harvard, of course, a very different kind of school, and then Bentley, a business-oriented college. And in all those places, there are teachers who are good because they know their own particular students and they love those students and they really have an optimism about democracy that gets them again and again to go in there and take students who are not initially interested in this topic and get them excited about it.

MM: Is there a good philosophy curriculum?

MN: I think there shouldn't be any single such thing. It would be foolish. I think you have to know your own particular students and where they're coming from and what's likely to get them excited. Because the main thing is to get students drawn in.

MM: You can't just say, here's a good curriculum—everybody should be teaching this.

MN: Any general curriculum indicts itself by its very generality. No, the good courses are the ones where people have thought, let's say, my students are religiously conservative. They may think that argument itself is a subversion of their faith, so my job is to get them interested in giving reasons for what they do at all. Now that's one kind of curriculum. A very different kind would be at a place like Brown, where I taught for many years, where students are all too familiar with arguments and they're cynical about it and they think, well, an argument is just a tool of imperialism. And so then they, too, need to learn to care about arguments but from a rather different direction. So good teachers have got to be teachers for the particular students they have.

MM: Okay, so ultimately it comes down to good teachers? Are good teachers good philosophers? Are good philosophy teachers good philosophers?

MN: I think they're good philosophers. They don't always write a lot. In fact, they don't always publish a lot, but I don't care about that. I mean, they think well and they teach well.

MM: You know a lot of people look out there and they say, let's not introduce them to a philosophy course because it's all logical analysis. I don't want, I don't need to know any of that stuff.

MN: Well, of course, if you just say, here's a course on formal logic, that's a very dumb way to approach students who haven't taken philosophy before because it doesn't get them excited. But, on the other hand, let me just go back to this course at Bentley. They started by talking about Socrates and his life and death and then they actually showed a film about Socrates. And the student who I followed most particularly got really hooked by this movie and he said, I could just see that funny man just walking around and asking questions. And he was reading Plato's *Apology* and *Crito* when I met him. And I should add that I met him because he worked in my health club and I was coming in to use the gym and I saw this guy reading Plato and I thought, this is interesting. And I think I'll talk to him and so I did all the way through the course. Now, after Plato they did do some formal logic and they did it in a way that was not too protracted, but they just gave them some basic techniques of inference and he actually loved it because he found that he could do it. He had never respected his own mind before. He thought, I'm a dumb guy going into business and he could figure out these patterns of inference and then he got a sense of self-command and self-regard that was really very touching when I talked to him. And then after that they put that to work analyzing newspaper editorials, political speeches, and saying where is there a fallacious argument in this speech? And finally, they went on to have debates about issues of the day and he was assigned to argue against the death penalty, although, in fact, he favors it. And that, he said to me, gave him, for the first time, the idea that you could argue in favor of a position that you don't hold for yourself and that was really illuminating to him because, as you know, you can imagine kids brought up on talk radio, Rush Limbaugh, and so on, they are going to think that is what an argument is. You make your claim and the other person shouts you down, you shout louder, and so on, so he got the idea that there is a thing that's understanding the position on the other side. So all of that was done with enough formal logic to make it work because you have to talk about that, you can't get very far in philosophy if you don't talk about valid and invalid arguments. But, of course, if she had just come in there and said here's a logic text, now let's go through it, that would have been deadly. And it's deadly for students at all levels.

Martha Nussbaum

MM: Let me ask you about another Greek notion that might be obsolete, especially these days, the concept of virtue. Does virtue matter at the end of the twentieth century?

MN: I think we have to ask what it means, first of all, because there are lots of different conceptions of virtue and some of them are very antiphilosophical and some views of virtue say you become virtuous by subordinating yourself to an authoritative tradition. You become virtuous by developing habits that you never question. Now all of the major philosophical conceptions of virtue say that virtue requires constant reflection and critical questioning of tradition. Actually that's why I rather strongly object to the title that's been given to this World Congress, Paideia, because I think in the Greek tradition, that word was strongly linked with the authoritative, don't question, just get acculturated kind of education. And the philosophers were big critics of Paideia because they thought virtue is something else. It requires more inwardness, more taking charge of your own reasoning. So I think virtue matters if you think about it in the right way. But, I would not . . .

MM: Virtue is not morality?

MN: Well, there are different conceptions of morality, so it cuts across. I mean, my conception of virtue is one that involves quite a lot of critical reflection and therefore requires us to get to know the history of our society, that image which needs to be criticized and so on. And I think the reason that it's important for philosophers today to talk about virtue is that if we talk only about which actions are right, we miss the fact that what we're doing is forming the whole personality of a person, that what morality really consists of is a way of life. It's a way of shaping your emotions as well as your actual choices. So the emphasis on virtue in the ancient Greeks brought with it the idea that not just the actions but the inner life matters for morality and that you can shape your inner life. You can become a person who doesn't hate people of another background, let's say, or you can become a person who doesn't take illegitimate pride in your wealth and your status. Those were the things that the philosophers who I work on were particularly obsessed with. Because the Stoics, for example, saw that they lived in a society where people would kill each other for being on the wrong side in gladiatorial games and everyone was obsessed with manly honor. And so they wrote, again and again, about the damages of anger and excessive attachment to honor. And they thought that virtue consisted in weaning yourself from those bad attachments, learning that honor and money don't matter as much as the society thinks they do. So it was the whole inner world that could become enlightened by philosophical reflection. I think that's a very promising evaluative idea.

MM: Well, let me ask you, do we live in a virtuous age? Do we live in an age of morality? I mean, you can turn on the news and it seems that if you're a sufficiently famous celebrity and have the right legal team, you can murder your wife.

MN: Well, of course there's never been a virtuous age in any of human history. I think our American society has a lot of resemblance to ancient Rome in the sense that we're very hooked on reputation and honor and we're all too likely to get turned on politically by hatred of people who are different. But more important, I think, than the virtuous individual—I mean it's always nice to have virtuous individuals, but you will never have a society entirely composed of virtuous individuals—is the virtue of institutions and social arrangements. That's another thing that the Greeks thought about. They thought that a good political society was one that gave all human beings enough support to be capable, if they should choose, of a certain group of major human functions, such as let's say being well nourished, being able to exercise practical reason and planning your own life, being able to participate in politics. Now what I'm concerned about is that no society that exists in the world today is a virtuous society in that institutional sense—that is, providing people with what they need if they are to be capable of the major human functions.

MM: Are we on a virtuous cycle? Is it getting better, or are we on a vicious cycle? Are we spinning down or spinning up?

MN: Well, I think there are good ideas and there are bad ideas and I would like to think that philosophy can play a role in moving us in the right direction by providing better concepts of what it is to move up. We have to have a concept of development—development is the area I work in. But if we are to make any contribution to development economics and development policy, we have to have a concept.

MM: Did the Greeks give us a model for that?

MN: Yes, I think they do. I think they gave us the idea that what we have to think about is not just gross national product per capita, not just satisfaction even, but rather how are people capable of certain central human functions? What are they actually able to do and to be. To me, this is the idea that Aristotle really contributes to modern thought about development. I've spent a number of years working on development projects, principally focused on India and on the situation of women. I've advocated this idea of human capability and human functioning, as an alternative to the impoverished and simplistic conceptions that development economics keeps trying to use, such as saying that the good country, the developing country, is the one that has a higher GNP per capita. Now you can see that that doesn't even tell you about the distribution of wealth and income. Far less does it tell you about other aspects of a human life that are not always well correlated with wealth and income.

MM: Well, let's talk about the women's rights in India. As I understand it, at the opening of the movie *The Bandit Queen* in Bombay, a movie essentially about a woman who's raped seventeen times and then becomes a bandit and wreaks revenge on men. In the audience, women cried during the rape scene, men cheered loudly. This strikes me that we're a long way from women's rights in India.

MN: Well, the situation of women in India is very bad on a number of dimensions. Thirty-two percent of women are literate and that's a major determinant of life's opportunities, employment opportunities, ability to even control your own fertility. There's compulsory education by law in every province but in a lot of the provinces, there aren't even enough teachers, or they don't show up. In a lot of rural areas there aren't even any schools. Where there are schools, girl children often don't get the chance to go to school because their families need them for child labor and the government hasn't done anything intelligent about that, or just because people think girls shouldn't be educated.

MM: Well, that sounds like a job for politics, not for philosophy.

MN: Well, the thing is, politics needs to have some sense of what norms it's moving toward. I actually think the Indian constitution is an admirable document that contains a lot of ideas that, as a philosopher, I would want to defend, so politics has had some good ideas. But, unfortunately, when economics gets into the picture, the simpler pictures of the social goal that are thrown in by neoclassical economics are likely to become dominant and we think that things are better just because GNP per capita is increasing. So the team that I have worked with has tried to put into this world of development policy a richer conception of quality of life based on an idea of human capability that comes, ultimately, from Aristotle. And, of course, it's not just a question of talking about education or political participation, but even of basic nutrition itself. The sex ratio in India is now 92 women to 100 men. It's generally thought that when women and men are given equal nutrition and health care, you get a sex ratio of 103 women to 100 men, so you figure there's a large number of what my colleague Amartya Sen has called missing women—that is, women who we think probably would have been there if they had had nutrition and health care equal to that given to men.

MM: Well, let me play devil's advocate a moment. I'm the CEO of a global corporation and I'm going to open up a plant in Bangalore and I say to you, it's nice we talk about politics, we talk about philosophy, but I'm going to build a plant there and we're going to hire women. And if you want to improve the lot of women, then get more plants like mine there because we're going to get them out of the house, we'll give them a job, we're going to give them economic independence. They're going to learn on the job and gain skills. Spare me all the philosophy, let's talk commerce. If you're going to get these people out of this, these women out of this predicament, it's going to be commerce that does it.

MN: Well, I have no objection to economic growth and I'm certainly far from being one of the people who thinks that growth is bad and that we should focus only on other goals and forget about economic growth. But I think there has to be an intelligent partnership between people who are promoting economic growth and people who have their eye on other human goals that are not always well correlated with growth. Now, if you look around India and do comparative regional studies, you find out that there are some regions that have promoted growth very successfully, but that have done nothing at all for literacy and basic health. And other regions, for example, Kerala in the south, that have done extremely well in literacy, you have 99 percent adolescent literacy in both women and men, and very well also on basic health. But Kerala actually has done very badly on economic growth. I think it would have been nice if Kerala had had a wiser economic policy in various ways and had more growth because then there would be more jobs. If you, as a manager, came to Kerala, you wouldn't stay, because the unions have driven wages up so high that often businesses move elsewhere—that's the source of the problem. But if you did come, I would welcome you if I were a policymaker there, but I wouldn't think that that by itself solved all the other sorts of problems.

MM: Let's make you a policymaker. As a philosopher and a writer, what can you contribute to what is a millennium-old question and problem in a particular society?

MN: Obviously, I have to learn a lot about real life and that's why I spent a lot of time going around to women's development projects with activists. I try to see and talk to as many people as I can because I don't think I can do philosophy well if I'm just sitting in my office in Chicago, trying to dream up what would be good for women in some distant part of the world. But in the end, you know what I have to contribute is a fairly abstract level of reflection that has to be responsive to practice, but the idea would be to provide a rich conception of the foundations of some basic political principles of human well-being that can guide public policy.

MM: Which takes us back to the Greeks again, the idea of a good life.

MN: That's right. I mean, the Greeks were in a developing country and people forget about that. We often think they were modern Europeans, but in fact they were living in an extremely poor country and Aristotle talks about things like how we should get a pure water supply and how far from the coast should we build the city. Both Plato and Aristotle were city planners.

MM: So is a good philosopher a good social engineer?

MN: I think a good philosopher needs to work in partnership with a lot of different people, that is, people on the ground who know the local conditions, people who are policymakers who can implement what the philosopher will do and then, also, they need to know some economics and work with people who know more economics than they do. But they shouldn't be uncritical of what they hear from any of these sources, and they should retain a certain critical independence that comes from their own reflection on their alternative theories of justice that the tradition offers. I think that what I put out, I hope that I will be able to write it well enough and vividly enough that someone gets interested in it and that it means something to them, so that people of these many different sorts will then be influenced by it and take it up and do with it something that I myself couldn't possibly do, because I'm not a politician.

MM: I'm curious about something. We're both professional writers. Are you a writer more than you are a philosopher or the other way around? If you had to give up one for a while, which one would you give up?

MN: For me the two go together very deeply. I mean, I do philosophy in writing, so I couldn't do philosophy orally. That just isn't my way. I might adjust to it.

MM: One difference between you and the Athenian tradition.

MN: No, I mean Socrates didn't write, all the others did. I think Socrates had some interesting reasons for not writing, but in the society that we're in where writing is so important in reaching people of different backgrounds, I think it's very important to me to write and for me also, I think it's important to use language in a literary way in order to grab people's imaginations. That's—for me—how I reach out and how I'm able to communicate something to people who live at a distance.

MM: So you're doing the same marketing of philosophy that the Greeks were doing against the other ideas and schools?

MN: Well I try my best and, you know, I learned a lot from studying the Stoics and the Epicureans because they're the most similar in the sense that they lived already in a culture that was widely dispersed. I mean the Roman Stoics were living already in the Roman Empire and they're thinking, how shall I write Latin in order to reach people who come from Spain, who come from Armenia, who come from Parthia, but Latin is what they all know something about. So how am I going to write in order to grab them and get them to think about why they should question their culture? Now they talk a lot about this and they say that you have to arrest the person, you have to give vivid examples written in highly colored language. Well, I tried to do something like that.

MM: What Cicero said, you have to paint the statues with blood so people remember them.

MN: Well, yes, and you know at the beginning of all their treatises there are usually vivid descriptions of the bad thing that they're trying to rebut, or as it may be, the good thing that they're trying to promote. And I try myself, the way I do this is just to talk about particular women. I will tell some stories of a woman and try to make her life come to life, so that all the different elements that I'll go on to focus on in the philosophical part of the writing will be there in people's imaginations.

MM: She stops being a cipher. You subjectify her. You make her into somebody we can identify with.

MN: Somebody that we can identify with because I think our philosophical culture has forgotten about good writing. That wasn't always the case: William James, Dewey. But, of course, many people in the tradition before that were wonderful writers. Bertrand Russell was a great writer when he wrote about politics. There was a tremendous style that grabbed people's imaginations. But, in our graduate programs that's not rewarded, that's not what the journals will publish. I think we need to think of ourselves as playing two roles: one inside the Academy and one when we try to reach a broader public and sometimes you can combine those quite well. I always think that I can try to write both for the academic and for the broader audience, but then there are times when you want to do two different kinds of writing. But whatever people do, I think they shouldn't forget that they're part of a world of human beings who are out there and whose lives can be changed by philosophy. Some people do this simply in their teaching, not in their writing. And I deeply honor those people because I think they do a tremendous job and they change our country for the better. I myself, of course, I teach also, but I reach more people through writing than by teaching. I think we need all those kinds of philosophers. We must always remember that we're not just talking to each other in the Academy, but we have a duty to use some part of the relatively privileged lives that we have to make human life better.

MM: Let me ask you a question, as a classicist. I've noticed a surprising number of people are reading Gibbon right now. As a classicist, I know it's a cliché, but our time seems to be more Roman than it does Grecian. Do you buy that?

MN: I find that I recognize us in the Romans.

MM: We have a shining example of Periclean Athens and we've been haunted by that for thousands of years now, like this lost paradise. And yet we don't seem to be even heading toward that...

MN: Well, first of all, we don't know much about Athens. I think one reason the Romans seem familiar is we have their letters, we know something about their family life, we just know a lot more about their daily life than we do about the Greeks. And if we knew more about the Greeks, I don't know, would they seem more familiar or less? As a woman, I certainly find that in Rome there was much more discussion of women's opportunities and women's role and there was much more interest in equal education of women. Women were playing a much bigger role in the political life and marriage was more of a companionate affair in Rome. So in those ways, as a woman, I find it much easier to identify with the Romans. But I also think that our vices are, in some ways, Roman vices: excessive money making, excessive attachment to honor, and excessive anger. Now maybe Greek political culture was marred by those same vices but we don't know quite as much about how pervasive it was because the Roman philosophers have just told us so much about the vices of their culture. So I think it's easy to identify with the Romans in many ways.

MM: You've written that for thousands of years women have been called emotional and that's been used to exclude women from full membership in humanity and to shape often in ways detrimental to their own flourishing the moral education of men. Has that changed? It doesn't sound like it's changed in India. Has it changed in the United States?

MN: Well, I think in India, you can't make any generalization. I would want to insist that there are many men who are profound feminists and, of course, the people I work with are among them, and so I wouldn't want to make any generalizations on that score but...

MM: But you can render large judgments. You're a philosopher, that's your job.

MN: No, I don't think you should say things that are untrue. Why should you? But, men, I think, have often in many cultures been brought up to think that sympathy is soft or that compassion for the weak is beneath the manliness of a manly man, and so on. And I see that in some of my law students who I teach in Chicago. I'm sure it's also the case in some of the men in politics in India. There's a certain amount of saber rattling and macho posturing that's going on in the surroundings of their nuclear debate.

MM: Is that all culturally created or is some of that hardwired in?

MN: Well, I think that we don't know. I think that what John Stuart Mills said in 1869 is still true today—that is, that we're just not in a position to say what natural differences there may be between the sexes because no one has ever done the work that would separate out the influence of culture from whatever biological difference there may be. We know that very young children are already held differently, played with differently in accordance with the sex that people think the baby has. There's so much good research along those lines that we know that culture creeps in very early and women are led to be one thing and men another thing, regardless of what natural difference there may be. So maybe some day we'll have information about that, but we certainly don't right now.

MM: Now, let's go back to Greece again. Greece is not a monolithic story. I mean, there's Periclean Greece, there's also Peloponnesian War Greece. There are golden ages and there are times of the barbaric. As you look at our time, with all the cues you have from the ancient world, where are we and where are we going?

MN: Well, I think that we have an opportunity to move in a more Periclean direction, meaning making a democracy more genuinely deliberative, making it more an exchange of argument and less just an exchange of rhetorical posturing. We have an opportunity to move more in the direction represented by Cleon and the decline of the Athenian democracy, that is where people just trade slogans and rhetorical postures and they don't really deliberate at all. And I think technology can help or hurt; it can be a deliberative instrument, but it isn't right now, at least TV isn't right now. A lot of intelligent thinking is being done by people who think about the media, about how we can influence it to be more of an aid to political deliberation. I just hope some of that thinking prevails because it's a very important issue.

MM: How about you, Martha, when you wake up at 3:00 A.M., what world do you think we're heading into? Are you optimistic or pessimistic?

MN: When I wake up at 3:00 A.M., I like to think about something concrete. I'm more likely to think about some particular woman whose life might get better. I think that what is important is that people, one by one, should have better lives and I would be very happy if anything I write makes anyone's life better. I'm not so concerned with cosmic visions of progress or decline really.

MM: I have a question about something you wrote once. Love looks different from different angles. What do you mean by that? Should a philosopher look differently at love than everybody else?

MN: Well, what I meant is that when you're writing philosophy, that's often a posture of reflective detachment from a concrete experience and, it's no accident, I think, that philosophers who write from that perspective are often rather harsh toward romantic love and critical of it. What I was suggesting there is if philosophy's aim is to describe the truth, then it has to be willing to immerse itself in the messier, darker aspects of human experience, and to write partly from within that experience. Well, of course, remembered, recollected, whatever, but, you know, philosophers often refuse themselves that immersion in the messier emotions because they think that it's bad form or it's not really philosophy. So I was trying to nudge and goad our profession to go back to where I think Lucretius, Seneca, and some of the ancient thinkers wonderfully were— that is being willing to talk about fear, love, anger as people who had experienced that and who understood what that was like on the inside.

MM: Now, we're going back to the Greeks again. Was the old, age-long question the tension between reason versus passion? That philosophers given a chance will run from passion as fast as they can and hide out in reason?

MN: Well, I think that contrast is a very inaccurate, misleading contrast and a lot of my effort is to say that there is no such thing as a contrast between reason and passion because if you think of the passions right, they are intelligent modes of evaluation. They contain thoughts. When you fear, it involves the thought that something bad and significantly bad is going to happen to you. When you're angry, it involves the thought that something that somebody has done is damaging. And so on. So the passions are not unintelligent. And insofar as the ancient Greeks contrasted them with reason, they thought they were contrasting one kind of reasoning with another kind. That is, the contrast was between reasons that ascribe a lot of importance to attachment, outside yourself and, on the other hand, reasons that ascribed very little importance to anything outside your own thinking and reflection. So when the Stoic said, get rid of the passions and cling to reason, they thought that meant get rid of this particular train of reasoning and cling to this other one. And I think that's the right way to pose the problem. I don't come out in the same place as the Stoics on the conclusion, but I think they set up the problem of the emotions in the right way. And the question they pose is, how much room in a good human life should I allocate to attachments that pose a lot of my good in something outside me that I don't perfectly control?

MM: You talked about experiencing the world, experiencing the darker, messier things. Philosophers in the past oftentimes came from the outside world, you know, you could be a Caesar, you could be Marcus Aurelius, or even an essayist like Montaigne, you come home from a lifetime fighting wars, settle down to a time of meditation and writing. Are we training our philosophers today wrong? Should we say, go drive a cab?

MN: Well, I say something next to that in something that I recently wrote. I think our generation is particularly vulnerable to this ivory tower lack of experience because we were the first generation of philosophers that hasn't had to do military service. I say that because I think everyone who I knew who tried to get out of the Vietnam war did. I, of course, was not in that position of even having to think how to get out of it. So we didn't even have that occasion to learn about other occupations, other ways of life, people of different social class, different nationality. So I think we're a very ignorant lot and we must, if we're going to write political philosophy anyway, go out and see more of the world from a different angle. I'm very moved by Cicero, who in 44 B.C., shortly before he died, was so dedicated to the job of philosophy that while he's on the run in the countryside, while his enemies are trying to find him to assassinate him, he's also writing off to his philosophical buddy saying, send me this manuscript of Posidonius because I need it. And he wrote the work *On Duties*, which is probably the most influential work in the history of Western political thought, work read by all statesmen from so many countries. By the way, in Africa, Joe Appiah, political leader in Ghana, had two books on his bedside table, Cicero's *On Duties* and the Bible. So it's a work that's had tremendous worldwide influence. And Cicero was writing this while he himself was doing politics, trying to escape from his enemies. I wish we had more philosophers like that, combining the two worlds, because I think that the reason that work is good and has had that influence is because it's real and statesmen read it and they know it's real.

MM: It's got the sweat and the dirt of real life. Okay, my last question: what do you like best about what you do?

MN: I like it all. I don't like these questions about one thing, but I suppose the writing I like best is based on experience.

MM: I knew you were a writer at heart.

MN: Well, I mean I would if I had to give up teaching, I probably would be willing to do that, so writing by comparison to teaching and certainly serving on committees I could do away with immediately. Answering the mail I could do away with yesterday. But, the writing to me is only worth doing if it comes out of something else that I also do and that is going and learning about people and what their problems are so that whole parcel of things, the work before the writing and the writing, that is what I like.

MM: Martha Nussbaum, thanks for joining us.

TU WEI-MING

*The Complex Bridges between
China and the West*

Tu Wei-ming, Director of Harvard-Yenching Institute, Professor of Chinese History and Philosophy, Department of East Asian Languages and Civilizations at Harvard University. Professor Tu, one of the foremost Chinese scholars outside of China, has previously appeared on a Bill Moyers program and gives an enlightening portrayal of Chinese world relations, touching on such topics as Confucian humanism and the public intellectual.

MM: Michael Malone   **TW:** Tu Wei-ming

MM: Okay. Wei-ming, let me read you something that's absolutely extraordinary. "We are estranged from our cultural traditions and estranged from our own communities. As we become increasingly subjectivistic, individualist and narcissistic, we can neither remember the old nor instruct the young. We are politically isolated and spiritually alone." Pretty strong words.

TW: Strong, but I feel strongly about it.

MM: It's true for the whole world?

TW: Oh, it's the new human condition. That is depressing. Part of the reason is the emergence of a very powerful modern consciousness which seems to be so arrogant, so self-centered that the rest of the world, the history, other forms of existence in the world are all marginalized.

MM: Now, there's one more sentence on this quote, which strikes me as a rather devastating critique of philosophy. "Yet, in our early scholarly endeavors, we assume that we have to take an impersonal stance in order to reason objectively."

TW: Well, I also feel very strongly about this. I first came to the States in '62 to study philosophy at Harvard. The three areas of philosophy that I considered important and legitimate and that I personally found very meaningful were ethics, aesthetics, and religion. Ethics, the whole question about how we live our life. Aesthetics, how we relate meaningfully and find beauty in the world around us. And, of course, religion, our ultimate concern. These three areas were considered not only marginal; they were not meaningful. Professional philosophers were only interested in epistemology, logic, philosophy of language and mind. But mind is very much still conditioned by the Cartesian idea of thinking, abstract ideas rather than the concrete way of living.

MM: Every philosopher I've talked to, I've asked the same question: Why did this happen to philosophy at a time when it was needed the most in the twentieth century, during this incredibly bloody century? Where does philosophy go?

TW: There was a major change. After the First World War, some of the most creative minds in the West were fascinated by cultures outside of the West. Some of them became interested in the *Book of Change*, the Taoist text that teaches us that learning is the accumulation of knowledge. But the pursuit of the Tao is to unlearn, to try to purify our mind, to purify our soul. And some great thinkers, like the theologian Martin Buber, the psychologist Carl Jung, and quite a number of other scholars, were fascinated by these ideas. But, after the Second World War, a certain kind of complacency set in. The feeling was that the West is the area where most of the great ideas occurred. Therefore, there's no need for us to learn from other civilizations. And also there's a quest for purity, a sense that the real method, the real important issues, the thing that can be argued and empirically proved. Anything that cannot be demonstrated by some kind of narrowly defined methodology is considered either meaningless or irrelevant.

MM: Was this because science just seemed so damn successful?

TW: That's part of it.

MM: Why not follow that model?

TW: Try to emulate science or try to say, well, that philosophy is the handmaid of science. You know, originally philosophy, as a comprehensive vision of our human flourishing, opened up all kinds of new possibilities. But, in the post Second World War period, there was this kind of closing of the philosophical mind and an effort to emulate what the scientists could do. And that shift, I think, whether you call it a scientific turn or later a linguistic turn or even a pragmatic, if not disastrous, a significant narrowing of the philosophical mind.

MM: So what message does Confucianism bring?

TW: Well, one deep concern of the Confucian tradition is learning to be human but not as an isolated individual, nor as an island. A human being is always understood as the center of relationships. So there's a relationship between the center and human relatedness.

MM: Confucianism talks about improving the self through knowledge. It's a different self.

TW: It's the self. It's a complicated issue, but the self, as we experience it, as we understand it, it's not simply the *cogito*. You know, the famous Cartesian notion that if I think, if I reflect, then my existence is based upon the thinking self. This is an abstract universal understanding of the self. But the Confucian idea of the self which is embodied, the idea of the self includes feeling, willing, thinking, sensing, all of them. Learning to be human is to learn how we can interact fruitfully with other human beings.

MM: So, it denies the very notion of dualism, the ghost inside the machine?

TW: Certainly. But, also, it denies this whole notion that there is a clear separation between the mind and the body, or a total separation between the sacred and profane or between spiritual and material. These kinds I call exclusive dichotomies. Of course, there are dichotomies, we cannot think without dividing things into different kinds to try to understand a relationship. But if we simply say it is mental, therefore, it's not physical; if it is spiritual, then it's not material; if it's sacred, then it's not profane, then the whole idea is impoverished because what we need is a fully embodied, not only the body, but mind and heart and soul and spirit. The learning of the human involves all these dimensions.

MM: And this is where we bring in the idea of harmony and balance?

TW: Right. But, I think it's often misunderstood. Harmony is often misconstrued as inability to deal with conflict, with tension. If you look at the world today, even though we have a global village, it's not an integrated village. It's a village ...

MM: In this dissonant, noisy, 24–7 Internet-linked, high-speed world, I don't see a lot of harmony and balance.

TW: Not at all. And the world is divided in terms of wealth, in terms of power, accessibility to goods, to information, all kinds of things. So the harmony that Confucians look for, try to stress, is not any kind of conformity. It is an ability to work through contradictions, conflicts, and tensions, to see the balance, the possibility of balance. It's not even the Greek idea of the golden mean or moderation. In other words, if you can imagine two forces, powerful forces fighting against each, yet they just stand still. The situation, may be tension ridden, but, there's a certain kind of equilibrium. This is what the Confucians look for. It's high energy. You have to be mobilized to do things. You have to be able to take charge. You have to confront all kinds of challenges from the outside and yet you do not lose an inner equilibrium based upon your understanding of the outside world.

MM: Does this surprise your students when you talk this way? Because I would think that the Western stereotype is much more meditative, almost passive.

TW: Of course. I appreciate the whole notion about philosophy as reflection, as the contemplative mode of life. But, don't forget, the great Greek philosophers, such as Aristotle, put a greater emphasis on practice. The contemplative mode is not at all separate from the engagement in the world here now. Now, for the Confucians, a real thinker is not someone who can only reflect without being engaged in the process. That's why I use the word embodiment. There's a beautiful term, *ti*, which means the body. But, that word, *ti*, can also be used as a verb. It means just my body, but also to embody. The embodiment is a process of understanding other human beings experientially as well as intellectually and spiritually. So, in that sense, the conflict and tension that we experience ought to be harmonized at a higher level of integration. So sometimes the word *harmony* may not be as good as the word *optimization, maximization*.

MM: That's an interesting word.

TW: The optimization . . .

MM: As a business writer, I mean, it sounds like, that's a business term.

TW: It's also an engineering term.

MM: Absolutely.

TW: The notion is that, in a finite system, you take advantage of all the forces, conflictual forces, and try to work on the best solution. Of course, every one of us suffers from the veil of ignorance. There are so many things we do not know. So many factors we would not be able to fully understand. And, in this finite situation, we consider all the possibilities to come up with the best solution. It is simply contradiction for contradiction's sake or whether there's a harmony which is to undermine the various kinds of conflictual forces. Therefore—marginalize others? No. It is a way of understanding all these conditions and putting them together. That optimization is real harmony.

MM: Now, in a world, though, where there's a hamburger fast food place on every corner and cable television and web sites and all of these things, it would seem that philosophies like Confucianism are in retreat from this fast-moving technological, scientific, empirical world.

TW: Yes. On the surface, we may think that the globalization based upon finance, multinational corporations, even tourism, and, of course, even disease, that this kind of rapid transformation is so overwhelming that we can only react to what has happened. And the kind of reflective mode, the kind of thinking about world issues is too much of a luxury. But, now, the question is different. There's a tremendous sense of urgency. If we allow this process to continue without reflection, we confuse information with wisdom. We confuse knowledge with human flourishing, because, you know, this whole notion of educated incapacity will become highly informed, will become very knowledgeable, and yet we do not live meaningful lives. We cannot interact fruitfully with other human beings. We do not understand ourselves. And now the big question is how we will be able to understand and develop ourselves by cultivating human relationships that are meaningful and understanding that we are an integral part of a much larger universe, not just a human universe, but a cosmic process, how everything is linked together. One thing that Confucians very early on developed is to see at least four dimensions: the self, community, nature, and heaven. These four will have to be integrated between the self and community. They ought to be continuous, fruitful interaction. Community, of course, is variously understood as a family or even the global community. Then, the whole human species, the relationship of human species to nature. Hopefully, there is a sustainable, harmonious relationship. And there's also the human heart and mind with the Way of Heaven. Hopefully, there is mutuality or responsiveness. So, it is in this sense there's some, on the surface, idealism. But I think each one of them is so important that we have to pay special attention to it if we want to live a meaningful life in the world or even if we simply want to survive.

MM: Make me your student here for a moment. Explain to me the differences between things. Taoism seems to be sort of the romantic, beguiling side and Confucianism much more the conservative philosophy. Well, give me the differences. Distinguish them for me.

TW: Within Chinese philosophy, there's a major debate between the Confucians and the Taoists and yet we have to understand that the two traditions merged, not totally integrated, merged into a whole to develop a character we call the Chinese mind-set. From the Confucian point of view, we are in the world here now. We are engaged. This worldly. We have to work through the power relationships, the social political structures. We cannot totally abandon the world and say, let's create a spiritual sanctuary out there and let's just live the meaningful life separate from humanity. Confucius said, "I cannot herd with birds and beasts, I have to be a man among other human beings." So there's a critical choice of being an integral part of the world. The Taoists say, no, you don't have to be. It's possible for you to cultivate your inner spirituality outside of human relationships. Now the Confucians say, look, you really have to take politics seriously. Human beings are political animals. Even though you don't like all these politicians, you don't like the status quo. But yet you cannot afford not to become an integral part of a political system, but you do not accept the status quo. You change it from within. You become committed to some broad humanistic ideas. The Taoists would say, almost like Thomas More, if you get soaked in the rain, no matter how you try to do it, you will not be able to clean yourself, so get rid of politics. You don't have to do it. And the Confucians say, look, family relationships are so important for us, especially the parental relationship, but all five relationships, husband and wife, sibling relationships, friendship, or even the relationship between ruler and minister—by implication, between those who are in control and those who have to serve. But, the Taoists say, no, you have to get rid of these relationships. The only relationship that is meaningful is the relationship between you and nature, to be consanguineous. No, the Chinese mind-set is shaped by these two conflicting trains and, yet, somehow . . .

MM: Is there a hybridization taking place?

TW: It's not hybridization. Of course, you can say failed integration is a hybridization; it's eclectic. So some people say you become weekend Taoists. When you have to teach, you have to work, you have to be a Confucian, then you become weekend Taoists. Some people say when you're young, engaged in the world, you are a Confucian. When you retire, you become a Taoist. When you are in the office, you are Confucian. When you are out of the office, then you become a Taoist. I think this is a rather superficial understanding of a kind of a hybridization. The other one is to say the human condition is such that there are occasions that we need to be involved. But that involvement does not necessarily lead to total obsession with the world. But this interested experience, which is philosophically sound, it's not uninterested, just disinterested. And that spirit, to look at it from a distance, to reflect, to understand it, to see the interplay, to be contemplative but, at the same time, you are passionately engaged in transforming the world. These two modes can actually shape an integrated personality with powerful inner resources. Unfortunately, in modern China, many young people have no access to the great traditions. They become totally overwhelmed by the market, by the quest for simply one's own fame or one's own glory, and some of the resources are being marginalized.

MM: Well, then, let me ask you if we look at the People's Republic of China and with this fifty years of a sort of a secular religion called Communism . . .

TW: Socialism, Yes.

MM: We look at Hong Kong with its rampant free-market capitalism. Can we see both of these as suggesting a failure of Confucianism?

TW: To a certain extent, yes. It failed miserably in terms of modern Chinese transformation because it was marginalized; it was no longer taken seriously.

MM: Okay, can we see this as a failure of Confucianism?

TW: On the surface, it not only failed, it failed miserably. In a comparative cultured perspective, the Confucian tradition.

MM: So what, why didn't they have enough robustness to counter this, this twentieth century trend?

TW: Well, on the surface they have failed, but if you look at habits of the heart of the people—in other words, how they react to forces from the outside, how they find personal gratification, what are some of the values they cherish in the privacy of their home, how they deal with friends, deal with relatives, and so forth, and how they faced up to the challenge of the outer world, and how they relate to not only their family but to their school, to their village or to their society as a whole—they managed to tap into all these cultural resources to help them to develop some kind of stability of life, a certain kind of motive force for social transformation, for the transformation of themselves. So, even though for fifty years Confucianism was somewhat marginalized from official ideology, in terms of how people behave, some people say the cultural DNA is not being wiped away. It's still there. Not just waiting to re-emerge, it's still functioning. People judge others' characters; they judge politics. For example, when the students demonstrated against corrupt government, they didn't think they were isolated individuals. They thought they were members of an elite or even a social conscience. They tried to react to the challenge of the state as a group . . .

MM: The Tiananmen protesters—were they speaking the language of Confucianism?

TW: Very much so. Some of them were conscientiously doing that.

MM: In the West, how would we have read that? I mean, it wasn't self-evident to us they were using those terms.

TW: Actually, they do if we say they use many, many examples from Chinese history. They used the example of righteous ministers. Examples of students, student demonstration are a major feature of Chinese politics. The Han Dynasty, the first established Chinese dynasty in, say, the third century B.C., to third century A.D., collapsed partly because of a student demonstration. The house arrest of the intellectuals was one of the serious mistakes made by the dynasty. In the eleventh century, student demonstrations inspired some of the citizens and more than 300,000 people surrounded the court demanding the corrupt officials be punished. And the dynasty was in grave danger. But, one of the most important academies in the seventeenth century, called the Donglin Academy, and they criticized the government. There's a beautiful couplet: see the sound of the wind, the sound of the rain, and the sound of reading classics, each sound, entered into our ear, the affairs of the world, the affairs of the nation, or the affairs of the family, each affair is our personal affair. This couplet was used during Tiananmen all the time. Everybody could recite it. The students consider themselves as the conscience of society or conscience of the people.

MM: And, the government knew . . .

TW: The government knew about it.

MM: But, in a sense, they were operating from the same history and the same base of knowledge and the same residual Confucianism.

TW: Precisely. Absolutely.

MM: So there was a debate going on in Tiananmen that we in the West, we weren't even privy to.

TW: In the debate, I would call it politicized Confucian rhetoric, which is a kind of authoritarian mechanism of control. You should be, you should consider yourself youngsters. You should respect the old, respect authority, respect solidarity of the country. Don't mess up the situation. We're still involved in the development of the economy. Students said the corrupt government was against the general welfare of the people. We're not fighting for our own narrowly defined self-interests. We're fighting for the future of the country, also fighting for other walks of life because, students, as students, ought to be responsible not just for the meaning structure of the society, but the well-being of the society as a whole.

MM: It seems to me that's a perfect example of the opaqueness of the conversation taking place in China for us in the West—it's opaque to us. We hear things but we don't hear the encoded meanings behind it.

TW: Yes. There are a lot of fascinating things going on.

MM: And, for example, the recent press conference between the leaders, you know the President of the United States and China's leader. The language being said had Western connotations. But you had the sense that the connotations of those words were different in China.

TW: Right. Yes. One fascinating thing in the exchange was China's clear misreading or misunderstanding of Tibet as a cultural universe. And this, of course, is a very complicated issue. The mind-set now is for scientific development, for modernization, for economic progress. The ruling ideology is to say everything should be understood in terms of the national commitment to a modernization defined in terms of economic and political terms. But the broader issue is to say, at what cost? What kind of process? What kind of life? What is a good life? What is the true meaningful way of being Chinese? Now, the reason why it's difficult for the Chinese leadership to understand Tibet is because this mind-set, which I call scientism, is a commitment to modernization and Tibet is immediately understood as backward, as a case purely defined in terms of economic and political relationships.

MM: Is this the communist idea of the perfectibility of man . . .

TW: No, not just the perfectibility of man. The whole notion is also very powerful in the Enlightenment mentality, that is, human progress from religion to metaphysics or philosophy, then to science. And there's a powerful sense of social engineering. The leaders will be able to organize everything according to a unified system of ideas. But this, of course, Havel has argued is very devastating for the human spirit. So, if the Chinese leaders, I'm hopeful, begin to appreciate some of the cultural resources—for example, in India and by broadening their cultural perspectives—they would begin to understand Tibetan Buddhism, religious Taoism, or Taoist philosophy and Confucianism. These religious traditions, powerful traditions, in fact, still help us to understand what is the meaning of being human. What is the meaning of a good life. And they would then look at Tibet not simply as a serious political issue, but also as a cultural concern, as shareable ideas about human flourishing. Now it's an attitudinal change. Some people say you're too idealistic; they will never change their mind. I don't believe that's the case. If they begin to appreciate that what Tibet symbolizes is a beautiful culture that has its right to not only survive, but to flourish, this will be beneficial for China.

MM: Isn't it ironic that the scientific West is the defender of this traditional culture? And it's personified by, you know, His Holiness the Dalai Lama, while China sees it as this anachronistic state that needs to be modernized.

TW: You're absolutely right. You see, what is happening is that within the defenders of a scientistic point of view, you cannot find too many of them in Cambridge, Massachusetts, or in Berkeley, or, for that matter, in Oxford or Cambridge. But you do find a great deal of them in Beijing, in Hong Kong, or Taiwan. But the situation is changing very rapidly because within the core of the Enlightenment of the West, there's a very serious concern about human spirituality, about religion, about human flourishing. It is in this sense that in the English language community, the Dalai Lama is understood as a holy man, as a man with incredible spiritual force and commitment. Whereas, in China, he is understood as a political separatist, as someone who is very deeply committed to an outmoded form of life. But China is going to be changed. When China opens up to all kinds of possibilities, the intellectual community will begin to see new possibilities and there will be a new negotiation and I'm quite hopeful that the Confucian tradition, you know, humanistic . . .

MM: So you're saying that the Confucian heart of China understands. But the political superstructure of China does not yet?

TW: I would not put it exactly that way. I would say a highly politicized Confucian mode of control, which is linked to socialism, to a modernization project, is now in conflict with Confucianism as a broad humanistic concern for human flourishing. That, even though there's a conflict, there are also areas of communication. In other words, if the Chinese leaders begin to appreciate not just technological competence, but cultural competence; not just economic capital, but also social capital—you know, through communication and so forth—not just cognitive intelligence, but also ethical intelligence; not just material conditions, but spiritual values as well; and to understand what some of our colleagues call the soft power, the soft power is to allow other people to appreciate your values. If people appreciate your values, your influence becomes greatly extended. Now the Confucian tradition in China, among other things, has created an arena in which power and wealth are not necessarily the most influential forces in the world. In other words, a group of people who are neither powerful in the political sense, nor wealthy in the economic sense; still, because they are educated, because they are reflective, because they are concerned about the broader picture, they are still extremely influential. That's the reason why the scholar officials, the literate in China, continue to be very influential. They are neither powerful nor rich, but they are influential. The influence is moral influence, spiritual influence, cultural influence. China understands that. How to exercise that influence, even Mao Zedong understands it. But it could be demonized. It could be mobilized for the wrong reason and I hope that, by now, some of the Chinese intellectuals have begun to appreciate their own power by changing their attitude and trying to challenge, I think in a very good sense, the official interpretation. Also to broaden the Chinese concern for their own society, especially for the marginalized, for the underprivileged.

MM: As someone with a unique vantage point of being able to look from the outside in: What does your gut tell you? Where does this conflict go? How does it end?

TW: I was born in China, raised in Taiwan. But, since '78, I've been back to mainland China and I taught at Peking University in 1985, for the first time in thirty, forty years, a course on Confucian philosophy. And I told them that I'm going to teach it sympathetically. I tried to argue the point that I felt very, very strongly about this. And they accepted it. And that was the beginning of opening up a new public space for debate on these kinds of issues, because I see the authentic possibility—even though it is extremely difficult to be realized—between fruitful interaction between Confucian humanism and liberal democratic ideas in the context of the socialist country in China. We have to remember that after the collapse of the Soviet Union, there are still a few socialist countries in the world. China is one of them, Vietnam and, of course, the bad example of North Korea.

MM: With 1.3 billion people, we don't forget.

TW: No. I disagree. For years and years, it's quite possible for some of the best trained American minds at Harvard, at Yale, at Berkeley, to have no knowledge whatsoever about the Pacific Ocean. You know, they travel more from the two sides of the Atlantic Ocean through a continental market. They have no knowledge about the issues of the Pacific region, their leaders. If you look at our congressional leaders, look at academic leaders, look at our business leaders, business is changing because of the power of the Pacific Ocean, but our ignorance of the outside world, especially of the Pacific region, is taken for granted. This is sharply contrasted with the situation for more than 150 years in Asia. East Asian intellectuals have been devoted students of Western learning. You know, look at the Japanese.

MM: Sure.

TW: Dutch learning, French learning, British learning, German learning and, more recently, American learning, particularly since the Second World War, America has become such a powerful center of influence, and we have become a teaching civilization to the world, especially to east Asia. Unless we now transform ourselves from the teaching civilization to become a learning civilization again, not just vis-à-vis Europe, but also vis-à-vis the Asian Pacific region, our future will not be as bright as it ought to be. I think, in this sense, it's a very serious matter. Over 1.3 billion people could be totally silenced, could not represent any kind of voice anywhere, if we do not pay special attention to the cultural resources.

MM: But you noticed a change in the last two or three years, if nothing else, by fear. The notion, the realization that this is, this may become a bipolar world again and the other superpower is China and China has 1.3 billion people and it has nuclear weapons and it has a multimillion man army. There's no denying it. So the question then is—back to your gut feeling. The great fear is every time China has gone through the end of a dynasty it's also undergone enormous internal convulsions. So, I'm asking you, what do you feel? How is this one going to end? This transition.

TW: First, let me point out that ever since the Opium War until the founding of the People's Republic, for that very long 100 years, every ten-year period was major change. Convulsive change in China. The Tauping Rebellion, the internecine warfare relating to the warlords, and, of course, the confrontation with the Communists and the Nationalists, of course, Japanese aggression, and so forth. Since the founding of the People's Republic in '49, gradually China became stable and, yet, every five years there was some kind of change. Cultural Revolution, the great leap forward, and all these calamities happened in China. The neighbors were not affected. The Asian Pacific region was not aware. And the Western countries, America, became totally oblivious. But, since '79, China's linked to a very large global community. And anything dramatic that happened in China will have major impact on China's neighbors, the Asian Pacific Region, and so forth. So what we want to see is not China purely defined in terms of economic power, political power, or military power. But what is the message of China's entering into the family of nations? One possibility is that we move from a bipolar confrontational world to a multicentered wholistic world. All these civilizations begin to take each other as reference points.

MM: Does Confucianism help us get there?

TW: Absolutely important. In the eighteenth century, the Enlightenment began. The most brilliant minds in the West—Voltaire, Leibniz, the encyclopedists, the physiocrats, took China as the most important reference society and Confucianism as the most important reference culture. Many of them would become very much attracted to Confucian ideas of rationality, of social transformation, and so forth. In the nineteenth century, most European thinkers, including Hegel and others, did not take the East Asian cultures seriously at all. And, now, in the twenty-first century, China will re-emerge as an important reference point, but not just China. China only represents part of East Asia. Japan is extremely powerful, Korea and Southeast Asian countries, then South Asian countries, India in particular, but also Pakistan and many other countries, Latin American countries, eventually, even African countries as well. So what we see now is that the modernization is assuming different cultural forms, so we begin to talk about traditions in modernity. This is certainly not simply the modernizing process is going to overcome all the traditions and compel the world to become a homogenous whole defined purely in Western terms.

MM: So, Wei-ming, what's your role as a philosopher in all this?

TW: Well, to help people to think about that and to provoke the discussion, to open the public space so the people will not be simply obsessed with limited concerns so that they can have broader humanist vision about what we can become and what we ought to do. And I think we philosophers are yet to become public intellectuals, which means our concerns must extend beyond the Academy. When I define a public intellectual, I mean a person who is politically concerned, socially engaged, and culturally sensitive and informed, and is willing to address issues not in the narrow confines of their professions.

MM: So the philosopher of the twenty-first century must become more Confucian.

TW: They have to take the Confucian problematic, the Confucian idea of engagement, of transformation absolutely seriously.

TW: One thing I find fascinating is the culture message of China is not simply to say now there's another possible superpower, now we have a chance to humiliate others, to say no to the United States. This will be disastrous. I do mean it. But, there's another possibility—that is to say, look, since we've been humiliated, we suffered so much in modern history, no matter what we do, we don't want other people to suffer because of us. This is the basic principle of reciprocity: Do not do to others what you would not want others to do to you, the Golden Rule stated in the negative.

MM: Having been the victim, you don't want to become the victimizer.

TW: Right. And this is intimately linked to the idea of humanity: In order to establish myself, I help others to establish themselves. In order to realize myself, I help others to realize themselves.

MM: In order to free others, I have to free myself?

TW: Yes. That sense of mutuality, you know, interconnectedness, is to say, look, precisely because my own dignity of the person is so important, I respect every other human being for their own dignity. This is the Kantian notion that you take every person as an end, rather than simply as a means to an end. Now that sounds idealistic, but once you begin with that attitude, then you know that no nation, no matter how strong, powerful, can dictate. We can discipline Haiti, we can probably discipline Iraq, we cannot discipline any other country larger and more powerful. We need to transform the politics of domination into the politics of inclusion. And we have to learn to negotiate, to communicate with all of them. I think that sense of self-restraint is very, very powerful and important. I think we're in that stage.

MM: Wei-ming, I want to thank you for being on the show.

TW: Thank you.

JOHN J. McDERMOTT
Trumping Cynicism with Imagination

John J. McDermott, Distinguished Professor of Philosophy at Texas A&M University. Professor McDermott is one of the leading scholars of American philosophy and a renowned educator. A riveting, animated speaker, John McDermott demonstrates a vast knowledge of the history of philosophy from Plato to Dewey and the remarkable ability to apply these great thinkers to a modern context.

MM: Michael Malone   **JM:** John J. McDermott

MM: Okay, John, I've been wanting to ask you a question. I've been waiting for you to come on to ask you this, because you're the great pragmatist. Here we are at the end of the twentieth century, 100 million people dead, probably the bloodiest century in human history. The Holocaust, the great famine, all of these events, what exactly has philosophy done to help get us through all this? It seems to me philosophy has been off in a corner devising new language and symbolic logic.

JM: Yes, but no, the difficulty is that current philosophy has lost its purchase and consequently even things which are helpful have not received attribution.

MM: What do you mean by that?

JM: Well, philosophy is the lodestone for the wisdom tradition and it has been much less ideologically burdened than religion and politics. And so philosophy has been able to have a living, accruing, creating tradition which has much to say of great significance to the overall questions, but certainly less so since the thirties.

MM: Because of the Vienna circle.

JM: The Vienna circle, but also since Oxbridge analysis and since they adopted the manners of sciences—not the best of the sciences, not the intuitive character of the sciences, not the experimental sensibility of the sciences. But of the quest for certainty, as Dewey would say. That part of the sciences.

MM: But why did philosophy suddenly fall so in love with the sciences?

JM: Because in philosophy, there's a deepened insecurity in the twentieth-century intellectual which generates arrogance.

MM: Okay.

JM: And so this insecurity, wanting to get this right and so on, when as a matter of fact if you really return to tradition, you discover that ambiguity is everywhere. It is true that the Cartesian move was a move in the direction of certitude, but it was a very modest move because it didn't involve the body, it didn't involve sensorial foundation. See, he was smart enough to know that. So I want to get back to the business about the Holocaust and so on; it has to do with authority and absolutism. This does not have to do with inquiry. It has to do with taking positions before there was any evidence. And so it is the reverse of everything we believe in philosophy. There is no inquiry characteristic of the Fascist movement, whether it's on the left or on the right. The Fascist movement is a move which is a function of absolutism. And it is a function of nonreflection.

MM: So did philosophy fall victim to absolutism at the beginning of the century, too, in a sense that they looked around, they said, look what Rutherford's doing, look what Einstein's doing. They're coming up with answers. Maybe if we turn scientific we'll come up with answers, too.

JM: That has been said and you can say that. But let me say something else to you. I think that there was a reluctance to confront the fact that the really powerful questions are never going to be answered. And so what they did is they backed out, you see, into language. One of the lines was that the task of philosophy is not to diagnose experience, but analyze language. Now that line is I think a line that takes us nowhere. If I keep the first part of the line, to diagnose experience, I'm constantly confronted with setback, with mishap, with ambiguity, right? I'm confronted with, ah . . .

MM: Failure.

JM: Yes, yes, with failure, you see. And if you think that failure is not part of the meaning of growth and the meaning of the human spirit and so on, well, then, of course, you are looking for smaller and smaller versions of which you are more and more sure.

MM: But philosophers, of all people, should have been the people not afraid of failure, by definition. Is that because of the Academy? Once you go inside the walls you've got to publish, you've got to . . .

JM: Well, that's another question and it's a question which is in all realms. It's a small question compared to the one you opened up with.

MM: Yes, well I'm asking because now we're at the brink of the twenty-first century. Is anything changing?

JM: No, things are getting worse and universities are infinitely more pompous, more bloated, more insensitive, more unaware of what it was supposed to be about, and less involved in what we would call pedagogy. So the American experiment, which is the greatest of all the experiments in the history of the world, was to strive for equality across the board. That is to take seriously that everyone is educable. You know Royce once said, the popular mind is deep, knows a thousand times more than it knows, and the task of pedagogy is to enable people to see. Or in Buber's phrase to the man who challenged him in Jerusalem in '47, listen buster, you are able. You can do it, you see. I believe that; I mean, it's hard to believe that in a world in which you see less and less that's that significant. Huh? So, the university is no help.

MM: Yes.

JM: All right. I mean, the university is no help. More and more, it looks like corporate life. Less and less does it look like the agora, does it look like the monastery walk, less and less does it look like, you know, Emerson's stuff or whatever. So, more and more, I see myself and others like me, my friends, too, and all these people and so on as a remnant. It's really quite extraordinary, Mike. But then in the last . . .

MM: Do you see yourself just as a remnant?

JM: Don't say just because that's a very deep term.

MM: No, but I mean, you're talking to an Irishman.

JM: Ah, as if I didn't know.

MM: Yes, but there came a point when there was just a handful of Irishmen keeping the tradition going. Hanging on the coast.

JM: That's right.

MM: So is that what you are? Do you see yourself as that—is your duty to carry it?

JM: But, you see, the difference is that they [Irish] were keeping something right for our future.

MM: Yes.

JM: You see, we aren't keeping something that has been bypassed and remanded and absolute. It's very different.

MM: But it always comes back; it's waiting out there to come back.

JM: Well.

MM: People need it. If, because official philosophy hasn't done the job, people have looked to philosophy in other ways. They've gone to other sources. But still there is a need. You've always said, philosophy comes down to a handful of simple questions.

JM: Right.

MM: People ask those questions every single damn day. They're asking them in the offices out here in Boston right now.

JM: That's right, that's right. Well, you see, you say they look for it in other ways. Now here's my sadness, okay? I think that there's been this move toward movement toward pop stuff, quick fixes, right? And yet it's sort of a cheap and even spiritually salacious road. When, certainly you know this, but the deep things are irresolute, okay? There's a lot of trouble even in this room here, a lot of suffering, broken stuff, and so on. Now I think, you see, that I can do much better than that stuff by teaching the meditations of Marcus Aurelius. Or, for example, open with the line from Epictetus, "You should live life as if it were a banquet." Marcus Aurelius says at one point to the centurion, look, he said, see the mouse? Ah, you, me, it's all the same. How long would you live, Mike? Six years, sixty years, six hundred? What difference does it make? My friend, life is a warfare and a stranger's sojourn and after fame is oblivion. That's all there is. So warriors are frightened by this; the centurion is horrified. So he tries to do something with them. That's that whole doctrine of a stoic bond and my position is that each of the powerful philosophers has a diagnosis of this wound, you call it what you want, the fall or, I call it a walk-on, DNA, everybody has their way of doing it. Now the task is what can I do? So then you reach for healing metaphors and these healing metaphors don't have to be chintzy, I mean, they can be built into deep stuff, like a metaphysics.

MM: Yes.

JM: Spinoza says that I have an adequate idea of the mind of God. William James says the whole thing runs in a current, it's all in a flow. Dewey says, basically, we're tied to nature. We have to just see this stuff as a kind of problematic and do the best we can, and each of these, you see, they've got forty people out there. Ten said Dewey's might work, right? Okay. And then they have something to move onto. Once I teach in such a way as it's arcane, that no longer is it something that they can in any way tie to the quality and nature of their own experiences, they drop out.

MM: Right.

JM: Okay, but that's what's going on. Somehow the philosophy crowd thinks that I'm less if I'm understood. How'd we get into that—will you explain that to me?

MM: Well, it must be doubly troubling to you as a pragmatist because you know you can look out there and say, well, the whole principle of pragmatism is, pick what works, and this obviously isn't working, but nobody's dropping it.

JM: Okay, that's very good.

MM: Nobody's putting the thing down and picking up something else and saying, well, let's try this, maybe this is going to work better.

JM: Well, just for clarification, I don't use the term pragmatist for myself. I mean, I'm basically a guy who's interested in diagnosis of experiences, so I'm just as much into Camus as I am into Dewey. But you're right, you use the term *works*. And that was a term that James used, that's a beautiful American word, right? You know, in the thirties, my old man was out of work, I lived in the depression, so in the line they would say, hey, Mac, did you get work? And when, even in the forties and I was going to school and this and that, they'd say, do you have a job? Did you get work? I'm going to school. I didn't ask you that—did you get work? What does work mean? Work means, you see, this way, in which possibilities, consequences, I mean, hopes, aspirations, expectations that there's some kind of organic way in which the thing works, that's what it means—it's a beautiful word. Yeah, you're right, it's not working.

MM: We have another phrase, too. Which is, you manage to accomplish something together. Whether it's a car motor or it's your life. And it's barely going, but people point that out and you say, what the hell, it works.

JM: Exactly, exactly. And you cobble, see, that's nice, life's a cobblestone.

MM: Yeah.

JM: You say cobbles, right. You get through it, not smooth, not smooth. It's like the streets in the Bronx, right, they're not smooth. See, but you can get on them. So you're right, now. I mean there's this thing about enrollment is dropping. People aren't interested in philosophy, you know, nobody is, they just keep going. But I think another thing you see is that we, you know, John Smith, my friend, used to say that ideas die in England and come here to be reborn. And we seem to be having this thing about the intellectual. I mean, we don't seem to see it in this Emersonian, Deweyian way. Do you see? I mean, for example, Whitman opens his *Leaves of Grass* and he says, hey, he says, Mike, would you like to be taking a walk with me, and he said, remember, I don't want you to be seeing what I see. I want you to see what you see.

MM: Yeah.

JM: And that's the famous *Leaves of Grass,* we take this walk. And so, the task of pedagogy is to have you come with me, right? And then, you know, after a while you begin to see what you see. And then you tell me what you see and I say, wow. Well, we've lost a lot of that, you know that.

MM: Sure.

JM: Right. What's the word, what is the word that persons use when they say how do you feel about going to school? Boring. That's the word. You see there is no eros.

MM: Yes, boring.

JM: Well, the possibilities are extraordinary. For example, take the canon. My position is you keep the canon and you fire it. You just, throw it wide open, right? So I mean all the blacks and the women and everybody goes in the canon, you know what I mean, wide open, and so. And I would say . . .

MM: See what works.

JM: Yes, exactly, exactly. And I'm teaching Eugene O'Neill's *Long Day's Journey.* And I'm going around and so on, and this young female student, she puts up her hand and she says, I'll tell you where it is, page whatever, it is, you know, sixty-one, I think. When Mary Tyrone says, well she says, it's not his fault. These things happen to you. There's nothing you can do about them, and then you've lost your own true self. She says, that's what happened to me. Okay? Now, for someone else, it's a paragraph in *Go Tell It on the Mountain,* for someone else, it is a paragraph from Carson McCullers. For someone else, you see, it is what

Aeschylus says: wisdom comes only through suffering. I mean, I don't know, but you create this theater of possibility. Well, then, why philosophy at all? Well, because, you see, the philosophers have this girth, you know what I mean, you understand? They're not just ... there's girth here. You see. So you do the *Meditations* and they say this is serious business—you can't do this overnight. There's girth and there's a seriousness. And that takes away, then, you see, the whole "pop" aspect of it. They say, what are you going to do this weekend, Mike? Say, I'm going to read the *Meditations* of Descartes. I say, I'll see you in a month.

MM: Going in the steambath with Descartes.

JM: Okay. All right, see, and that seriousness is important because when mama dies, right? When the little one gets run over, you know what I mean. When they foreclose the house and so on, that's serious.

MM: And serious is important because life's important.

JM: Exactly. Life is serious.

MM: Yeah, it's damn serious, it's deadly serious.

JM: Deadly serious.

MM: So behind the pop side seems to me is a manifestation of the craving for somebody to help give people answers to these things, help me deal with this thing, help me take these terrible problems in my life and deal with it. Cause they're ... I'm not getting it at school.

JM: Right.

MM: I'm not getting it from the academics. I'm not getting it from the people who are supposed to be giving it to me.

JM: Right.

MM: So, let me ask you then. Take all the craving that's out there—250 million people. Is there still uniquely American philosophy hidden behind all this that's not being taught? That we're living?

JM: Well, you know, yes, that's a controversial issue. Rorty I think is a brilliant guy and he worries about the jingoism of this thing, you see. I don't worry about that because I think all the great cultures have their version of the world, I mean cultural anthropology is a discipline of the twentieth century. And so everybody does this differently. And then it gets into other questions as you well know, being Irish. I mean, guilt, they say. You know, relationships and so on. Yeah, I think there's—I wrote this forty years ago, what I call an American angle of vision. I mean, it's like what we would call on the street a take—you got a take on this, John? I got a take on this. What's the take on this? Okay, you ready? The take on this, have you ever thought about why there's no Hegel in American thought? Have you ever thought about why Marx never took? Have you ever thought about why we don't like, you know, hierarchy and Roman Catholics and so on? Right. Because, basically, you see, we're a three-generation people. Margaret Mead said we live in three generations. We are a group of people, you see, for whom the fabric of history is episodic, and it's built in. The genealogy is tight. And that's a very bold, spiritual move. There's no canopy of explanation. We ain't going anyplace else, you see? Now what's the negative upshot of this? The negative upshot of this is that when we trash somebody, it's all that they have. They're not going to get, you know, worked out some other place, some other time. You see.

MM: Right.

JM: Now Dewey has a marvelous sense of this. This is a very serious calling. This work is very serious. Really? Because these students, my children, you know, my relationship, spousal, whatever they are, and so on, this is it. Okay. So, that's, you see, why you have this extraordinary, intense kind of literature and certain kind of philosophical tradition.

MM: And that's the American take?

JM: That's the American take, the American take. See, no eschatology, no ultimate goals, and so on. And, of course, it's very dangerous because it also means you don't look to the future. I quoted this thing from the Iroquois Confederation this morning, that every time we make a decision, we should think in seven generations. We never think in seven generations, right? We think in how to clean up from the last generation, you see.

MM: Right, right.

JM: But those of us, who maybe we think in two or three generations. I have grandchildren, six grandchildren now.

MM: Yeah, that'll do it to you.

68

JM: Well, obviously it means I'm going to die soon. It does. It means, I'm coming to the end and so I'm beginning to see this thing now in terms of expectations and losses, and you know, suffering, sadness, joys, and so on and I get this American thing. There's nothing else working, man, this is it, you see. This is it. And I think that at our best, the tradition of literature and philosophy in America, for example, Royce, that nobody reads at all, that's powerful stuff about this business of the community and so on. So the take then is the utter, irreducible, illogical seriousness of these events in our time and of this conversation with you, my friend, right? This is what's going on right now in my life.

MM: That's why we have to get it right, because you ain't going back.

JM: You're not going back, I got to go ahead. And the thing is that there's no wager, no Pascalian wager here. This is really up front, and . . .

MM: That's the wager. Well, you might as well lead a good life just in case there is God.

JM: There's none of that, no. There's none of that in the best of American thought. See, the best of American thought is the secular religious tradition— what I call secular spirituality. And its chary of all institutions and hierarchies and bishops and all that stuff. What it has to do with, you see, is the community. It's the old New England bequest of the face-to-face community and it's what we used to do in the schools, it's what we used to do in the university. It's what we used to do in the grocery store, it's what we used to do in a ballpark. It's what we used to do at a local bar. It's what we used to do in a funeral home. You see, it's what we used to do.

MM: You're teaching down at Texas A&M; they do it in Texas a little bit.

JM: They do it in Texas a little bit.

MM: You walk in to a 7-Eleven and get to know somebody behind the counter in thirty seconds.

JM: Well, yes, and I'll tell you this, that those people are totally disenfranchised from the university, completely. I was talking about this this morning. This is a great university, land-grant tradition and so on, so I mean Mr. and Mrs. Texas should not be disenfranchised from the, I mean, there's a lot of yahoo stuff, but I'm talking about deep—see what I mean? We are not open, right? See, I believe every university, every school, should be open twenty-four hours a day, seven days a week, and that people should be able to come and go. All the time. So, if the Wal-Mart's open, the school should be open. To be able to go in there and take Philosophy I at two in the morning, if you're a fireman, whatever you are and so on, two to three in the morning, you go in . . .

MM: 24–7 school.

JM: That's right, twenty-four hours a day, the whole thing you see, and that credentialing should all be functional in terms of all these needs, and they just cut everybody off. The whole thing is quite scandalous; it's sort of like a European high-culture model dropped on a democratic ethos—it doesn't make any sense.

MM: And underneath, underneath it though, like at Texas A&M, it's still that old land-grant model, which it was that, wasn't it?

JM: It was beautiful. Oh yes, it was. Of course, but it's not only that, you see, Morrill, in the Morrill Act, this guy was great, he says, look we're going to have this act. We're going to have this act for the young people in the Plains states, man. And he said we're not going to be narrow like the big shots, Harvard, Yale, and so on. He said, they teach Latin and Greek, but they don't teach the mechanical-agricola arts. He said we are going to teach the mechanical-agricola arts and Latin and Greek as well. And when Texas A&M University opened up in 1876, Latin and Greek were required. You see? He got it. You see what I mean. Now that's all gone, that's just everybody's nostalgia, man. So the degree has been, has become a $50,000 bill. Do you understand what I mean; you don't carry it or you cannot get it, right? And I see no way to deal with the spiritual crisis in America. Except that every community, as we used to say, every hitching post, right, is a source, you see, of this thing.

MM: Is it happening? Is it not going on anywhere in America?

JM: No, no, because I mean corporate capitalism is not going to let this happen. I mean, you know, Marx was right about this. He was right about this, you know.

MM: What about entrepreneurial capitalism?

JM: Well, they're not going to let it happen either.

MM: Look at those little start-ups and those are like little families.

JM: Yes, but, you see, I see the only way this can happen is, that's why Rorty used that phrase, "Achieving Our Country," which comes at the end of James

Baldwin's essay. I mean, it's not my phrase. My phrase, you see, would be the Jewish teshuvah, which means recovery. I mean a recovery of the real meaning of the democratic ethos. And the real meaning of the democratic ethos, to do a paraphrase of Rousseau's famous line: If you are not free, I'm not free, and so on, you see. My understanding of this is if everyone doesn't have access—I don't mean on the Internet, I mean access your right through the community with sanctions, you understand? With sanctions, but if everyone doesn't have access, then the kind of conversation we're having and the words that we're having and so on, then we're not going to make it.

MM: Let's talk about the Internet then. Is that a hope?

JM: I don't know, I'm not . . .

MM: It's another way. Another linkage. And it's access. It's access to all of that out there.

JM: Right, but as Dewey says, all, everything, depends on the quality of the experience which has happened. You see, I am not at all impressed. As a matter of fact, I'm distressed by information pileup.

MM: Yes.

JM: Look, in philosophy, there's just a couple of questions. One question which is a tough one and nobody knew what to say: Why is there something rather than nothing? One question is, are we in on something which has meaning beyond our ken or are we responsible for the meaning, right? The third one is, you know, what should I do? I mean, Kant had this right. What should I do, what should I know, what can I hope? And so these are the only questions. They're variations on a theme. They're really aesthetic variations. I mean, in a deep sense of that. So the question—I have my version, you have your version. So if we turn toward them, we would have two different versions of really the same thing. Well, basically, you know, the question is, what the hell's going on here, man? You see, it's like when my little ones were growing up and so on, and you know the youngster, she gets acute leukemia, thirteen years old, she goes, hey, dad, what does this mean? Now what does that mean? I mean, what does all this mean? I don't know what all this means. But then we enter a community, right? You go with the parents and the siblings and talk and that's community. The meaning then, you see, emerges from the situation.

MM: You walk together in the woods.

JM: Yeah, exactly.

MM: Right, and grandpa can show them things, but hopes that they'll see it their own way.

JM: That's right, that's right. But, no one, no one in a democratic politic should be cut off from the best that can be for their lives. In other words, I mean, no one should be walking around not knowing that Hobbes said it may be, right, that we can't do it without authority. Nobody should be walking around without knowing that Locke says maybe if we sit down and work out a contract, we could do it, right? Nobody should be walking around not knowing that Dewey said, if you hook your strap on your horse to the ridge there, and what is known in New England as horse shedding, you see you're face-to-face with someone, you can work some of these things through, and on and on and on. I mean, all of that, to me, should be available to everyone. It should all, all the way from the beginning.

MM: The questions are simple.

JM: They're very simple . . .

MM: Then you can teach the questions in first grade.

JM: I could teach Royce's famous third term, which he took from Peirce, and so on, the triad, all that stuff. Here it goes, like this, you're seven or eight years old. Say, what do you think the best way would be to resolve a dispute? Well, you know, bop! Well, you sit down and talk it out. I know what; I got an idea. What's your idea? My idea is that if there were a third person here, so this third person is a person who is an interpreter. Why do we need an interpreter? We all speak the same language. I said, spiritually we don't. Some speak the language of hate, some speak the language of jealousy, some speak the language of insecurity, some speak the language begotten by trauma. This person, this third one, you see, is going to help interpret this, okay. So we're all going to meet here. Well, I could show the passage in Royce, it's very difficult, but that's what it is. And I think you can teach it to a seven year old. And you want to know something else, as you well know, they'll understand it. Of course they will.

MM: Sure he will.

JM: Sure they will. I gave this thing at Bainbridge Island, that's outside of Seattle, a guy teaching philosophy at the high school. So anyway, I get up early at six in the morning and take the ferry over there. I get over there, there are 150 high school students sitting on the floor and I talked to them about the difference between Plato and Aristotle. Half of them walked me back to the ferry. You know, they wanted to come on the ferry and go back and keep talking. Why? Because I told them, I said, look, there are two big ways to do this. One is maybe there's a secret, Plato. The other way, there ain't no secret—you know, you just look at that stuff and say I want to talk about that man. They wanted to talk about it. Or another way is, do you move through the world with your hands or with your eyes? Do you move with your feet? Woodbridge said to Dewey, you know, the trouble with you, he said, you're always talking about the hands and not the eyes. And Dewey said, I take that as a compliment, the thing with the hands, right?

MM: Right.

JM: Descartes is the eyes. See the seventeenth-century guys were optic guys. In the nineteenth century, they are hands guys. All that stuff is teachable to everybody, Mike.

MM: What are twentieth-century guys, word guys?

JM: Very deeply constipated, man. Yes, we're chronically constipated, you know. I think it's more and more complicated.

MM: All right, if you can teach this stuff to seven year olds, how come when you look at a philosophy library on campus and there are 250 books of symbols and logical languages and all that. Why aren't they out teaching that to the seven year olds? Teaching the good stuff to seven year olds?

JM: Well, I mean, you know, the philosophy of children crowd teach logic and so on, but you know, Buber says how we're educated by children and by animals.

MM: Or grandchildren in your case.

JM: But, here's something, let's talk about this for a minute. See, I don't believe that directness and simplicity of articulation necessarily betray depth or complexity. I don't believe that. Now, that doesn't mean I'm a wise guy, in other words, I don't think you could take Kant's *Critique of Pure Reason,* you know, and just pass it around. I have as much trouble with that as the next person. But I happen to be the kind of guy who likes to read that, you understand?

MM: Yeah, yeah.

JM: And that's okay. I'm not talking about that, you understand. But, what's behind that, you see, is quite extraordinary. It's in the dissertation of 1770. The only dissertation that's ever been written—the rest of them were all . . . just forget it. There's only one ever been written. It's the dissertation of 1770. And in there, he says, I got to tell you something, Mike. What do you have to tell me, Kant? I have to tell you that space and time are made up. And you say, what? Right. Now some of us can do the deduction of the categories and all that sort of stuff. I'm not asking everybody to do that. But I do want to say this. I do have to say to him, now look, why did Kant say that this had to do with Copernicus? What does Copernicus have to say to us? Well, I say what Copernicus has to say is things will never be the same. They'll never be the same. We used to think we could get it together. Now we can't get it together—just try that, you see. So I think that, just as there are only three or four or five questions, there are three or four or five very deep things to worry about. You see, deep things to worry about. And my own death is one. The death of those people I love is one, and sadness and brokenness and inequity and, you know, all this stuff.

MM: Yes. How about doing the right thing?

JM: Well, doing the right thing, you know, that's Spike Lee. It's also a line in the 12 and 12 of the AA program, and, by the way, you know where I first found it? It's in Emerson. Yes, it's in Emerson. I'm sure it's in some Chinese philosopher too, but anyway, it's doing the right thing. What does it mean to do the right thing? Well, who knows what the right thing is, you see? And that's where the American stuff is interesting because you'll know pretty soon, because there are consequences.

MM: Well, we've seen the consequences of twentieth-century philosophy. What's the right thing for philosophy to do in the twenty-first?

JM: Well, the right thing for us to do is to not tie being real, real smart with pedagogy. In other words, the right thing, you see, is to begin to develop a pedagogy of pedagogy.

MM: Yes.

JM: It's really remarkable that there is no effort made in the graduate schools to teach people how to teach, not to be smart, you see. I did a seminar at Stony Brook for many years and they would teach and we would just . . . and it's really quite extraordinary . . . say wow. But it's not just how to teach in a classroom. I mean, it's how to, I taught in a medical school, you know, I've been teaching in medical school fifteen or sixteen years and a guy once said to me, what do you know, he said, you don't cut anyone. He was going to be a surgeon or something. I said, I don't? I said, let me tell you something. I can cut. Mike comes to me and he says, McDermott, I'd like to go on to study philosophy and I say to Mike, you don't have it, Mike. I mean, there ain't no surgery equivalent to that.

MM: Yes, the deepest cut of all.

JM: Deepest cut of all. I don't do that, by the way, I'd never do that; God forbid I would do that. But, Michael, that's done all the time. Do you understand? You see, so that being smart is dangerous, you know what I mean? So when you say, what's it to do the right thing? Well, to do the right thing, see, is to re-enter the community.

MM: Well, let me ask one last question. In the time you have left, what's the right thing for you to do for philosophy?

JM: Well, I have to avoid one thing. I must avoid cynicism because all the evidence is there, Mike, right? So I guess what I have to do, you see, is, like old Dewey, just keep going. And you hope that the cry for help, that the passion for inquiry is taken up by others. But, I'm not burned out, I'm not giving up. But we're up against tough odds here because the intellectual life has become conflicted, insular, self-centered, arrogant, and suspicious.

MM: We've got to start working with our hands, again.

JM: You bet, you bet.

MM: Thank you.

MARJORIE GRENE
The Trials and Tribulations of
Philosophy and Farming

Marjorie Grene, Professor Emeritus of Philosophy at the University of California–Davis and Honorary Distinguished Professor at Virginia Tech. Professor Grene is the "dean" of women philosophers in the United States and the first woman selected for the distinguished Library of Living Philosophers Series. A vibrant eighty-eight years old, Professor Grene is renowned in some areas in the history of philosophy and in the philosophy of biology, but well prepared to speak to any issue.

MM: Michael Malone   **MG:** Marjorie Grene

MM: Marjorie, tell me something. For 400 years, philosophy has been in the thrall of Descartes and you come along and you say, no, he doesn't do anything for me. So, first of all, what do you have against Descartes?

MG: Everything. Well, he's unfair to children. But the main thing is, he's got this thing about knowing yourself as a secret inner something. That's Wittgenstein's phrase, secret inner something, that's what he said philosophers always wanted to find. And, then, on the other hand, an external world is just spread out and doesn't mean anything and, as Whitehead put it, he made philosophy, or science even, a mystic chant over an unintelligible universe. And that's pretty bad stuff. I mean, I've never known myself as just something like that without any relation to what makes me what I am and what's outside me and what impinges on me.

MM: So he sent philosophy down the wrong path for four centuries?

MG: I think so, but it isn't only Descartes. Obviously, people wanted that and things were going that way. On the other hand, the funny thing is that when you really look at the history of philosophy in some detail, you find that, in France anyway, now, of course, they think Descartes is marvelous and I remember years ago an interview in the *New Yorker* with some, I think it was some people from the Comedie Français—French actors who came here—and they explained we're all Cartesians. But, in the eighteenth century, Descartes was frowned on because he "succumbed to the spirit of system," as Voltaire said. A lot of people said that about him. And the eighteenth century, God help us all, the French wanted to be Lockean—that's much worse than Descartes.

MM: Now, you also thought that Descartes was mean to animals, too.

MG: Well, of course. He abolished them. He didn't think there were any.

MM: Oh, well, you know what W. C. Fields said about people who hate children

---

and animals, they can't be all bad. Well, he was pretty nasty to some of his friends, too. He just wasn't a fun guy, but he was influential.

MG: Very influential. But, the funny thing is, as I said, when you look at the details of what happened in French intellectual life, there seems to be a very brief moment when people were Cartesians. A colleague of mine has done a lot of work on the condemnations of Descartes in the seventeenth century. He was condemned all over the place and people got in trouble for following him, not only because of his view of transubstantiation, that is, of the Mass, but, in general, all the same, it is the case that modern philosophy has been very much shaped by the moves he made. But, as I said, people were waiting for it. It was coming.

MM: Now, let's get to this Cartesian dualism. You've written about something called positionality. Now, what do you mean by that?

MG: Oh, that's not my term. That's Helmuth Plessner's. And that's got nothing to do with the question. Well, it's one of the answers to it. Actually, Plessner was a German sociologist and philosopher who wrote a book called—what do you call it in English—it's *Stages of the Organic in Man,* and that's where he introduced this concept. Nobody paid any attention to it. But this was supposed to give you an account of a characteristic of all living things. And what it means is that any plant or animal, and that includes us, of course (animals, I mean, not plants) not only is somewhere, like your cameras that I'm not supposed to look at, but it sets a boundary between itself and the rest of the world. So, in a way, it isolates itself, but in relation to the outside. And Plessner distinguished between open positionality, which is what plants have, plants that can reproduce vegetatively, they just kind of go on by sprouting, and closed positionality, which is what animals have. They set themselves against their environment somehow in a more closed or positive way. But we have what he called eccentric positionality. We not only have this kind of somewhat set apart relation to the external world, but then we can reflect, we can look at that and consider it. So we're animals with this ability to reflect. Now, that's not what Descartes wanted to say; well, never mind, let's not go into that. It's very complicated. But the mind–body relation in Descartes is something else again.

MM: It's been suggested that you were, in doing philosophical biology, you were an environmental philosopher . . .

MG: Ecological, if you like.

MM: Before there was even that term.

MG: Well, I published a book which I'm now ashamed of, at least of one chapter, in, when did it come out, sixty something. And I thought, at the time, of saying this is an ecological epistemology. And then I thought, oh, that's too much of a fashionable word, I won't say that. But since then, J. J. Gibson and his wife, Eleanor Gibson, have developed what's called ecological psychology, which I very much subscribe to and think ought to be very influential in philosophy, though it isn't. There were three people I thought would develop it. One of them didn't get tenure at Yale and went into the development office at Princeton. One of them betrayed the whole thing by trying to make it into an old-fashioned representational theory and the other one died. So I don't know who, if anybody, could do that. I'm too old. But since I've realized there is this view of perception and, therefore, of the way we are in the world as perceivers, that's now been developed, I could have called my view ecological epistemology, sure. That's what it is. Emphasizing the fact that we are expressions of an environment which we have also helped create by being an expression of it. If you want a little tag from my research lecture at Davis, I tried to talk about what a developed human being is and—how did I put it—a person, a mature person is . . . a personalization of nature through participation in a culture. So we are animals, were part of nature, but we get our funny difference by being formed in a culture which itself is part of nature.

MM: Is there an implicit hierarchy in all this—does man sit above?

MG: No, it's a circle. We're in it. But we're inside of nature and the culture is inside nature and we're inside the culture. And so it's a set of circles. I don't think it's hierarchical.

MM: Now, one of the things you can help me with. I've talked to a lot of philosophers here and there's a number of schisms, it seems to me, in the field.

MG: Oh, there are . . .

MM: One of them between analytical philosophy and people saying we've got to get philosophy back to the people. We've got to start writing.

MG: That's not the same thing—that's two different things. I'm not very fond of the former. But I never have spoken to the latter. I don't know who they are. My friends and colleagues who teach ethics certainly deal with questions like abortion, and questions like when do you turn the machine off, questions like gene therapy and so on. So they are doing something the public is concerned about. But I know nothing about it. I say sometimes I'm an immoral philosopher; at least I'm not a moral philosopher.

MM: Well, so, that's one split, this one group saying analytical philosophy and the other half saying, no we've got to, you know, go back to the original principles, ask those first questions and help people.

MG: The people in bioethics who are doing these things that do help people are analytical philosophers and not anything else. They're using analytical philosophy and applying it in these cases.

MM: But what some of these people I've talked to are saying is, what has philosophy done for mankind in the twentieth century? We have this . . . maybe the bloodiest century in human history. Well, where was philosophy through all this?

MG: It wasn't any help.

MM: Why not?

MG: One of the most eminent philosophers on the continent of Europe was a Nazi—Heidegger.

MM: You met him as a young woman, didn't you?

MG: I went to his lectures and his seminar, yes.

MM: I mean, it seems like the twentieth century, the philosophy of the twentieth century seems to hinge on Heidegger . . .

MG: Oh, no. I hope not.

MM: Why did such an eminent philosopher, twenty-four centuries on in philosophy, end up a member of the Nazi party?

MG: He was a patriotic German and he resented the fact that he couldn't be an active participant in the First World War because of some health problem. So he was just fanatically patriotic. I mean, that's my view now.

MM: Yeah, but why didn't his philosophy collide with his careerism or his emotions at some point and say, wait a minute, this is the wrong thing to do.

MG: Because that wasn't that kind of philosophy.

MM: Well, there you are. Should it have been?

MG: We're getting in a circle. You can't say what it should have been. You can't say what anybody's philosophy should have been.

MM: But, if philosophy is about the great questions, it seems to me this should have been . . .

MG: Wait a minute. I don't know what you mean by the great questions. Heidegger was asking the question of being. I suppose that's a great question. But he was asking it from within a situation where he was supremely confident of the superiority of his own tradition. Now, that's only Heidegger. Jaspers was no Nazi, he was married to a Jewess. But he truly believed, like Heidegger, well, actually, sorry, let me back up. Heidegger believed that you could only philosophize in two languages, ancient Greek or modern German. I don't think Jaspers even counted ancient Greek. Since I came back home to Harvard, or to Radcliffe, which was where women had to go in those days, and studied philosophy here, I've been an adherent, a very strong adherent of David Hume. Well, Jaspers said a little bit about Hume when he was lecturing on Kant, about Hume's trivial little squirrel cage of an argument compared to this great circular, transcendental argument of Kant. These people just sneered at anything that wasn't in German or Greek.

MM: You've even written that all of Heidegger's philosophy betrays this sort of Teutonic point of view.

MG: Yes, it does.

MM: So, whom do you read? Who's important to you besides Hume?

MG: You mean, in the twentieth century, who's important to me?

MM: Go back, go back.

MG: Oh, well, Plato, Spinoza, not because I believe in him but because I admire him immensely. I'm passionately interested in Descartes because the whole story is so subtle when you study it carefully and because he's a magnificent philosophical writer. And I'm still fascinated by Kant.

MM: Who else in America? Only Peirce, and I don't know him well enough because the edition that was done at Harvard years ago was said to be very bad and there's going to be a good one but not in my lifetime, so I can't study him. Now, you're not real keen on Dewey? What do you have against him?

MG: He's a slob.

MM: How so? An intellectual slob? He's a sloppy thinker.

MG: Yes. And it's always the same thing about experience; besides, I think he destroyed our educational system single-handedly.

MM: That patron saint of public education?

MG: Exactly. The patron saint, gosh, have you any kids still in school? I've got grandkids in school. Anyway, the thing he said, for example, a man doesn't build (he didn't suggest a woman could do it) a house in order to live in it. He might die before it's finished. He does it for the joy of doing it. And I remember at the lab school in Chicago, which he founded before he left Chicago in 1890 something, friends of ours, colleagues of ours, sent their child there and the first day they were told, we never start at all until we're sure all the children really want to. Now, what kind of a school day is that going to be?

MM: I would have been instrumental in a very long recess.

MG: Exactly. No, it's always the same thing, experience. He means well, but he's really a slob.

MM: Who else, who in the twentieth century matters to you?

MG: I admire Merleau-Ponty. Because, he did, even though a Frenchman, go beyond what Plessner called the Cartesian alternative. Because in *The Primacy of Perception*, he undercuts the traditional view that we have these little secret sensations and somehow we make up the idea that they refer to an external world. He puts us there in the world. His chapter, I think—well, I thought it was a chapter, but when you go back to look at his book, he writes appallingly. He never finishes a sentence. He never finishes a paragraph. But what I thought was in his chapter on the body as speech, as it's called, showing how embodied language is undercutting this idea that here we have this artificial language stuff which is quite different from anything real, and he shows that speech, after all, has to be either spoken, heard, made oral, or touched, if you are blind. I mean, there's no way to have speech without some embodiment. I think that was a very great move forward. And his notion of the *cogito* in the next-to-last chapter also involves a great change. It's not this little inner moment. It's the sort of stretch in which you recognize where you are as well. In fact, I've relied in some of my work on something he says in a much more boring thing he wrote, *The Structure of Behavior*. Both of these things were his dissertations; *The Structure of Behavior* is the first one. It's in *The Structure of Behavior,* which is otherwise a rather dreary book, that he distinguishes three different worlds. Now, am I going to get this right? What it amounts to is things in general, what physics studies, or chemistry, the animate world and the human world. And, again, as I said, these are contained in one another. There's nothing separate. We don't have any human world that isn't part of a natural world and an expression of it. And I think he made that distinction very well there.

MM: You know, listening to you talk, you may not be a pragmatist, but you're pragmatic that your philosophy demands that you've got to be in the world.

MG: Well, of course. But you're not necessarily doing anything active in it. I was a farmer for more than twenty years. It's an experience of activity . . .

MM: Well, I was going to ask you about that. There's this hole in your résumé.

MG: Yes, because I got fired when I was an instructor at the university in Chicago in 1944.

MM: So, this is 1944. You don't work again in philosophy . . .

MG: Until 1959. That's right.

MM: Fifteen years.

MG: Yes, that's right.

MM: So, what'd you do?

MG: It was twenty-some years not teaching in this country, which, if I may put it that way, if there had been a good God, is this what he would have made me for? I mean, teaching in America, I'm not a great big patriotic zealot otherwise. But teaching in our college system, there are some rotten colleges and universities, but, you know, our system is just streets away better. I've been a visiting professor in Germany and I've taught in the British system. Not the real posh ones like Cambridge, but in the provincial universities, and we're just streets away more interesting. In Belfast, the students would never ask questions. There's no use teaching philosophy to people who won't talk back to you . . .

MM: So, they quietly take notes while you talk to them?

MG: Well, that or fall asleep or something but, I mean, you know, that there was no idea that there was conversation.

MM: Tell me about those fifteen years. What did you do? Get your hands dirty, go out and . . .

MG: Well, my then husband was both a classicist and a farmer. He always wanted to do both. So, we farmed in Illinois and I had never liked living in a city. I used to think, you know, why do they have all these houses one after the other?

MM: Where did you grow up?

MG: Madison, Wisconsin.

MM: Oh, okay.

MG: But, at any rate, I was glad to do this. I mean, you know, belonging to the second-oldest profession gives one a sense of continuity, if one believes in being in the world.

MM: So, you had a family farm. What'd you grow?

MG: Oh, we had eighty very bad acres of a soil called Clarence Row in northern Illinois, in Cook County.

MM: In Cook County.

MG: The edge of Cook County, twenty-six miles from the University of Chicago campus. And, you know, we grew what you had to, corn and oats and I've forgotten—barley? And we had pigs and poultry and cows. We weren't set up to ship to a dairy, but we shipped to the creamery and you do remember those little—you don't, you're too young. Those little books about Momma and baby, this and that animal, and you turned the page?

MM: Yes.

MG: I made up one to prove that the principle of tragedy was circular, not as Aristotle said it was, which went: When Momma cow eats soybean meal, she says moo moo, how well I feel. But when she hasn't any such, the milk she gives, it's not so much. But then she gives us cream, you see; we ship it to the creamery. The mailman brings a check, and then, we buy some soybean meal again. So, it never made a profit.

84

MM: No?

MG: In farming. We farmed in Illinois for twelve years . . .

MM: Is that a philosophical lesson for you?

MG: Yes. No. It's a lesson, it's not philosophical, it's practical. Then, we farmed in Ireland and the year my husband left, I made twelve pounds profit. The first time we ever made a profit.

MM: In how many years?

MG: We moved to Ireland in '52 and he left in '61—twenty-one years.

MM: So, in those days, in twenty-one years you made thirty bucks profit? Did that contribute to your philosophy at all, these experiences?

MG: Well, as I have said in the intellectual autobiography I wrote for this living philosophers series, I was trying not to talk about my personal life, but I must admit that both farming and maternity taught me something.

MM: You're a grandmother now.

MG: Well, of course. And if I'd married when my college friends did, I'd be a great grandmother.

MM: What does motherhood do? To philosophy.

MG: It teaches you a lot about the relation to another person. When you have somebody growing inside you.

MM: It's the ultimate I–thou?

MG: Who's part of you. It isn't even I–thou, to hell with that I–thou. I don't think there's much to Buber. But anyway. No, you have this person who's part of your body and then independent and then really independent in a few years, gradually more and more so and it's very instructive, I think.

MM: Let's talk about philosophy now. You, as a member of the Library of Living Philosophers . . .

MG: Right.

MM: One thing about reaching this venerable point in your career, as everybody looks to you for wisdom because you remember more.

MG: I remember a lot, yes. An awful lot of times when I'm asked to do something now, I produce my recollections.

MM: What do your experiences of philosophy in the twentieth century teach you about philosophy? What's the lesson of the twentieth century?

MG: Well, the lesson of the twentieth century is hard to formulate. On the one hand, what you see, if you look at the profession on the whole, is that it gets more and more trivial, more and more divorced from anything. In the little book I published with Open Court in '95, called *A Philosophical Testament*, I invented a philosopher's room, like John Searle's business of the Chinese room where you're inside and nobody speaks anything but Chinese and how do you understand anything. In the philosopher's room, you have a chamber that's sealed; all the doors are shut firmly against reality. My daughter's a scientist and she says you can tell when philosophers start talking. There's no connection with reality. And, inside, all that's allowed, apart from the philosophers that are shut up in it, is the last two issues of the *Philosophical Review* and the *Journal of Philosophy*. It's this self-contained game. And an awful lot of it has no connection with anything. And I don't understand, well, I think sometimes I don't understand most people. I don't understand how young people get interested in this whirligig of nothings, although, some of them are terribly clever. And a few of them I like listening to because they're just so damn smart, but they aren't talking about anything at all.

MM: How did the profession start out so grounded in the real world, in the problems of everyday life and then . . .

MG: That's easy. Well, in all of this, I'm sorry, I'm not talking about ethics. I don't know about that. And it's interesting that in the Library of Living Philosophers, there's never been a moral philosopher. I don't know why not. But the kind of thing I'm interested in is really what it is to make a knowledge claim. What I've worked in mostly, though, is conceptual problems about biology and problems in the history of philosophy. There is some good work being done in both those areas. But, in general, there just is less and less connection with anything in what philosophers do. As I was saying, I don't understand why young people want to do this. But they do.

MM: So where did philosophy make this left turn and go off . . .

MG: Oh, now, I'm sorry. That's easy. It isn't a left turn, it's just that all the subjects left us. Philosophy for Plato or Aristotle and long after was just knowledge, or at least the search for it or for wisdom.

MM: So, you mean, biology spun off, physics spun off . . .

MG: That's right. And, finally, psychology. I took my prelims at Radcliffe the last year that you had to do psychology as well as philosophy and then psychology split off and as, I think it was Davidson said last night at the roundtable, it moved to the second floor of Emerson Hall and we were left with the ground floor. Now, philosophy has the whole, and I'm sure psychology has some huge domain in the science buildings. But that left us, the social sciences have left us. Plessner, for instance, who, we said a little earlier, was a sociologist and philosopher and I don't think he had any different chair when he did the one or the other. But that was a half-century ago.

MM: So, can we then say that philosophy did its job?

MG: No, it didn't.

MM: It spun these things off and now it's this empty husk . . .

MG: It didn't spin them off. They spun themselves off.

MM: And that's fine. Okay. So where does philosophy go, then? What's its job now?

MG: Its job, well, that depends how you look at it. In one sense, philosophy is a conversation over time, a certain tradition—that is, Western philosophy. I'm afraid I don't know other philosophical traditions. I think you have to know their languages in order to know them and I don't. My only languages are European. But our tradition is a conversation that goes back to the sixth century B.C. in which any of us can take our place. In the history of philosophy, you want to try to talk to some of these dead minds. But you've got to learn their language and understand whom they were talking to and what they were doing in order to do that effectively. And, since we have a very great literature, and since, as I believe, we are our histories, our past has something to do with what makes us what we are. I think this is very much worthwhile to study. It is also worth studying the philosophy of subject "x" if you know "x." For instance, there are some people who are excellent philosophers of quantum mechanics. That's connected with reality. And there are excellent philosophers of biology and there may be some excellent philosophers, I don't know, of art, maybe.

MM: A lot of those arise from the professions themselves, not from philosophy.

MG: Usually they arise from philosophy, but the philosophers have to know the other thing. It's the philosophers who are just doing philosophy without any connection with anything else who seem to me to get into these circles, and there are an awful lot of them. And, unfortunately, some people who do history of philosophy do it that way. They want to know about our problems. And then they take stuff out of the past without trying to understand what it was then and just use it.

MM: So, having seen most of philosophy in the twentieth century, do you have hope for philosophy in the twenty-first?

MG: Well, no and yes. I think, as I said yesterday evening, that, on the whole, most of the cognitive science movement is just disastrous. It's still Cartesian in a sense that there's the brain, you study it just sort of molecularly or physically or what not, and then there are these little subjective somethings, consciousness. Everybody's talking about consciousness now. That's just hogwash. If that's an Irish term, I'm sorry. I lived for a long time in Ireland and I sometimes don't know when I'm not using an American idiom. But, anyway, it's maddening. You either mechanize "mind" totally or you make it totally subjective. All I see of that is very depressing. And, the whole business is also too big. That's part of our education problem, too; it's not just John Dewey's fault. The whole thing is so massive that it's very hard to make it, to keep it alive. It just gets so governed by rules and regulations. But, on the other hand, there is a lot of good work, for instance, in the history of philosophy which is more contextual, where we really are getting into the people that our major people talk to and the problems they were really concerned with. And there also is still a lot of interesting work going on in the philosophy of biology and some in the philosophy of science.

MM: Has it all been worth it—the philosophy part of your career?

MG: Well, again, this time I'd say yes and no.

MM: This is the kind of question you also get at, you know ...

MG: Yes and no. Philosophy is a wonderful teaching subject. If you get young people interested in these fundamental questions, what's real, what's truth ...

MM: It pays better than farming, too, apparently.

MG: It pays better than farming. It doesn't pay, you know, oceans. Actually, my pension from the University of California went up this year $29 a month. Isn't that exciting?

MM: That's more money than you made in twenty-one years of farming.

MG: That's right.

MM: So, is it worth it to you; has it been worth it to you?

MG: Well, yes. Insofar as I was teaching and also I'm afraid I like writing and I like talking, as you can probably tell.

MM: That's the best part. Marjorie, thank you very much.

MG: Not at all.

SEYYED HOSSEIN NASR
Islam and the Philosophy of Hope

Seyyed Hossein Nasr, a native of Iran, is the University Professor of Islamic Studies at the George Washington University and the youngest member selected to the Library of Living Philosophers. He has made numerous appearances on television, including a Bill Moyers program. With extraordinary breadth in both the history of science and the humanities, he has broken new ground in his discussion on religion, philosophy, and history of science, history of art, and Sufism. Professor Nasr explored cross-cultural topics comparing the world of Islam with Western and Asian cultures.

MM: Michael Malone **SN:** Seyyed Hossein Nasr

MM: Let me ask you something—it's intrigued me for a while. Why is it that other religions, the other religions—Christianity, Buddhism, Confucius—why do they fear Islam more than any other?

SN: First of all, this is not true, let's say, of Confucianism, Taoism, or Buddhism.

MM: Just Christians?

SN: Yes, Christianity, and that's because of the very long history of the foundation of Western civilization during which the only "other" was Islam—that is, Western civilization, during the period of its formation. As you know, we always carry the memories of our periods of formation. Human life and civilization do the same. The Christian West did not know the Hindu civilization; it did not know the Chinese civilization; it did not know the African civilization. It only knew one other civilization, which was that of Islam. And there was always this constant fear also of being overtaken since Islam ruled over Spain, even up to southern France for a long time and had hegemony over the Mediterranean world, which had been the cradle of ancient civilization.

MM: So . . . we still have Seville and Constantinople in the back of our minds.

SN: Exactly, exactly. That is one reason. As far as Hinduism is concerned, that's also the case, to some extent, because although Islam and Hinduism lived together for over 1,000 years in India, since partition these two religions are confronting each other, both outside the borders of India and within India itself.

MM: Before partition, was there much tension? I mean, I know there wasn't, as the British colonialism ended, natural tensions arose. But what about 500 years ago?

SN: There's no place, of course, on the map in which there is a human society in which there is not tension. That's an impossibility. But, by and large, the Hindus and Muslims lived more or less at peace with each other. This famous Babri Mosque, which has been now destroyed in the name of building a temple for Rama, an event which has caused so much passion in India and caused the death of several thousand people a short while ago when the Hindu Raj tried to come to power, the land was given by the Moguls, that is, the Muslim rulers, to the Hindus to also build a temple. And, if you visited that site several years ago, the Brahmans would be the very first to speak with great fondness and fond memories of the Muslim rulers who had been there. What happened is that, when the British came to India in order to be able to rule over India, they decided to help the "underdog" overcome the group that was in power. And since the group that was in power was Muslims, they supported the Hindus.

MM: They played the factions against each other.

SN: Of course, played the factions against each other. It is still very unfortunate that the situation came out to be what it was. Perhaps, if the two groups—that is, Muslims and Hindus—had stayed together, which was the vision of Mahatma Gandhi, it might have been in the long run of greater benefit to both. But the way that the British had ruled over India had made that very, very difficult, if not impossible.

MM: I was intrigued in learning that European Jews found sanctuary in the Islamic world.

SN: Oh, yes. Until the question of the partition of Palestine came up, of all the different civilizations within which Jews lived, the most comfortable for them was the Islamic world.

MM: The Ottoman Empire was their greatest protector.

SN: And even before that. Not only the Turkish part of the Ottoman Empire, but other lands such as Egypt, which in a sense was also a part of the Ottoman Empire. But I'm a Persian or Iranian; when Cyrus the Great freed the Jews from captivity in Babylon, which is mentioned in the Bible, many of them migrated to Persia and they're still there. And there they have lived for over 2,000 years. Many of them are merchants; many of them are musicians, excellent musicians. Persian music has been very much enriched by them. They speak the Persian language very well and also this is true for the Arab world. And I said not only the Ottoman Empire because we have, for example, also Morocco, where many Jews settled when, in 1492, the Jews and Muslims both were expelled from

Spain. In fact, the word anti-Semitism began at that time as being anti-Arabic and not only anti-Jewish, since both are Semites, of course.

MM: Right.

SN: Morocco was not a part of the Ottoman Empire, but many of the Jews settled in Morocco.

MM: Expelled from Spain.

SN: That's right. Others, of course, went to Istanbul and to the heartland of the Ottoman world.

MM: What I'm curious about is, I've talked to a lot of philosophers here. Most of them don't want to talk about religion. In fact, it's ranged all the way from saying that religion gets in the way of good philosophy to religion is superfluous to philosophy. How does religion affect your philosophy?

SN: Well, you could turn it around and say that many great civilizations have lived throughout history all over the world without having the kind of philosophy which is divorced from religion, and it was philosophy that was superfluous. There has been no human society without religion, but there have been human societies without non-religious philosophies.

MM: So the essence of religion precedes the existence of philosophy.

SN: Absolutely. I think this is a historical fact. But philosophy in the sense of wisdom, of seeking of the truth *agatheia,* in the Platonic sense, of course, is a part of all the great civilizations, as we see in Chinese philosophy, Islamic philosophy, Indian philosophy, Japanese philosophy, even among the primal people who did not write books, but had a very profound philosophy expressed in symbolic forms. Now this phenomenon that you talk about, if this conference were held in any other civilization in the world, although communist China is an exception, because there the Confucian thinkers are not allowed to speak and it's supposedly to be Marxist. But, putting that aside, that is in . . .

MM: Marxism is a religion in its own way.

SN: It's a pseudoreligion of sorts. In India, in Japan, in the Islamic world, in Thailand, which is Buddhist, you name it, you would not have found any philosophers who would have made such an assertion.

MM: So it's the secular West that's ...

SN: That's right. And the West was not always like that. When the Greco-Roman world died, and what you call Western civilization was born, with the coming of Christianity to the West, of course, for 1,000 years, philosophy and religion were very closely related to each other.

MM: Sure, Prometheus ...

SN: Until the time of the Renaissance. The separation really came with the rebellion of reason against revelation, on the one hand, and against what the Medievals called intellect—that is, that divine faculty of knowledge that is identified with the heart, on the other. And this did not occur in any other civilization in the world.

MM: But other civilizations had their kinds of Renaissance—why didn't the schism occur there? Why did it only occur in Europe?

SN: I don't like the word renaissance very much for that very reason, because it embraces too much to have a specific meaning.

MM: But some sort of secularization occurred ...

SN: Yes a transition occurred, but you have both "humanism" and "renaissance" in the sense of the revival of culture, the arts, literature, and poetry, but it always occurred in other civilizations within the context of the dominating worldview, the dominating religious world view, but not outside of it. Whereas the European Renaissance was the revival of the Greco-Roman paganism against existing Christian civilization. Of course, it couldn't ...

MM: And then driven home by the Protestant Reformation.

SN: Reformation. Of course, the Protestant Reformation was itself based on the Bible. But, by rejecting 1,500 years of Christian history, in a sense also helped the process. Although Luther and Calvin were pious Christians, they helped indirectly this process of secularization to take place. And this type of ...

MM: The irony would have killed them, you know, to realize the secularization of the West.

SN: Exactly. Which is not what they wanted to do. They wanted to undo some of the excesses of the medieval church, but that's what happened. At once, you

Seyyed Hossein Nasr

say, all right now, we throw out medieval philosophy, we throw out medieval science, we throw out medieval Latin literature—what are you going to put in its place? What you put in its place, and this is what happened in the West, was no longer Christian, it was outside of the Christian world. Of course, many philosophers were still Christian. People like Fecinno or even Descartes, who was a pious Catholic. But his philosophy was not a Catholic philosophy. That is, it was not St. Thomas of Aquinas or St. Bonaventure. And that event did not take place in other great civilizations of the world.

MM: So, without the schism, is there a distinct Islamic philosophy that you . . . that's obviously different from Western philosophy? Because of this religious element?

SN: Yes, there are so many different Western philosophies.

MM: Yes.

SN: The West, in the thirteenth century, created on the basis of the translation of texts from Arabic of the Persian philosopher Avicenna, of the Arab philosopher Averroes and others, a synthesis associated most of all with St. Thomas Aquinas and scholasticsm, which continued to be the official philosophy taught in all Catholic universities, like Boston College right nearby here, until the 1964 Vatican II and this philosophy is even now powerful . . .

MM: It still haunts the process, yeah.

SN: It's been a very powerful philosophy. So that kind of philosophy also survived in the West. But the mainstream of Western philosophy separated itself from the concerns of Revelation and religion, especially after the seventeenth century, a trait which distinguishes it from Islamic philosophy. Yes, there is such a thing as Islamic philosophy. And what is interesting for the West is that it is heir to the same sources. And that is why it's also so much neglected philosophically. I have always said jokingly, it's as if you were heir to a fortune and suddenly a man opens the door and comes in and says I'm your brother, I'm heir to this fortune also. Of course, you don't want to accept that.

MM: Sure.

SN: Because Islam inherited the Greco-Alexandrian philosophical heritage. Muslims know Plato and Aristotle not only as well as the medieval West, but even better. That's why the West wanted to receive Aristotle with commentaries of Islamic philosophers. Islam also is based on the revelation of the Koran, the sacred scripture of Islam, and is a sister to Christianity and Judaism. It belongs to the Abrahamic world. And so the major influences in the West, which are sometimes said to be Jerusalem and Athens, or the world of the Abrahamic patriarchs, the Semitic patriarchs, and Greek philosophy, Islam is just as much heir to them as the West. And, for several centuries, they grew in a parallel fashion and in Spain, there was a lot of concordant relationships, with Jewish philosophy playing a very important role as the bridge between Islamic philosophy and Christian philosophy. And then philosophy in the West went its own way and Islamic philosophy went its own way. They didn't die out; they continue to this very day.

MM: So it begins with the same roots, but this element of spirituality remains interpenetrated . . .

SN: That's right. There are two major elements that remain connected with Islamic philosophy, which gradually departed from the mainstream of Western philosophy, not all of Western philosophy. One is, of course, the element of religion, Revelation, spirituality. The other is what could be called in the original sense of the term, gnosis—that is, a kind of knowledge that illuminates, which certain medieval Western philosophers and Christian philosophers such as Erigena and Bonaventure or even later on people outside of the mainstream of Western philosophy believed in, such as Eckarthausen vonBaader, people nobody hears about precisely because they remained close to those elements. Now Islamic philosophy always remained very closely wed to those two elements. Islamic philosophy never divorced itself from the Koran and the Islamic religion and the particular philosophical questions and challenges which the Revelation posed—for example, that the world has an origin, the world has a creator, that human life has a meaning beyond the earthly, and so forth and so on. These remain questions which you have to answer. And also the intelligence, the very reasoning mind, never became secularized. We take it for granted in the West that there is only one kind of way of thinking and that's by the rational mind as we understand it. We think that the rational mind is like the mathematical mind. Two and two is four. Here, there . . .

MM: Thank you, René Descartes. Thank you, Francis Bacon.

SN: Exactly. But when we come to the world of philosophy and thought, thought is conditioned—that is, the very reasoning faculty is itself conditioned by many factors. It's conditioned by man's inner as well as external state. And the development of this Enlightenment kind of mind which sees reason as totally divorced from religion, from Revelation, from the spiritual questions and from spiritual discipline—that is, alien to other civilizations. Look at, for example, in Japan. Put Islam aside.

Seyyed Hossein Nasr

MM: Sure.

SN: If you want to be a Japanese philosopher—I don't mean the modern Japanese philosopher who is always studying Kant. That's not classical Japanese philosophy, but take a traditional philosopher who, let's say, becomes a Zen or a follower of Shin ran or another of the major schools of Japanese Buddhism. He would spend years and years in remaking himself, in gaining a new state of consciousness, not only going to college and reading books, but remolding himself so that the consciousness is transformed and then he becomes a philosopher. This wedding between philosophy and spiritual discipline came to an end in the modern West.

MM: So the Western view of a good life, as something in itself, as opposed to how other cultures say a good life is a spiritual life aimed at something beyond the physical world. I mean, that's a profound difference.

SN: That's a profound difference. But even if you look at the West and say the good life, how do you define this word g-o-o-d? What is the content of this word?

MM: Well, that's one of those basic questions. Right?

SN: Exactly, but if you really look at this philosophically . . .

MM: In Islamic philosophy, you must ask the same question.

SN: Yes. And in Islamic philosophy it's very clear: The good is what God has defined as good in the Revelation. And the philosophers also believe that God has given us the intelligence to be able to discern that truth. They give a positive turn to intelligence. It's the nature of intelligence to be able to understand that God has commanded the good. But supposing you don't believe in religion, you don't believe in the divine origin of things. Ask the question: how do we know that something is good? It is the question, famous question, asked by Dostoevsky, in *Crime and Punishment* where a person kills a person who seems to be useless. He's of no use to society—why shouldn't we kill him?

MM: Right.

SN: And so, the question is . . .

MM: Was it Chesterton who said that if people who will believe in nothing will believe in anything?

SN: Exactly. Exactly. So even people who claim, who say they're ethical philosophers but have no interest in religion ...

MM: Can you construct an ethics without ...

SN: I do not believe so. What is really the content of that ethics has not come from simply rationalism. Otherwise, you have a lot of rationalists in Stalin's Russia and Hitler's Germany and many other abominable situations, but also ...

MM: Dostoevsky's person who doesn't contribute to the world, doesn't deserve to be a person?

SN: Exactly. Yes, the idea that reason itself is sufficient to determine the content of the good life, what is the good life, that I, as a philosopher, do not accept. And I believe those who do are really heirs—let's say to what Socrates had said was the good life or Plato said was the good life—but such people do not realize that those views are not based on pure reason. They were men for whom reason was affected by the intellect, by what Plato calls *nous*, which is not simply reason or *ratio* in Latin. It's a faculty which is able to, in a sense, know the divine truth in its immediacy.

MM: So, the goal is to live a good life as revealed to us by God and to live to the greater glory of God? That's a medieval view.

SN: Yes. But it's close enough, it's close enough. But I'll go one step further as far as Islamic thought is concerned. The highest good is to be able to know the Supreme Reality. It is knowledge, philosophical knowledge in the oriental traditions, Islamic, Indian, Chinese, Japanese, the different forms, of course, different emphases, that lead ultimately to freedom, deliverance. But deliverance from ourselves.

MM: Deliverance from ego, from self ...

SN: From the ego, from the passions, from all the limitations which contingencies of life on this earth impose upon us. Only in this way one becomes able to know fully. We, today, believe that knowledge brings freedom on a horizontal level, and so we invent more and more things and we think, therefore, that we become more and more free.

MM: Physical freedom.

SN: Physical freedom. But we realize that is not so even on the physical plane.

Seyyed Hossein Nasr

This world boomerangs back upon us. Are we more free really than in the eighteenth century?

MM: And you have to wear these bodies around all the time.

SN: Not only that, but if you were living in Boston in the eighteenth century, you didn't have all the knowledge of airplanes and so forth and so on; it was more difficult to travel to London. But, in other times, from another point, it was much easier, you would just take a boat and go. Now you have to get a passport, you've got to get a visa, the plane has to do this, you have to have a whole group of people to get the plane ready, and so forth and so on. So this kind of freedom is not really freedom. It's a pseudofreedom.

MM: So what's real freedom?

SN: Freedom is to be independent of contingency and limitation. To become, to be able to transcend all limitation is freedom.

MM: To transcend the physical world and the . . .

SN: And the psychological world and the passionate world. There is something within us at the center of our being which is beyond and above all the temporal and spacial contingencies and limitations of human life with which we identify ourselves, usually. And the role of the philosopher is to be able to reach that center, the divine center within us.

MM: When is that revealed to us? How do we sense its existence, this place?

SN: It depends who we are. It could be revealed to you as a teenager, it could be revealed to you when you are seventy years old. But it is accessible.

MM: Is it revealed through philosophy?

SN: It's revealed through religion and the philosophy that is within religion, philosophy in the sense of *Sophia,* of wisdom that is within religion. Religion has two levels, two roles. One is that it provides an ethics for everybody. Not everybody is meant to be a philosopher. No civilization has produced a society in which there are only philosophers.

MM: Right. Somebody's got to put the saddle on a horse.

SN: Also, of different temperaments. Even not only putting a saddle on the horse; people might be artists, poets, pianists, workers in a mine, all kinds of different things. There are different types of human temperaments, different types of human vocations.

MM: Does God tell us what our work is?

SN: Well, in a sense, He gives direction, gives meaning to that. You also have the doctrine in the Catholic church. That's why you have a patron saint of almost everything, precisely because there is a kind of saintly, spiritual element that is connected to traditional work. But that level of religion is for everyone. But, in addition to that, from the Islamic point of view or the Hindu point of view, there is also metaphysics, knowledge of the nature of ultimate reality, associated with the inner dimension of religion.

MM: There's another term you don't hear much in philosophy anymore—metaphysics.

SN: Exactly. And which we used to hear a lot, for 2,000 years in the West, but you don't hear about that very much today. Well, I'm a metaphysician. I'm primarily a metaphysician, although I began in the field of physics while studying here at MIT and Harvard. But I'm a metaphysician. I went into the field of philosophy with a love for metaphysics.

MM: I'm amazed by how many people I've talked to who are philosophers now who started in physics.

SN: That's right.

MM: Is there something in physics that lends itself to moving, moving into philosophy?

SN: Well, first of all, the chair occupied by Sir Isaac Newton, which still is at Cambridge University, which Steven Hawking now holds, is called the Chair of Natural Philosophy. Physics was natural philosophy. The term physics is a very modern term. It goes back to the eighteenth century.

MM: There's another figure to go with Descartes and Bacon, is Newton.

SN: Of course.

MM: God is the watchmaker.

Seyyed Hossein Nasr

SN: But from a very different, very different perspective. Newton was a profoundly religious person who was tortured by his own discoveries. People do not realize that more than half of Newton's works were concerned with commenting upon the scriptures, with alchemy, with the numerical significance of the Book of Daniel, with predictions based upon Gematria and Cabalistic interpretations of the sacred text and so forth and so on, which is quite amazing.

MM: Do you think he was, at some point, revealing God, too, with his calculus?

SN: There are many later writers and poets who felt that he was, in a sense, revealing the mind of God. That I will not go into because it is a very complicated issue. In a sense, anyone who learns anything about God's creation is gaining vision of an aspect of God's wisdom.

MM: So is that what happens—is that what you found, that the more you looked at the physical world, the more you find yourself drawn toward God?

SN: What I found was not quite that. Because I was a very gifted student in the field of mathematics and the sciences. I received one of the highest grades anyone ever received in one of these math exams even before I came to MIT. Everybody thought I was going to go into this field. But I believed that, when I studied physics, I would discover an aspect of the nature of reality, at least physical reality. I was right here at MIT one day and Bertram Russell was giving a lecture. I had a philosophical mind and I was studying philosophical things. And he said, do not think that in studying physics, you're going to learn about the nature of reality. You're going to learn about a construct concerning pointer readings. And that was really the straw that broke the camel's back. I decided to leave the field of physics, although I still was an undergraduate. I spent several years finishing my degree and even getting a Master's degree in the sciences before I went to do my Ph.D. in the history of science and philosophy at Harvard. But, right there and then, I realized that in physics I am not learning something about really God's wisdom, and that modern science is not interested in God's wisdom. That is, modern science creates a form of knowledge which is exclusive of the divine principle.

MM: Though, lately, half of the physicists out there seem to be catching up with . . .

SN: Ah, that's the point. That's the whole point. That is, it's really impossible to do serious physics unless you don't want to think . . .

MM: Well, there's a few. I talked to Steven Weinberg.

SN: Yes.

MM: He said we don't need God in all this.

SN: Well, he's an atheist. But there are many others. Even Steven Hawking is not an atheist. He talks about discovering the mind of God.

MM: Apparently not any more. His writings have changed.

SN: Have changed a lot. They've changed a lot recently, but there are a lot of physicists who realize that to do serious theoretical physics, unless you don't want to think beyond the lab and just turn off your mind and come out, if you're doing serious physics, you're confronted with questions which are deeply philosophical and theological questions, not only philosophical questions, but also theological questions. So, paradoxically, what's happening in the West is that, as mainstream Christian theologians, most of them, not all, are turning backwards to be second-rate physicists, in a sense, trying to make theology more malleable; to be in accordance with modern science, many physicists are turning to theological issues and are becoming philosophers and theologians. And Western philosophy, since Kant, has really been the handmaid of physics. And now, gradually there is a movement within the philosophical world in the West to try to be a critic of modern science as well as simply trying to explain its methods.

MM: Was the twentieth century the last attempt of Western philosophy to try to become Western science?

SN: I believe so. I believe so.

MM: We have the history of the Vienna Circle and all these groups.

SN: You see, there you have people as different as Martin Heiddeger and Richard Rorty. Two very different philosophical positions, both saying that Western philosophy is reaching a dead end. Of course, it is not Western philosophy which is dead, but this kind of philosophy which simply seeks to be the handmaid of an empirical science and which is based upon analysis after analysis after analysis and which has destroyed the metaphysical edifice of Western civilization. The word truth is no longer mentioned. The word beauty is no longer mentioned. Reality is operationally defined and so forth and so on. There has been very little interest in ethics. Now it's coming back because we're destroying the world very rapidly thanks to the application of the science, which itself is related to modern philosophy. I think that kind of activity is on the decline and I think in the twenty-first century . . .

Seyyed Hossein Nasr

MM: Where does Western philosophy look? Does it look into its own past or does it look to Islamic philosophy and other philosophies?

SN: I think that is a very good question. I think it's going to look to two places. First of all, to take its own tradition seriously, not only as history of philosophy, but as philosophy. That is, Aristotle is not only interesting because he's in the history of philosophy, but because he's Aristotle. And, secondly, I think it will look more and more to non-Western philosophies. Until now, some have looked upon Indian philosophy. I mean, drawn from Hinduism because the term Indian is a bit vague, and some to Buddhist philosophy, very few to Islamic philosophy. Henry Corbin was one great exception in France. But now more and more people are beginning in that direction. I think that in the future, these twin sources—that is, the West's own earlier philosophical tradition looked upon as philosophy and not only history, and also non-Western philosophies will be all important.

MM: So will this be the second time, then, that the Islamic world has held onto these treasures and then given them back to the West?

SN: That's a very good question.

MM: . . . years ago.

SN: One of the most eminent American philosophers, Huston Smith, who is a good friend of mine, when my Gifford lectures came out in 1981, was very kind and said this book will be remembered like the translations from Aristotle in the thirteenth century which brought something that was held in the Islamic world to the West and brought about a major philosophical change. We shall see. We shall see. But I think that may happen.

MM: Let's play out the scenario a little bit. What happens if the spiritual comes back into Western philosophy? Does it collide with the sort of crowning achievement of Western civilization, which is the scientific method? Do they run into each other?

SN: I believe there is no such thing as the scientific method?

MM: Oh, really?

SN: I believe that science is what scientists do.

MM: Yeah?

SN: I mean every child knows that Einstein said that *E* equals *mc* squared. What does that have to do with the scientific method? Einstein is a young man looking at the formulas of Newtonian physics and said something's wrong with this. And he came up with the theory of relativity. Without any experimentation and all these things we talk about as parts of the scientific method. I believe that there are many scientific methods. But this pure empiricism which we identify with the scientific method is a more philosophical understanding of science than science itself. Yes, it will collide with that philosophical interpretation.

MM: So, what happens then?

SN: You have to have a multiplicity of methods, multiplicity of looking at the world of nature, even. We must develop more than one science of nature. This one science we have developed, if you don't develop other sciences, is going to kill us all the way we're applying it.

MM: But the reductionist view of Western science is: there's only one way of looking at the natural world, through science.

SN: That's right. And, of course, I reject that completely, but I think that in the future it will be rejected more and more, especially because of the incredible crisis that is coming up on the horizon which is due directly to applications of modern technology to society. And on the basis of a kind of managerial logic, which has developed, we seek to manage the environment, manage this, manage that. This is an extremely serious matter—I mean the environmental crisis.

MM: But Islam has a tradition of managing the environment, too, doesn't it? I mean, that man is the most, is the most cunning and clever of creatures, so . . .

SN: Not in the same way.

MM: He is the custodian of nature?

SN: Well, yes, custodian is very different.

MM: Than manager.

SN: You see, what happened is that, in the Renaissance, I blame Renaissance humanism to a large extent for the pollution of the Charles River. In my recent book, *Religion and the Order of Nature,* the lectures I gave at the University of Birmingham . . .

MM: Erasmus might not like the . . .

SN: Exactly. He might not like it, but that's just too bad. Because what happened in the Renaissance is that, in a sense, Western man absolutized himself. He took the absolute away from God and put it in himself. Henceforth, everything human is absolute. Now, it is true that before that also men had domesticated animals, they had donkeys and horses that drew water from wells and so forth and so on—obviously. But the rights of man were not absolute. The rights of God were absolute and that, to some extent, protected the natural world. Now what happened in the Renaissance made the rights of man absolute, which we still accept, and hence we're destroying all the forests of Oregon in the name of those rights. They say, but if you don't do that, we'll lose jobs. So jobs of 12,000 people are more important than the lives of all the owls and other animals, of all the beings that we're destroying, and destroying the virgin forest. Now that kind of transformation did not take place in the Islamic world.

MM: But how do we know what God wants? Through Revelation?

SN: Through Revelation. But that religion has always taught. Despite the fact that some people in the West blame Judaism and Christianity for the environmental crises because Genesis said that man has dominion over the world, it is not religion that is responsible because that man who was given dominion over the world was also the man responsible as God's representative on earth to protect the world. I believe that the idea that we have a kind of absolute right is false. Through a kind of scientistic, not scientific worldview, any future in the spiritual sense has been taken away from us. So all we have is love of this world. We must try to live two years longer, no matter what happens, no matter how we impose ourselves upon the natural environment . . .

MM: Because there's nothing else.

SN: Who says there's nothing else? Since the soul is turned away from all of its spiritual associations and joy and is turned toward the world, people have to acquire more and more wordly things to keep themselves going every day. And yet they're unhappy with themselves inwardly and have to buy things all the time to forget themselves. They have to destroy nature and consume and consume and consume. So this is really a very deep spiritual malaise. And all that is not caused directly by Western science. Western science could be developed without even applying it. But, in combination with technology and the concept of man that grew out of the Renaissance, all of these things have combined together, creating a very lethal potion which threatens to destroy us all.

MM: So how do you keep from being very pessimistic?

SN: I think the spiritual person is never pessimistic. Pessimism and optimism are sentimental. I believe that . . .

MM: But if you sense a catastrophe coming . . .

SN: I think that the only hope for humanity is a catastrophe caused by modern technology; otherwise we'll all die a slow death. I think the only thing that could jolt the conscious of people not to continue this destructive way of living is a catastrophe not in Nepal and India, which nobody thinks about, for as Indians die—so what, you go and turn on your television and watch football. But something close enough to home to help everyone to realize the devastation that might come about later, to prevent us from continuing on this path. If we don't have a small catastrophe, we're going to have a big catastrophe. But, in the ultimate sense, I'm a Muslim. I'm a Muslim thinker and philosopher and, like a Christian or a Jew, I believe that there's always God's help as a divine source in the universe. In that sense, I'm not pessimistic, but I'm certainly very pessimistic about the way we're racing down the road like this at 220 miles an hour with hands off the wheel and turning on the radio and blowing the whistle as if nothing is happening. And no matter how one shouts and what one says, nobody cares. Nobody cares. Just to cite an example, we open up the Alaskan wildlife areas for oil, raising the temperature of the earth, when we really don't need the oil and could live with less. And it's not only in the United States now, of course. Japan has already depleted many of the forests of southeast Asia. It's mostly Japan, which has done this, taking much of the forest area in Malaysia and Indonesia and just cutting the trees, causing erosion. Japan is a powerful industrial nation. Now the Japanese are trying to take more care of their own natural environment while putting their hands on Brazil's Amazon Basin, Malaysia, Indonesia, etc.

MM: Is that what the fundamentalism is in the Islamic world—is it a defense against this Western influence?

SN: There are people who use the term fundamentalist; I don't like this term very much, but it's been used now, so we also use it. In the Islamic world, there was not too much awareness of the environmental crisis at the beginning, but there arose forces to defend society against the cultural changes which were coming very rapidly through the radio, through television, through the movies . . .

MM: And the secularization that came with it.

SN: That came with it . . .

MM: And the absolute-ism of man.

SN: The absolutism of man, and certain jarring actions, especially among the young and women, which was too jarring for the societies in question. And, therefore, there was this reaction of trying to protect one's identity. That's what it was. But many of these forms of what we call fundamentalism then picked up the most violent aspects of Western thought and history. The very notion of revolution, for example, is a Western idea, a nineteenth-century Western idea. It really goes back to the French Revolution, which came at the end of the eighteenth century, and the American Revolution . . .

MM: So, ironically, by resisting the West, they ended up adopting the methods of the West.

SN: Indeed. But there are other movements afoot for which, again, I don't like to use the word fundamentalism, which are not doing that. Look at what's happening in Algeria today. The two sides are participating in the same kind of atrocious warfare which is against all the teachings of Islam. One side says the French secret police is helping the Algerian government. The Algerian government says other countries are helping the other side and so forth and so on. But there's nothing Islamic in the equation. In other parts of the Islamic world, although some people have adopted Western ways of thinking about ideology applied to Marxist ideas, even models of Lenin coming to Russia in 1917 and so forth in the name of Islam, in some places, there are deeper movements and currents afoot which try to protect the cultural identify of Islamic society.

MM: And is that where the message will be found that eventually will be rediscovered by the West in those movements?

SN: Yes, from those elements which, in a permanent, traditional way, have preserved the Islamic form of life and wisdom found in Sufism, Islamic philosophy, and theology, many different currents of Islamic thought which even now have gained many interested parties in the West.

MM: Stop right there and we'll say good-bye.

SN: All right.

JOSEPH MARGOLIS
The Marriage of History and Culture

Joseph Margolis, Laura H. Camell Professor of Philosophy at Temple University. Joe Margolis, author of more than thirty books, is a "gentle giant" in the world of philosophy. In the midst of calm repose, he expresses profound ideas while drawing on his tremendous knowledge of human history. With his belief that culture and history are intertwined, he expressed that to understand history is to understand culture and ideally this will lead to a greater understanding of the bridges between cultures.

MM: Michael Malone   **JM:** Joseph Margolis

MM: Joe, let's talk about history. You've been thinking and writing about history for half a century or more. And one of the more memorable things you've ever written was that to theorize about history is to theorize about reality. What do you mean by that?

JM: Well, usually, when people think about history, they just think about narratives over time. But you can also think about history as the process of thinking. That's to say, not only are there events that we think about and organize in a narrative way, but thinking itself has a historical structure—that is, we don't think the same way from one age to another.

MM: Our consciousness changes?

JM: Yes, I think it does. I don't mean to say that it changes radically—because there is one interesting general truth about the human race, which is a stunning fact: namely, that every society is a society of bilinguals. There is no known society for which there are no people who don't speak the language of that society and the language of another society. There's never been a human society that was not bilingual.

MM: Really?

JM: And to be bilingual also means being bicultural. That is, if a people speaking any language are bilingual, then they also have a way of understanding some culture other than their own. Now the way in which we think, I believe, is a function of the changing practices of the society we learn the language in. And, consequently, the way we understand ourselves and understand other societies is a function of the historical change in the life of that society.

MM: Now these shifts in thinking are due to changing metaphors? Changing senses of time and space? By technology?

JM: Well, in a way, technology is closer to the truth. That is, as I see it, human experience changes, and one of the reasons it changes is that our technology changes. Many other things as well—political events and so on. And so the concept that we internalize in infancy and in learning language carry with it the changing history of the culture. Our thinking about the world actually changes historically, but never so radically that we exceed the limits of bilingualism and biculturalism. You see what I mean? There's a conservative element there. We cannot change that fast that we couldn't understand one another and we can't fail to change or be that slow in changing that we aren't accommodating the rate of change in the culture we live in.

MM: Are all these changes still embedded in our history?

JM: They become sedimented.

MM: Sedimented, okay. So we think in layers.

JM: Yes. See what I mean?

MM: Yes.

JM: Absolutely. And so, for example, one interesting thing is that the parent generation and the generation of the children tend to notice in some way that they don't quite see the world in the same way. But they don't see the world in such different ways that they cannot quite fathom one another from their own point of view. Okay?

MM: Yes.

JM: Now, in that sense, understanding history in this deeper way of understanding the historical structure of thinking is understanding that the world which is intelligible to us also changes from that point of view.

MM: And what about these great paradigm shifts—like going from hunter–gatherer to an agrarian society, or 1795 with the industrial revolution, or 1876 with the second industrial revolution and then now, with the digital revolution?

JM: Yes. Well, I think those are, so to say, radical changes seen in retrospect. They're *all* gradual. They cannot fail to be gradual because if they went too quickly, human beings would not be able to make continuous sense of their world.

MM: In the middle of one of these transformations, could you look at the disparities between parent and child and see that they're greater than they usually are?

JM: Well, you know, there is this general theory that human history does not seem to have changed at the pace at which we now see it changing. Prior to the emergence of the Industrial Revolution or prior to the development of political society in the modern sense, distinctions are made between so-called traditional societies where the technology is extremely, shall we say, natural in terms of hunting and gathering and that kind of thing, as opposed to technological changes of the kind we're now familiar with. When that happened, particularly with the emergence of technology in the modern sense, the pace of change and, therefore, the pace of thinking accelerated. And so, the discrepancies between generations are more noticeable in our time.

MM: But we can still talk to the past, can't we?

JM: We can.

MM: We can still read the Gilgamesh Epic.

JM: Exactly.

MM: Which is 5,000 years old.

JM: Well, that, in a sense, is the point of what I was driving at by emphasizing bilingualism. Put it this way: The problem of bilingualism is not only the problem of one culture understanding another or one language understanding another, but also within a culture or language. It's in our own society as well as between societies.

MM: So we not only communicate with our contemporaries in society, but we also converse with the past.

JM: And even with ourselves, in a sense, if we look at things that we produced under earlier days, we may find it difficult to understand not only what we meant at the moment, but what the concepts were in terms of which this was being processed.

MM: What about the role of translation?

JM: Well, translation will follow the same pattern.

MM: In a sense, don't we retranslate all the important texts to understand them?

JM: Yes.

MM: In our own worldview?

JM: That's right. Well, that is one of the consequences of what I'm calling historicity—by which I mean the process of the historical movement of thinking and, therefore, of the intelligible world which is, so to say, the accusative of that kind of, in a grammatical sense, the accusative of that kind of process of self-understanding. So translation moves the same way that self-understanding moves. In fact, it's just a form of self-understanding. We have to reinterpret our world in the terms we regard as current. We change over time in the same way.

MM: Now what about not history itself, but histories. Doesn't each generation revisit history and rewrite it according to its needs?

JM: Yes. Well, I think if you take events like the French Revolution or the First World War, or Second World War—it's clear that the Civil War is a good case—there is no obviously single correct way of construing a history. There are even contemporaneously many alternative and competing views and certainly, over time, the events are seen in terms of what are taken to be the consequences of events that couldn't have been foreseen. And they're not simply tacked on to the events, they begin to color the description of the earlier phases of those events. And so the history of histories changes. That is to say, the histories are narratives constructed retrospectively by people whose own historicized imagination keeps changing over time. There's a sort of a double element—namely, the real events are read differently over changing history and our capacity to read them changes for different reasons.

MM: So history then, as you said about objectivity, is consensus.

JM: That's my view. But by consensus, I don't mean taking a vote. I don't mean consensus as a criterion. I mean consensus is the space of social life: that people can tolerate the account that's given, can regard it as acceptable even if it disagrees with another account—divergence and so on.

MM: So, in our time, this lack of interest in the great man theory of history . . .

JM: Yes.

MM: And much more, the average person theory of history . . .

JM: All right.

MM: And that's just happened within the last fifty years.

JM: Yes. So it is the case that there are changes in fashion in history, but it's also the case that there's not simply a selection with respect to a sort of fixed array of possibilities, but the space of the possibilities keeps changing. And it changes not only with new experience, but it changes under the pressure of interpreting the changes that have taken place in the interpretation of history.

MM: Let me tell you why I wanted to talk to you about this. I was very interested in talking about this. I've been a daily beat reporter, I've been a feature reporter, I've been an investigative reporter, and then I've written books of contemporary history.

JM: Okay.

MM: And people ask me what the true story is.

JM: Oh, well.

MM: And the only answer I have for them is, when I wrote the breaking news story that day, I thought I had the truth.

JM: Yes.

MM: And then, two weeks later, when I wrote the big roundup feature on it, I realized that there was a truth behind the truth.

JM: Yes.

MM: And then, six months later, when I did the big investigative story, I realized there was a truth behind the truth behind the truth.

JM: Yes.

MM: Five years later, at a cocktail party, someone comes up to me and says, "Let me tell you what really happened."

JM: Yes.

MM: And I now have another truth behind that.

JM: Yes, very good.

MM: And, ten years later, I write the history of it and, in retrospect, pondering everything I've heard, I realize there's yet another truth.

JM: Right.

MM: I've never found it. Unless they're all true.

JM: Yes. Well, I wouldn't put it quite that way. I would say that our picture of what it means to be objective has changed. I mean, the usual view has been that the objectivity of history or description of social events and so on follows the pattern of the description of nature, which doesn't have human significance in the same way. So there is a theory—whether it's right or wrong can be debated—but there is a theory that, with respect to natural phenomena, there is a uniquely correct description or explanation that's going on. So people suppose that the same thing is true in the world of human culture and history. Now it seems to me that, under the pressure of understanding the effect of "historicity," we realize that objectivity, in that sphere, has to accommodate the variety of possibilities of interpreting history within certain limits. Not everything goes. But it is the case that many things that are incompatible with another may be part of the picture part of an objective account.

MM: That gets almost into the aesthetics of history.

JM: Well, the interpretation of an artwork is, in my view, a sort of metonym or paradigm for how we understand ourselves in terms of history. The logic is the same.

MM: So perhaps the only points of view where you could actually see history objectively is either the eye of God or the innocent eye test of art?

JM: Well, I think neither one of those is possible, in a sense. That is, if God sees it in a certain way, human beings would still have to interpret what they think God is doing when he's seeing it that way.

MM: It still has to go through us.

JM: Right. And the innocent eye is a construction from an idealization of some kind from the variety and scatter that I'm talking about.

MM: This isn't very comforting. You know that.

JM: Yes. It isn't, or it is?

MM: It isn't comforting. It is not comforting.

JM: Oh, in the ordinary world it is regarded as not comforting. It is comforting for me.

MM: Well, I was hoping you'd give me this paradoxical thing of the truth behind the truth, you know, constantly just receding into the distance ...

JM: Yes.

MM: But I have to operate as a historian.

JM: Yes.

MM: As a journalist.

JM: Absolutely.

MM: You have to operate on the belief that you can find objective truth somewhere in there.

JM: Well, I'm saying that what we mean by objective truth in the historical setting will have to accommodate this play of differences, whereas the sort of, the prejudicial view of truth borrowed from a frame of reference which is alien to human self-description insists that this couldn't be objective because it doesn't agree with the other. Now the key to the whole argument is that there are properties in the human world which don't appear in nature.

MM: Like contradiction.

JM: Well, like the significance of human events. I mean, nature does not have significative properties. I mean, if you pick up a stone, you say, "Well, what are its physical properties?" But if you, so to say, pick up a war, you say, "Well, what is its significance?" There doesn't seem to be any way to understand the meaning or significance of a war in terms of the way in which you describe the properties of a stone.

MM: You can't detach it from ...

JM: I think not.

MM: ... humanity.

JM: I think you can.

MM: In its interpretation.

JM: That's also why to understand history is to understand the world. If you see what I mean. That the nature of what we regard as the human world is simply the counterpart of what happens to our abilities to understand ourselves and our world.

MM: And that explains your line that thinking is a history.

JM: *Is* history. Exactly. Thinking is history itself. History is, so to say, the living process of human thought considered in its social dimension, moving through time with regard to understanding itself. How do we understand ourselves in time? That's history. And it's thought.

MM: But that means that there's no fixity out there.

JM: That's my point. And the radical implication of this idea is that, when people insist that there are fixed truths or fixed values or fixed norms, you realize that they are making an idealized selection out of possibilities in this world of flux, you might say, which suits their interests. Now I'm not quarreling with that, but the point is, it's an artifact. It's made at a certain time and there are people who monitor its validity and its acceptability and its right to, so to say, police people or something of the kind.

MM: So history has a mythical structure then?

JM: Well, by myth, I mean something slightly different, if I may say so. What I mean is, the vision of the whole, the idea that you not only look at the details of the human world, but you can have the picture of the whole universe of thought. Of course, the reason why you can't have that in any ordinary way is that everything we say is said in a certain context, as we say. And every context is located in a more inclusive context. And the universe might be said to be the context of all contexts. But, of course, if you take that view, then the universe is not an object of discourse because to say it is would mean to put it in a larger context and that would be contradictory. You see what I mean?

MM: Yes.

JM: So, in that sense, the way I put it is, in a kind of fussy way, is that to make an assertion implicates a mythic point of view. Because, whatever you say implicates the idea that you are talking in a nested set of contexts which ultimately belongs to the inclusive universe—which you can never specifically talk about or which you, so to say, parse as the whole domain within which you are saying what you say.

MM: I'm curious about something. Does this explain why the best histories are almost always like novels? They have a fictional structure. Because they recognize that nature of history?

JM: Well, I see your point and I think I agree with what you say, but I would put it a little differently.

MM: I mean, histories as lists are not interesting. Histories as charts are not interesting.

JM: No, of course.

MM: Histories as a story, like Gibbon, are wonderful. And we learn from them.

JM: Well, the only reason why I hesitated is that . . . I wouldn't say that speaking that way is producing a fiction. In other words, I think that human life has a narrative structure. That is, you live a life from birth to death.

MM: You live an epic novel.

JM: Well, not necessarily that, but you live a life that has a kind of purposive structure, which you impute to it as you live, as you become intelligent and reflect on growing up. You begin to see the shape of your life and you begin to see the implications of what you go on to do as somehow fulfilling possibilities of your life. So it has a narrative structure. History and fiction have the same structure.

MM: And, like history, you don't really understand the plot until you look back. In retrospect, you really only see the narrative structure.

JM: Well, what I want to say is, it's not so much that you don't see the plot as you constantly make and remake the plot. You're writing your own life, in a sense.

MM: And editing it.

JM: That's right. And there are constraints on it, just as there are alternative narratives for the Second World War, there are alternative narratives for your life and mine. They have exactly the same kind of structure in that sense.

MM: Now one of the rules of history is to teach.

JM: Yes.

MM: And to be predictive.

JM: Well, that's still possible. This frame of reference doesn't diminish either science or the plausibility of historical accounts.

MM: But, if we choose our history to fit our time, in a sense, then, we have narrowed our ability, haven't we, to predict the future? In a sense, we narrow to predict a future that's going to be a lot like now.

JM: Well, there is, you might say, there's a constant predictive element in narratizing our life. That is to say, the structure that you attribute to your own life already accommodates the likelihood that it will develop in a certain way. So it already has built into it predictive elements. I mean, even insurance, the idea of insurance, is based on the idea that . . .

MM: The actuarial table.

JM: Yes. Well, that the narrative account is entitled to give us a sort of expectation about how the story will fill itself out.

MM: I see. Blood pressure, certain point, nonsmoker, then the narrative says . . .

JM: Absolutely. Absolutely.

MM: . . . Okay, you get to live to be eighty-two years old.

JM: Those are all, so to say, atomic elements abstracted from some inclusive narrative.

MM: But none of those narratives account for a discontinuity. The prediction is, you're going to live to be eighty-two, but you get hit by the bus.

JM: Well, of course . . .

MM: The history that helps you predict the future doesn't account for the invention of the light bulb.

JM: Well, that's right. There are always going to be surprises which force you to reconstruct your history. But, under the conditions that things move in, let us say, an actuarially likely way, then the stories complete themselves in ways that we have effectively predicted. That's the way we see it. So, there has to be enough success . . .

MM: Yes. We keep rewriting the book right up to the last moment . . .

JM: Absolutely.

MM: So it looks like it was all planned in that direction, it was all going to end . . .

JM: Well, we might see it that way . . .

MM: End up with that resolution.

JM: We might see it that way, but I'm saying that we have to distinguish between, let's say, how we actually behave and think about our lives and the theory of what we're doing when we're behaving and thinking about our lives that way. My account is only concerned with the second question, not the first. But I'm trying to describe what it is people do when they are doing the ordinary thing with respect to their lives.

MM: Something major happens like the Industrial Revolution.

JM: Absolutely.

MM: Then society has to scramble very fast to rewrite its histories?

JM: No, because the Industrial Revolution is itself a narratized account of a very wide movement of history. It never happened at any moment. It's, so to say, the legible character.

MM: It's 100 years later, we put a mark on the time line that says 1795 . . .

JM: Exactly right. I mean, you know the old story that people in the Middle Ages didn't know they belonged to the Middle Ages. I mean, what's the point of that? The point is that that characterization can only be made from the future. So the future is, so to say, looking back and reconstructing the sequence of events.

MM: Well, let's talk about the future because you said an extraordinary thing. There is no form of serious inquiry that can survey our present options and guess satisfactorily what our options will be at the close of the next millennium. You're not talking about 2000, you're talking about 3000.

JM: Well, because when I wrote that I was anticipating the close of our millennium. But we know, I mean, if we take at all seriously what has happened in our relatively recent past, we know that the changes that take place, largely through technology now, are so radical, and that the introduction of those radical changes changes the pattern of our history and thinking, then we cannot possibly anticipate how those things will change in the future. That's also a mystery in our world.

MM: If we were in a castle in the middle of the Holy Roman Empire in the year 1000, there would simply be no way we could predict the year 1999.

JM: No.

MM: The year 2000.

JM: I have used the example of the cubists, the cubist movement. I'm rather fond of painting and the history of painting in a way. And now what I suggest is this: that if you knew everything that was reasonably claimed validly about art in the Middle Ages, you would not be able to foresee cubism. Not because you weren't smart enough, but because the connection between the work of the Middle Ages and the cubists is creative. That is to say, it introduces in some reasonably regular and impressive way changes which changed the whole world of our thinking. And that, therefore, only if we follow that pattern of change can we retrospectively see how cubism came out of, that is to say, the art of the Middle Ages. We can't see it in the forward direction because there's no retrospective there.

MM: There's no obvious causal chain until you look back at it.

JM: I think that's true. Because the explanation is given in terms of the conceived possibilities that were fulfilled in cubism.

MM: So we live in a very limited temporal domain.

JM: Absolutely.

MM: We can only look back so far in a sense that history has been changed so many times we can't imagine ourselves inside the minds of people a certain distance back.

JM: Well, we can begin to understand them, but that is from our point of view. But they cannot understand us from their point of view because . . .

MM: So, in a sense, our domain of knowledge goes a little bit into the future, but not very far. A few years, a few decades, maybe?

JM: Well, it depends. But let me see if I can give you some other examples that are even more elementary that confirm the same point. Nobody has ever managed to explain language in biological terms. There have been attempts. There is no known account that is convincing. There are attempts to sort of map language in biological terms. Chomsky is an excellent example, but there are serious limitations in his theory. Now, once we have language, we can look back to our biology and theorize about how biology has facilitated language. You see what I mean? So the same kind of retrospect . . .

MM: The same thing's true with natural selection.

JM: That's right. Now . . .

MM: Start with a horse and look back, but you couldn't start with an early horse and predicted the modern thoroughbred.

JM: Absolutely. Now, I say that the same thing is true in the physical sciences. That is to say, the idea that our universe at the present time evolved through the Big Bang from some initial explosion in a certain way only makes sense in terms of the emergence of creatures like ourselves who would theorize that way.

MM: Right.

JM: So that we construct the picture of how it must have been.

MM: So history is our mechanism for giving the world meaning.

JM: All right.

MM: We map it onto the world, make the world fit that model.

JM: Yes. That's another aspect of the point that the structure of thinking is inseparable from the structure of the world. The intelligible structure of the world is itself a function of the changing history of our thinking about the structure of the world, if you see what I mean.

MM: So, the world is structure-less until we arrive . . .

JM: No.

MM: To give it definition.

JM: No, it's not that it was structure-less, it's that it doesn't make sense to ask what its structure *was* independent of the conditions under which we do so. It isn't that the world either had a structure which we have not discovered or that it had no structure. It's just that it's meaningless to put the question forward except in terms of the history of trying to make sense of the world. Do you see what I mean? Now what that says is that what we call the intelligible world is cooperatively, you might say, built out of the constraints that the world imposes on our thinking so that we don't go haywire.

MM: Right.

JM: And the historical changes in our ability to do just that kind of thing. But to say that also means that there's no fixity there. There can't be. But, of course, human beings require fixity. They say, "You're wrong." I mean, there's a true law about how human beings should behave and nature works that way.

MM: Is there a freedom in that lack of fixity?

JM: Well, what I would say is this: There are theories that favor that. But what I say is, the basic idea of freedom is the idea of speech in the following sense. To be able to say something is to be able to affirm it and to deny it. That means that you can choose one way or another. There's no sense of speech which isn't already structured in some way that's related to the idea of freedom. But when we think about freedom, let's say, politically, we think that, well, it's not enough just to be able to say yes and no. You have to have this or that or the other thing. But what we mean by freedom is obviously a function of how we understand the possibilities of our world. Now certain things which used to be essential to freedom are no longer defensible in that way in our technology. I mean, for example, certain forms of privacy are clearly gone. Once you have a computerized world like ours, you cannot possibly keep your personal life secret in the way in which it used to be possible in things of that kind. Now either people will say, "Look, it's not relevant anymore," or . . .

MM: We've changed our definition of freedom.

JM: Exactly. We still have the basic idea that we can or can't do these things or those things, and it's important at this time to emphasize this new possibility rather than the old one. But the idea that there's some fixed set of conditions for freedom is completely insensitive to the problems of a changing technology. I mean, it doesn't make any sense. Do you see what I mean?

MM: I do. You've been a practicing philosopher for half a century. You've seen a lot of history being made.

JM: Yes.

Joseph Margolis

MM: Has philosophy contributed to the history of the last fifty years?

JM: My own personal view is that philosophy at the present stage is marking time. It's rehearsing the solutions that have been in the game for 400 years at least. In some cases, much longer. And the interesting point about the end of our century is that the concept of historicity has gradually been eliminated. Almost all official philosophy at the present time in the West has abandoned the idea of history. My idea of historicity has been drummed out, which is essentially, I think, the product of reflecting on the French Revolution and its consequences. So history in the modern sense, genuinely modern sense—because, after all, the Greeks had history, through Thucydides and Herodotus and so on—the modern sense, not only of history but of what I'm calling historicity, dates approximately from the time of Hegel. That is to say, the end of the eighteenth and the beginning of the nineteenth centuries. And the nineteenth century, par excellence, is the period of reflections on modern history. With respect to philosophy, in the twentieth century, particularly in Anglo-American philosophy, this idea of history was systematically and deliberately attacked. And, by the end of the century, it's been eliminated practically everywhere in the Western world. And that's absolutely extraordinary.

MM: So how do you stay optimistic? How do you stay engaged?

JM: Well, I like to say about myself that I'm doctrinally pessimistic, but biochemically optimistic. I'm by nature optimistic. But I think that the world is going to change again. Now, in the new century, I believe, the idea of history and historicity will have to come back because . . .

MM: It's been knocking on the door for a long time.

JM: I think it's there and I believe that the currents that have driven it out are gradually coming to the end of their tether. They'll be replaced. I'm absolutely convinced that that will be true.

MM: So it's not the end of history, it's the beginning of a new . . .

JM: No, no, no. There can't be an end of history without an end of the race. Yes.

MM: Yes. Thank you.

JM: You're welcome. Thank you.

ASHOK GANGADEAN
Global Dialogue, Global Peace

Ashok Gangadean is Professor and Chair of Philosophy at Haverford College, Pennsylvania, and he is founder-director of the Global Dialogue Institute. Throughout the interview, Professor Gangadean is especially concerned with exploring the capacity of human reason to move between worlds. Extremely articulate, he discusses the power and necessity of *dialogue* in tapping and clarifying the deeper common ground between diverse cultural, religious, and ideological worlds. Global peace and justice are obtainable, but must begin with global dialogue.

MM: Michael Malone   **AG:** Ashok Gangadean

MM: I'm curious about something—looking at your career, you started out as a logician.

AG: Yes.

MM: Thirty years later you're writing about spirituality. What happened in between to cause this transformation?

AG: As you know, logic is a science of thought, so it has a very illustrious history and it's seen as the primary science because if you could know the structure of thought and the laws of thought, you would then have a key and a code to all other disciplines because they all use thought. That's a classic line from Aristotle and Plato in the European tradition. And I was trained in that tradition as a logician at Brandeis University where I did my graduate work. Ah, but there was a wonderful revolution in modern logic with the work of the German mathematical logician, Frege. It was really a rejection of 2,000 years or more of the logical tradition of Aristotle, which had shaped the European imagination. And if Aristotle was wrong, it was really a deep critique of the entire tradition that relied on that logical paradigm. So mathematical logic with Frege, Russell, and Wittgenstein that spawned the modern analytic revolution turned on a deep change in logic itself, and hence advanced different ways of understanding human reason. That's where I grew up as a logician, between these two worlds of the modern paradigm and the classical paradigm. And I was not willing and able to reject the classical. And so I was asking how can these two powerful paradigms—that shaped modern culture and classical culture—both be right in some ways and yet each be limited. I couldn't dismiss either of them. It was a crisis personally for me because the ideal of reason is supposed to entail coherence and noncontradiction and nonpolarity in unity. So it shook me up because if reason itself is split, then, it seems, anything goes. And I realized at that point that this was a crisis Socrates faced as well, because when he came along at the birth of the European tradition, there was another contradiction that had matured between the two great thinkers, Parmenides and Heraclitus, one seeing that Being is the truth, the other one that all is constantly Becoming. And they were at odds. How can Being, Reality, be both being, eternal, and also becoming, radical process at the same time? And when you have a deep contradiction at the core of culture, it seems to open the floodgates to relativism. So Socrates got hemlock for trying to find a deeper foundation to reason. My career began with that crisis.

MM: So what did you do?

AG: In my first couple of years of teaching I faced this crisis and it was as if my professional life split as a logician because my heart and my deepest instinct was that there's got to be a unity to reason and the logic of thought. And that was a commitment. But what I found in my research was that there was a split in logic itself and there were deep polarizing crises across the paradigms of logic. It was even worse than that, because I realized at that point, too, that the greatest minds of philosophy had not yet solved a key question of our culture: How do we move between different worlds? How does someone, say, in the European culture understand the Chinese mind or the Hindu mind or the Buddhist mind or the African mind? I realized that we humans can do that. An anthropologist can go into Africa and, if they're good, not just impose a European grammar on a local worldview, but actually enter a different worldview, a different model of thinking.

MM: So you figure out a way to build that bridge in logic.

AG: Exactly.

MM: So if you can establish a dialogue between that new logic and Aristotle's logic, then you could do it for every other part of life?

AG: You've got it exactly. So my whole life quest became defined at this crisis moment for me. How do we solve the problem of human intelligence moving between worlds? I began to realize that there was a missing science of these dynamics where logic didn't go.

MM: You can't go to the library for that.

AG: No, of course not. I was in new territory and I felt very lonely and alone in my career and at that point I followed another agenda in my life, which was eventually to go to the roots of Indian culture. I was born in Trinidad, of Indian origin, and I grew up in the West. I studied Sanskrit. I went to India for the first time in 1971 for one year to study Indian music and learn the philosophy. And this was a mind-boggling experience for me. What Shankara did in the Hindu

tradition and what Nagarjuna did in the Buddhist tradition was profoundly different—those traditions were at odds and fighting amongst themselves in ways
which puzzled me so that even the meditative traditions had their deep disagree-
ments, obviously. But this is a key point. I began to see a pattern in the meditative awakening of reason. I never even thought of this before. That these teachers were seeing that you've got to pay attention to how you're conducting your
mind, which I didn't understand and which my own classical education didn't
teach me. Well, we look at the content of what we're thinking, but we never stop
to look at *how* we are thinking, the process of thinking. And what the meditative
traditions really saw *par excellence* was that there is such a thing as ego-centered
thinking, like a technology of the mind. They saw that ego thinking produces a
disaster in the human situation, polarizing it in all directions. The key point is
that egocentric thinking is a learned pattern of thinking that puts the thinker as
an independent entity centered in herself/himself looking out at the world as an
object, a content presented to it. It is not obvious at first that this way of thinking
creates fragmentation. That's the structure of egocentric thinking. And these
traditions saw it; the Buddha's great awakening was on that very point. He saw
that as long as you're ego thinking, you suffer. You can't have a coherent life if
things are split within and without. People are split between each other, your
world is split, space, time, mind, matter. All of these things are divided and split
into fragments, so the key that I learned in the meditative traditions from a logical point of view is that they saw that logic had to attend to how you're thinking.
And if you're ego thinking, you're participating in a fragmenting, dualizing, sep-
arating, isolating, tribalizing way that will always lead to pernicious splits. So the
lights went on for me: Could it be that ego-centered thinking had generated the
deep split in logic itself? The split that the meditative thinkers found? So that became a clue in opening the door for me as a logician and philosopher.

MM: And that's meditative reasoning?

AG: Well that took me thirty years of experimentation to clarify. Because I then
began learning and teaching Indian classical texts and my own world was, in a
way, "schizophrenic" in the beginning. I was teaching logic and presenting the
crisis in logic and teaching Hindu thought and Buddhist thought and Zen
thought as I learned these traditions and saw that the meditative traditions were
always critiquing egocentric thinking. And the great teachers, I began to see,
were all suggesting that we don't mature rationally, as thinking beings, unless we
get out of ego thinking into a more dialogical, meditative form of thought. I can
explain that later, but the meditative mind enters a unified field in which you are
not an object to me, you're different. Buber said it well. He said there's a difference between the I / It, which is ego thinking, and the I / Thou, which is dialogic
thinking. And the I / Thou way of thinking is when we're relational—in direct
relational encounter. For example, you are over there, you're different from me,

but somehow we are in a dynamic mutual encounter. And that's a dialogical mode and, to me, the dialogic clicked with the meditative way. For the meditative mind sees things relationally. The Buddha's enlightenment is that when you let go of ego and its pattern of fragmentation and you enter a dynamic unified field (they call it emptiness, co-arising, interactive, interrelational). Then everything is dynamically interrelational.

MM: Now most people will think, when they think of meditation, they think of entering into a space that has nothing to do with reasoning.

AG: Exactly right.

MM: That, you know, the intellect is at work—you know, the little man is inside the machine.

AG: Exactly.

MM: Running the thing, and then meditation is some sort of irrational space that we go to where reasoning, the rules of logic and reasoning, just don't co-exist.

AG: I started out with that type of prejudice myself. And it was not only that it's irrational, but it's extrarational, beyond reason in a way, not *irrational*.

MM: Nonrational.

AG: This is because rationality is almost seen by definition to be dualistic, you know, and based upon the subject/predicate duality and the subject/object split. So it took me years to really put these together to see that the Buddha and Shankara and these great other meditative traditions were really cultivating human reason and saying that reason is meditative; that reason is what happens when you wake up out of the ego thinking, which is what Socrates wanted to do. Plato and Socrates were talking about awakening—you know, philosophy as enlightenment. It has to do with awakening reason, and that reason is beyond mere egocentric reason. That's what was the key to me. That we should not and cannot afford to give reason, this great human achievement, over to ego-centered reason. So the distinction that was crucial to me is that egocentric reason is problematic and has not worked; it has become dysfunctional. But awakened reason, through dialogical, meditative awakening, is the maturing of reason and of the self. And that was like the flash that helped me to see what we really need in our evolution.

MM: And that's your reconciling mechanism?

AG: Exactly.

MM: Between opposing worlds?

AG: That enabled me to understand more deeply the polar split between the Aristotelian and modern logical paradigms. Meditative reason opened a deeper common logic that could heal this split. And the other clue was that I began to see that through the meditative experiments that they all showed that there must be a primal principle or field out of which all of these worlds are arising. And, ironically, that was what the great philosophers were all trying to do. There was always a quest to get to the first principle. I began to see that if you're in ego thinking, you're blocked from it and unless you step back somehow from that ego way of processing the world, you cannot arrive in that primal field.

MM: So what is this primal field? This common ground?

AG: Well, that's a good question because I couldn't even find a global name for it. For example, if you look at the Chinese way of naming this primal field, they would speak of the Tao. The nameless name beyond all names. Plato spoke of Goodness as the ultimate form, beyond all forms. The Christian tradition speaks of the Christ. The Judaic tradition of Yahweh, the first principle. Aristotle of the Prime Mover. Science speaks of the ultimate principle of Energy and Nature. The Buddhists speak of Emptiness. African tradition, such as the Bacongo, speaks of the Nomo or primal name. So we had so many different names for this primal principle that it required a breakthrough for me to say that there is a primal, global name, and a missing primal logic of this field. And so I had to introduce experimentally a name. I use the word Logos, from the Greek, which means the Primal Word, Reason, Speech, Language. It has many connotations, which makes it a good candidate for a global name. There was no global name. So that was a revolution in my own thinking—proposing a universal name for this primal field across worlds.

MM: And we do have the precedent of the notion of "word" as being this fundamental, primal thing.

AG: Exactly.

MM: And we have Christ as the Word. And we have Tao as the nameless thing.

AG: But notice the word Logos. Your question originally was how does a logician thirty years later start speaking of spirituality, because my logical quest ended in Logos, which is the essence of logic. Logic, deep logic, is the science of Logos. It's a science now that brings you to the Unified Field. And the lights began to go on because in science, in physics in particular, astrophysics, and with Einstein's legacy, you have the example of a man (Einstein) who spent his career trying to research the Unified Field. And scientists like Hawkings and others now are on the edge of tapping the "grand, unified field." So it's knowing that the essence of advancing science is gaining access to the unified field of relativity.

MM: Thus, the universe is the Word?

AG: And this, for me, began to solve a number of these deep, enduring problems. I began to heal when I entered into meditative reason. I saw that chronic splits in our culture, between science and religion and science and spirituality, were generated by ego thinking.

MM: Your two worlds again?

AG: Right. There are so many people now, awakening people who sense that there must be unity between the deepest pulse of science and spirituality, and they're right. Because if you tap this missing deep science of Logos, you find that Logos as this Infinite Word is the ultimate source of nature. So that nature is the play of Logos. But that is what the great scriptures are trying to get at.

MM: But can you systematize? Can you apply it as a bridge?

AG: Absolutely. Over these thirty years in my experiments, I had the opportunity at Haverford College to direct the Gest Center For Cross-Cultural Study of Religions and that was an incredible laboratory because it invited different worlds, different worldviews and religions, to come together and dialogue. So it was a living laboratory. Almost as a scientist experimenting, I studied the dynamics of interaction between Christianity and Hinduism. How does Christianity or Judaism interact with Buddhism or Zen or African ways of processing the world? And I began to see that this Logos is what generates dialogue between worlds; it was a bridge, it was a common missing link out of which different worlds arise, even though they haven't really recognized it sufficiently. So the question is: Can you really put it to work? As my career unfolded in this, I began to see that there is a missing logic or technology of thinking. Just as in the digital mode there is a technology of word processing, so too in minding, I see this Logos technology. How we are conducting our mind, moving from ego thinking to meditative thinking and meditative reason as a shift in how we're processing the world. These are two different technologies of minding.

MM: Let's say I'm watching this conversation here and I'm thinking to myself, how have I ever experienced Logos? Could I sit down and find it?

AG: Well, that's a great question. Let me give you a sense of how I explain this to my undergraduate students, which is an experiment in moving the student into this awakening consciousness. When I read the great Buddhist text where we see the Buddha's awakening and then try to take the student from ego thinking into this awakened thinking, students need to realize that they do touch it in their lives. So I find ways to help them see that there's a spontaneous access to the Logos in our high moments. For example, I give the example of a runner who has entered into what athletes now call "the zone," when you've somehow let go of the ego spontaneously. It takes a lot of discipline to do that actually. I try to help my students see that they've had those high moments. Poets have it, creative artists have it. I think obviously Einstein had it when he had flashes into the Unified Field.

MM: But when you're in the zone, first of all you don't know you're in the zone, by definition you're not thinking that you're in the zone, yet you're there. But when you leave the zone, you find you miss it terribly, but you wonder if you could live an entire life in the zone.

AG: That's a beautiful question, yes. And that is the intent of the great teachers, exactly. And being in the zone, living in the zone, is our heritage because if we're rational beings and reason is deeper than ego thinking and it really is the meditative awakening, then the great teachers were showing us the pathway into living in the zone, living in this awakened, mindful state. To me, that's the heart of education. A truly good education is helping our students to become human, fully human, and ego thinking is a stage we go through. As we naturally mature as rational beings to become dialogical, awakened beings, we become mindful in the moment. So I give my students one of the longest assignments he/she has ever been given. I say to them when they come into class: This is a laboratory in which you're going to be looking at your ego habits. Notice how you are sitting right now. How are you breathing? How many of you can attend to your breath without breaking concentration for one minute or two minutes, and they laugh because they realize they could not do it for even three or four seconds. I ask them to keep a journal. And when you come to this class you're going to try to be attentive and mindful of whatever you do: when you're walking with your friends, when you're sitting at a dining hall, when drinking water, when you are going to sleep, when you are playing, when you are playing with your friends on the soccer field, watch yourself. Be attentive. That, to me, is the awakening education and the heart of liberal arts, the classical liberal arts.

MM: So it's a lifelong homework assignment.

AG: Right. And they love it; they feel the challenge of it and it begins to work as they go through the semester.

MM: Didn't philosophy start out like this?

AG: Yes.

MM: So what happened?

AG: Socrates is one of my great heroes because he saw the crisis in culture and that the Sophists were the relativists who were saying that there is no fundamental truth. It's really a matter of your perspective and your opinion—a kind of naive relativism that isn't coherent and Socrates was attempting to give birth to a deeper awakening in philosophy, to deepening inquiry, which is the love of wisdom. And Socrates is a hero for me because he made the classical shift. He said unless you can recognize your ignorance as a prerequisite for advance, you can't advance in the level of wisdom, on the path of wisdom. So, for him, Buddha would say unless you realize you're ego thinking and therefore ignorant and lodged in a kind of sleep and begin the awakening process, you're not going to be educated and rationally enlightened and awakened. So this is the classical dream of philosophy and it seems we've lost it. And I think we've lost it because we cannot underestimate how much the ego patterns of thought have dominated our culture and our lives.

MM: We certainly feel secure in the ego world. I mean, going into the zone, once you realize you're there, you crave to get back to regular life, as appealing as it is, because we're comfortable in this world we know.

AG: I would disagree with that. I think we're very uncomfortable and insecure in the ego world because ... just think about it ...

MM: It's the world we know. The awakened world is not the world we know.

AG: There are different levels of knowledge. There is a primal knowing in which we know that is who we are and we forget it. All the great teachers thought that we forget it and go into ego thinking; we're familiar with it, but it's not very comfortable. And Buddha's great message is that you may not be fully aware of it, but when you're in the ego, ego thinking, you're in a quiet and sometimes noisy despair. Why? You're insecure, because what does the ego do? The ego is saying, "I'm a being unto myself." And that is a deep insecurity. When you create that fiction of "I" as a separate entity, it is the most insecure, ontologically speaking, place to be because you're separated, but you're not really. But you cut yourself off from yourself and this is the source of all sorts of anxieties and pathologies and emptiness of meaning, genuine meaning. You spend your life following certain rules that are maybe familiar in a prescribed life and you reach your midlife and you have a crisis. It's all a struggle for genuine meaning and people are hungry for that, and so I would say that, even though we're familiar with ego thinking, that it is a disaster in terms of the violence it creates between people and within the self. This is what Buddha meant in saying "Life is suffering."

MM: So you're suggesting the cause of most of the strife and the misery in the world is ego thinking?

AG: Absolutely.

MM: Is the Logos, then, the tool for resolving this conflict?

AG: I think so, but in the sense that you can't simply walk into the Logos. You have to be disciplined and equipped and skilled and educated.

MM: But you're establishing an organization to begin to look at it?

AG: Yes.

MM: This Logos is dialogic energy. It's the ground of the dialogue that you want to create between differing worlds.

AG: I would say that dialogue is the technology of entering the Logos.

MM: And that's where people from different worlds can meet. You and I live in a world of enormous conflict. Some people fight each other because they have absolutely antithetical worldviews. Some people, though, are killing each other because they pick up their fork with the wrong hand. They believe everything else. We have small conflicts—we have huge philosophical conflicts, both are violent. Can both be resolved the same way?

AG: That's a good question. First of all, it's important to see the many kinds of violence. I think one of my points is that we've not seen enough how ego culture itself produces and reproduces in our kids and our culture, the ways of violence. Violence has a deeper meaning than we realize. It is not an ego performing certain violent physical acts, but it is being in an ego way of thinking and making yourself is inherently a kind of violence that teachers like Ghandi and Jesus and Buddha have seen. It's projected because when you're an ego and you're in a violent act of being, you've cut yourself off from the flow of reality, which is unified and harmonious. I began to see that there are many levels of violence, but they're traced to the same way of thinking, at the core. Violence between cultures, interreligious strife which we see all around us, interpersonal strife in marriages, in families. But even more important, internal strife. Think about this for a moment. I show my students and they all chuckle, but they all realize it's true.

They come to college, they've been raised in a culture, they don't even realize that our culture is filled with multiple worldviews. I'm raised as a Jew, let's say, and I'm Orthodox. I believe in the biblical view, but I'm a scientist and I go to my physics lab and my teacher is showing me the Big Bang scenario and nature that doesn't have God in it. And I hear Genesis here, I hear Big Bang there. Then I go to see my therapist and I hear still a different story. You know, we live in different worlds and if we don't know how to put them together in internal dialogue then we may be split into different persona, or personalities or voices and so that tension internally keeps us fragmented, right? And there's a kind of quiet despair in not finding genuine personal coherence. So I'm stressing that living between the diverse worlds there may be existential stress: internal, interpersonal, intercultural, and interdisciplinary tension. We see it in all levels. And unless you can find a way as a culture to weave through it, then we can't get into this Logos field, which is what we've been trying to do for centuries—achieving the unified primal principle. And my point is that you need a certain technology of thinking, ways of thinking to access that field.

MM: And you can teach that technology.

AG: Absolutely. That is really what my teaching has distilled to. My own journey as a thinker has brought me to a point in my career where I also want to reach out to become a public teacher and to try and take this technology to a level of deep dialogue in the culture.

MM: So after all these years teaching at a university you discover that Socrates was right in the first place.

AG: Beautiful. Exactly. And Buddha and Jesus, and Lao-Tzu, and these great teachers of paradigms. So what I would stress is that what I am trying to articulate is not newfangled or novel in a sense—it's classical. I'm trying to tap the technologies introduced by Moses and Jesus and Buddha and Lao-Tsu and Socrates and Plato. Great minds. It has a long heritage, East and West.

MM: But what about this fear that everybody has if we move toward the common ground, we lose identity? Now maybe that's a residual thing of ego, but each of us has our worldview; we have our body of beliefs. To go into this common ground, do we lose all those things, do we lose our differences?

AG: You've just asked the most important question of the whole enterprise. Right now I think that our culture is in a deep crisis. There has always been a war—this war I've been talking about—two sides. We're in the midst of a deep cultural crisis between the forces of unity and the forces of multiplicity. And that's not a new crisis—that goes back to the Buddhist philosophy, and to Heraclitus who spoke of process, by which he meant constant change. If you look back over 2,500 years, we see we're living that drama now. Multiculturalism in the bad sense is the attempt to have mere differences, tribal differences, for the sake of difference. That is a cultural disaster, if we lose the common ground. And those who say we've got to have unity to have a culture, one nation under God, indivisible, can also look back and revert to an older way of stating that my Biblical ethics are the very ethics that should hold this country together. Both in a way are saying something important and right and vital. The Logos and dialogue heals that and shows a deeper way to find profound unity that encourages multiplicity. Hard to believe. You have to step back from your ego self to find yourself, but what the Logos does that's so powerful is that the Logos, the primal principle, being infinite, is the very source of flourishing multiplicity and diversity. I think both the East and West have provided great insights, but what is new for me is that this Logos shows the origin of individuality, our deepest individuality, once you get out of the ego. Think about what "individual" means, it's not divided—in dividual, not divided. And you can't find that in ego thinking. So in America we prize individuality as sacred, and we're right and it's the Logos and dialog that preserves and encourages it.

MM: But we only find our true individuality then when we get beyond our divided selves?

AG: Exactly right. Ego thinking is not the source of individuality. It's the opposite, it splits us, it divides us, and requires a rational awakening that takes us into the Logos. That's where we will find each one of us to be profoundly unique, a unique miracle.

MM: Is that why we find Socrates so compelling?

AG: Yes, because Socrates and Plato took us on this journey that the ultimate principle is Goodness itself. People never understood. Why do we call it "Goodness"? It's because it's the ultimate infinite force that holds things together. That's what the infinite power does and that's Goodness. Goodness is the unifying bond that holds things together. That's a love bond, communion, dialogue.

MM: And that's true happiness?

AG: Yes. And that's why philosophy is a quest for virtue and happiness and when we reach the dialogue of Logos and find the Logos within our own worldview, then we begin to reach fulfillment and satisfaction and all the great classical goals of philosophy—wisdom—begin to pour out.

MM: Thank you.

NANCY TUANA

The Science of Gender Issues

Nancy Tuana, Professor of Philosophy at the University of Oregon and co-editor of *Hypatia: A Journal of Feminist Philosophy*. With her provocative and educational discussion of gender roles and sexuality throughout history, Nancy Tuana is an ideal spokesperson for feminism. Some of the topics that interest Professor Tuana include the sexist bias of reproductive theory, feminism and the natural sciences, sexual harassment, and gender issues around the globe.

MM: Michael Malone   **NT:** Nancy Tuana

MM: I think the average person, when they think about philosophy, thinks of it as something sort of monolithic—or there is a philosophy and it has a certain set of rules. Is there a feminist philosophy as something entirely different from philosophy?

NT: No, it's not different. It's just that any time that you engage in doing philosophy, you always engage in it from a particular location. If I were someone who had been raised in China, I would be doing philosophy coming out of my cultural heritage. I would be doing philosophy coming out of the interests of my country at that particular moment.

MM: But I thought it was about basic principles. You go all the way down to the absolute corners, the handful of questions that keep getting asked over and over again. Aren't those the same questions everywhere?

NT: It's not quite that way. It seems that way because this is one of the pictures that has been offered of philosophy: We'll tell you what truth is; we'll tell you what reason is. But actually philosophy has many different perspectives. And not everyone thinks that's what philosophy does. For example, Simone de Beauvoir referred to philosophy as the art of living. That's about living well. It's not about finding ultimate truths or universal knowledge. It's about how I can be a good person, how I can think about living in a society that's a fair and a just society and how I can gain a lot out of my life.

MM: Does our sense of what a good person is change over time?

NT: Oh, I think very much so. If you think, for example, of Plato's time, you have a scientific theory and a philosophical theory that says people aren't all the same. We like now to think that all human beings are the same, we have the same basic nature—what we call genetic makeup. And, thus, that there is a single way of being human according to our worldview. But at the time of Plato and at least the story that Plato told, there were different groups of people that had different ways of being good, depending on what kind of person you were. I would be, I hope, in Plato's time, a philosopher king, the group of people whose particular skill was thinking about the meaning of life and ruling the city, but there were other people whose basic skills would be very different. Not all cultures have the same views about what it is to be human.

MM: Now in *The Symposium* Diotima teaches Plato about love. Is she the first female philosopher or the first feminist philosopher?

NT: Oh, well, there have been many women philosophers throughout history. We've lost a lot of them and, of course, you must know there are debates about whether or not Diotima was actually a true woman or a fictional woman. I think, actually, why you have the female voice coming in to this Platonic dialogue is that you have many traditions in which women stand for certain types of wisdom. There are many cultures in which male and female signify different principles. So, there'd be certain knowledges you as a man would be capable of and certain knowledges I as a woman would be capable of.

MM: So, male knowledge and female knowledge. Give me some examples of how that would divide up—male philosophy, female philosophy, arising from these different knowledges.

NT: There would also be different practices. In some of our indigenous cultures in the Americas the female holds the wisdom of the race, the male holds the wisdom of the culture.

MM: Distinguish between those two for me.

NT: Well, the race has to do with the heart of the people—in particular, the relationship between the people and the land, whereas the culture would involve the various different traditions practiced in that culture. But, let's look at the word "feminist." That's quite different from "woman." I mean, obviously, not all women are feminists and many men are feminists, too. So, it's not a gendered term. It's something that any person can be. It's an interesting question to ask: When did feminism start? Many people will talk about this particular time as being the second wave of feminism and now people are even talking about the third wave of feminism. Arguing that the first wave of feminism happened with the suffragist movement, here and in other countries.

MM: 1876 to 1920.

NT: Right. And the Seneca Falls Convention, trying to get the vote for women in the United States, for example. And, it was linked to the abolitionist movement, too. So there was a concern about human rights and about oppression. Feminists were looking around the world and saying, why are certain people disenfranchised simply because of their race or simply because of their gender? The "second" feminist era was so labeled because some people believe that feminism died and that it didn't get revived until after the war [WWII].

MM: *The Feminine Mystique,* Betty Freidan. Started with housewives in the 1950s.

NT: That's right. And there were, you know, very important changes happening in US culture during the '40s and '50s. Men had been going off to war and women were supporting the war in this country, for example, by taking on jobs that many didn't have prior to the war. Rosie the Riveter is the most common image of the type.

MM: Right. The hubby comes home and Rosie has to go back to washing dishes and doing the laundry.

NT: Well, what actually happened is that many women didn't leave the workforce at that point. There were economic changes in society that for some women meant that it helped to have a bit more income in the family. But, for other women, they found that they enjoyed having a job. What they did was shift the type of job. Women didn't work as welders so much anymore.

MM: So it heads out into the '60's, the '70's, the '80's. Now, all of a sudden, we look at *Time* magazine and they announce feminism may be dead again. What does that mean?

NT: Wishful thinking.

MM: Well, what was your reaction when you saw that? You're standing in line at the Eugene store and you see that *Time* magazine cover.

NT: Right. Well, for many people, feminism simply means that women should have the same opportunities as men. And they look around the world and they see women represented in most of the major career opportunities. They see women as CEOs. They see women professors. They see even women newscasters and they think, see, feminism is dead, we don't need it anymore; we've gotten the equality we want.

MM: We won—the war's over.

NT: That's right. But feminism is a lot more complex than that because as we begin to look at what it means to worry about gender discrimination, we realize that you can't really separate that from class discrimination, from race discrimination, and from the ways in which we gender many of our activities. For example, I have two children and it's very rare for my children to have any of their early education or any of their childcare done by males in our society. Even though it would be lovely to have males actively involved in the raising of our children, that's not done.

MM: That's the old "K–six teachers are all women and you don't see a male teacher until you get to junior high school."

NT: That's right. And, it's for a variety of reasons. Those salaries are very low. They're very hard to live off of. On the other hand, there's also a socialization that renders any man who wants to work with small children suspicious. Well, why would you want to do that? That's a female thing, it involves caring and it involves loving small children.

MM: I don't know if you have ever talked to a policeman—there is that automatic suspicion of any male teacher in an elementary school.

NT: Right. That continues to be discrimination. Now it's discrimination against men. We're setting up a situation where men don't have the same opportunities to be very much a part of the upbringing and play of small children. We have jobs, for example, that are not structured around family life, but are more structured around putting many hours into one's career, which doesn't provide much opportunity for really being a part of children's lives. So part of what feminists are saying is, we're not done if just certain groups of women start being able to compete equally with males in a job market that's set up in a particular way. We want to pull back and say, what are the values of this job market, what is it that we're trying to bring about and what types of lives are being privileged by this particular situation?

MM: Now where does philosophy come in to all of this?

NT: Well, philosophy has always been a part of it.

MM: Okay, but this sounds like policy, not philosophy.

NT: We can't really begin to think about policy until you're aware of the values that you're working out of and have a chance to really investigate those values and compare them to other sets of values. If you simply assume that you're starting from a neutral vantage point and can look around and determine what the best society would involve, you won't really end up engaging in interesting policy making. You begin by really thinking about the values we inherited from our culture because, indeed, growing up in a particular culture, you inherit a lot of values and a lot of beliefs. Philosophy provides a moment for seeing the ways in which we think about the world, how we respond to it, and how the kind of practices we engage in come out of our culture, but also how we're not the only culture. There are many other cultures in the world and there have been many different cultural practices, historically. So it provides a lens by which we can become aware of our background values. And, by becoming aware of them, we can make sure that they're the ones we want to continue to hold on to.

MM: Now let me ask you then, as you look through history, as you look through all these cultures, it's not entirely universal, but you can certainly say there's a great preponderance of gender differentiation along very common lines. Now does that arise from socialization or does that arise from organic chemistry and how do you tell which contributes what?

NT: Well, it's a very difficult question, but I think that we exaggerate the amount of gender difference there is because we look primarily at European cultures and some of the developed Asian cultures. But there are numerous tribal cultures in particular that had less gender differentiation in the sense of a hierarchization of gender roles so that whatever was the privileged gender role was given to the male. There were cultures, for example, in which you might have males and females doing different things, but that they were equally privileged and valued by the community.

MM: But, philosophically, once you determine that there are differences, isn't it natural to then begin applying values to those differences?

NT: Differences between men and women?

MM: Sure. Differences between any kind of group. You can't start that process and stop right there and say, we're just going to stop at differences and not actually render judgments on the value of each one of those relative to the others.

NT: Right. Well, the first thing you ask is, where do the differences come from? And where do you think those differences come from?

MM: Do we even know where they come from? I mean, has anybody systematically sat down and said, "is it DNA, is it testosterone, is it how kids are carried when they're newborns?"

NT: Well, the first thing you begin to think about as a philosopher is not only how to go about answering that question, but how the ways in which we answer those questions themselves come out of our cultural values. So, for example, in this century, for a long time, we had a story of human evolution that went this way: Peoples lived in small groups, you know, these are Neanderthal, early *Homo erectus*, we lived in small groups, the women stayed by the fire, they raised the children, the men were out hunting and we have images of men out in groups killing dangerous or large animals. And the argument was that because the men were engaged in activities that required cooperation, that they were the ones who invented tools because you'd need tools in order to bring down, say, a wooly mammoth, but that you'd also need communication among the men. Hence, the origins of language. And what do we see as bringing about a change from nonhuman animals to what we consider human beings? Technology, language. So that became our origin story. That was what we presented as our understanding of how we came to evolve. Well, what kind of meaning does that have for people today if you hold that belief? The meaning it carries back is, well, raising children is an innate activity. It's something women do because they know how to do it. So I'm equipped to do it and you're not equipped to do it. It's biological. It's innate. It's important, but it has nothing to do with culture. It has nothing to do with what it means to be human. Now let me change the story. And this is exactly what feminist primatologists began to do in looking back at early development stories. They said, wait a minute, wait a minute, why are we so captivated by that picture? Why assume that the men were out hunting? Let's think about what people were actually eating, and they developed a hypothesis that was based partially on some evidence that early hominids were actually spending a lot of time gathering and because their diet was primarily grains, roots, and such, not meat. Now gathering could be done equally by men and women. Women could very easily tie a child onto them and carry them around in a sling. And, what do you need for gathering, especially if you're gathering roots? You need tools to dig them up and you need to be able to communicate across the generations what is edible and what's not. Because if you dig something up that poisonous, you're dead.

MM: So the new notion is, then, in early man, the baseline caloric demand was covered by gathering, largely done by women? And then sort of the value-added protein addition came later and was supplied largely by male hunting teams going out and killing the mammoth?

NT: But the first development of tools and language would not be from hunting. That would have been quite a bit later. Now, that's a story. Right? Do we have 100 percent evidence of which one was right? No. We have certain evidence that supports each one. But the important thing is there's a compelling alternative narrative and that alternative narrative gives us a different picture of human practices. It emphasizes the ways in which men's and women's activities are more alike than different and it also indicates that men and women alike were responsible for the evolution of culture. Now then you have to ask the question: How do the values our culture currently has impact the kinds of theories we're going to develop? So, if you say, well, why is it that men are so different from women? What explains it—DNA, socialization? You can't answer that as if I can give you objective science and give you the answer through some objective practice, like science or social science. You also have to be careful because even those theories emerge out of a particular cultural understanding.

MM: So let me get this right. You're suggesting there's male and female science?

NT: Oh, not at all. I don't think men and women do science differently. What I'm saying is that there are going to be differences between scientific practices that develop in different cultures.

MM: So the choice of hypothesis to be tested could be colored by gender?

NT: Oh, it's colored by our societal values, not by gender.

MM: Okay, but now, once we get data and we get results, science, at some point, when it's done right, removes itself from that, doesn't it? If the hypothesis is wrong, the hypothesis is wrong.

NT: Well, it's often the case that the facts we have are not sufficient to completely determine one theory over another. With the example I gave about man the hunter versus gatherer stories of human evolution, there just isn't enough data available to say, oops, this one's 100 percent accurate and this one's wrong. That's not the way science works.

MM: Well, in paleontology, perhaps, but what about nuclear physics?

NT: Why are we interested in making high technology as opposed to finding solutions, for example, for worldwide hunger? That emerges out of a culture that is interested in answering certain questions and less interested in answering other questions. Now sometimes a gender dimension enters into that. Sometimes the questions we ask are coming out of male interests, but that's a relatively rare situation. For example, the recently published studies showing that there was a lot of research done on heart attacks in men, but little research done on women. So you weren't getting the impact of estrogens on heart attacks. That's a case where there was a gender bias. This is a case of what we call an androcentric bias in the practice of science. But, I'm not saying that's true of all science. I'm simply saying the kind of science we do, what questions we ask, what our conceptions of scientific method are, emerge out of a cultural context. They respond to the beliefs we have as a culture as well as what it is we want to do as a culture. That's why we need to have science much more democratic than it is right now.

MM: Okay. I don't disagree with you, the bias is built in. But let's talk about feeding the hungry—as I look at satellite data of farmland that's used by farmers who are driving their $150,000.00 tractors, using new biologic engineered seeds being put in the ground with microprocessor-controlled sensors, this is all a product of this hard technology that may have been created by a gender orientation. But when you talk about feeding the world, this is a useful contribution.

NT: It may not be a useful contribution because if you take those hybrid seeds—and this is what was done with the green revolution—and you import them to southern countries and change their practices of agriculture, they become dependent on those hybrid seeds. And what we're actually finding is what we call development actually is de-development of those countries. There's actually less food. It's not working. We have to look at who profits from these activities. Now we're moving away from method in science to the impact of science.

MM: Is capitalization male gender oriented?

NT: No. I'm saying it comes out of a particular culture. This culture isn't just a male culture. It's a very complex culture that emerges out of a long history.

MM: But wouldn't you say it's largely a patriarchy?

NT: It's a culture in which the people who have had the most influence on what we believe and what our values are are men. But not all of them have been men. There are also women who have been involved. There are also class issues. There are race issues. It's not the case that the dominant interests in our culture are men's interests because men are not homogenous. You have to bring class into play. You have to bring race into play. And if you just try to understand this in terms of male and female, you're going to get it all mixed up. Because then you're going to always give me counterexamples. Well, look, there's Margaret Thatcher, okay? But that doesn't acknowledge the way in which race and class intersect with gender.

MM: But if I choose to look at it through the gender lens, it's because I've been told that this is an important lens I'm supposed to look through because we now have feminist philosophy. So if I say, fine, we had that variable, let's hold all the others constant. Let's just look at that variable, can't we pull that out of the mix?

NT: No. That's one of the things feminists found.

MM: Then, why do we have feminist philosophy, if we can't pull it out of the mix of all of these other variables going on? If we have this field of things constantly in motion, why are we saying, okay, this is an area of study even though we can't distinguish it?

NT: We label it feminist only because it arises out of a commitment to paying attention to gender. But paying attention to gender doesn't mean you ignore everything else. What we discovered is that, in paying attention to gender, the only way you *can* pay attention to gender is not to hold everything else constant. My concerns and needs as an upper-middle-class, professional, white woman, is not the same as the experiences of a poor woman, or a Jewish woman, or a black woman. You can't hold everything else constant and say, "Let's just look at gender." It doesn't work that way. Some people—many of us—made that error earlier on. We thought we could just look at gender. Fortunately, there were many voices within feminism because feminism has always been a very diverse group of people examining these issues who said, wait a minute, wait a minute, you can't just look at me as a woman, I'm not *just* a woman. I'm also African American, or Latina, or lesbian, or poor, or Jewish. And we began to see that it's a misunderstanding of feminism to think you can hold everything else constant.

MM: Is that what the backlash was? Among women? The idea, I don't want to be categorized simply by that factor?

NT: Oh, no. The backlash didn't come in through that way. There was certainly a lot of discussion within feminist circles about whether or not feminism was appropriate to the lives of women at large and many groups of people started up parallels or alternatives, almost mirror images to the feminist movement. The womanist movement, for example, within the African American tradition, emerged out of the realization that there were many important aspects of feminism, but the experiences being captured within feminism were exactly the same as their experiences. A term that's coming into use now is "post-colonial feminism," as a way of looking at the experiences of groups of peoples who were colonized for long periods of time and how that—the impact of colonization—affects the experience of gender. It's an awareness that there's very complex interconnections between things. We can't just talk about a person's love of philosophy without understanding other parts of their lives. We aren't trying to be reductive and say, oh, we can just hold this constant and understand this. But . . . getting back to the backlash. The backlash, I think, came from a misunderstanding, whether it was willful or not, I'm not sure. It came from a misunderstanding of feminism. As you know, feminists are often depicted as irrational, man-hating. And you've got people calling us, to use a well-known phrase, "femi-nazis," that we were going to go around and do to men what men had done to us. If you actually know feminist philosophy, and there's a whole range of disciplines involved in the doing of feminist theory and feminist practice, not just philosophy, you can see that there's an incredible diversity within feminism and various different viewpoints about what it is that we're aiming for, of the role of men within feminism. Many women argue that men are, indeed, and always have been, a part of the feminist movement.

MM: Now, when I heard the phrase femi-nazi, I heard something entirely different and, far be it for me to speak for women executives, but I've heard it elsewhere, too. Which is that, behind it all seems to be an absolutist political point of view—anti-capitalists, anti-entrepreneurial, anti-being successful in a career. I heard that part of the backlash. And when I heard the phrase femi-nazi, that's what I heard was a totalitarian or at least an absolutist agenda buried behind all this.

NT: Oh, yes. Which I think is very much what you're supposed to hear. But the point is, that, again, it is based on a misunderstanding of feminism. Anyone who spends just a day reading through feminist literature will see how diverse it is, even just in feminist philosophy. This is one of the reasons that I developed my series of anthologies. I kept having my colleagues, knowledgeable people who know a lot of philosophy, saying to me, what would feminists say about this, or what would feminists say about that? What's the feminist stance on abortion? Well, feminists have lots of different viewpoints. To say I'm a feminist is simply to say that I'm aware of the ways in which gender oppression still exists. Its not the only axis of oppression, but it still exists. The day that we no longer have oppression based on gender, that day I won't be a feminist anymore. I won't need to be. But that's the only thing it means. It doesn't mean that I'm going to agree with every other feminist about whether or not abortion is right or wrong. There are pro-life feminists, there are pro-choice feminists. It also doesn't mean that I'm going to agree with, now to talk more about philosophy, here's the right way to do it. Capitalism is good. Capitalism is bad. Technology is good. Technology is bad. We all hold very different views.

MM: Let's continue philosophy a little. Is there a difference between a good feminist life and a good life?

NT: I think if we're going to talk about "the art" of living, which is the phrase I brought up before, from Beauvoir. It means that we have to be the best type of people we can be in the settings in which we find ourselves. We happen to find ourselves currently located within a society where there are complex oppressions, where our world is becoming more global, our actions have many impacts, both at the local level, how I raise my children, and beyond that. I think that you can't live well, you can't live a good life as a philosopher without being aware of oppressions. So I think that feminism would be a component of living a good life in any society that has oppression, but so would anti-racism, so would concern with the fact that there are children who don't have enough food to develop properly, to be able to get the basic ability to read and do philosophy like I do. A good life is a life that recognizes that and attempts to correct it. It's not a good *feminist* life. It's a *good* life.

MM: Now, when we talk about gender, it's inevitably bound up with issues of sex and sexuality. And you're a professor of sexuality. Well, what do you teach? What's the message? What's the changing nature of sexuality?

NT: Well, I teach a large lecture class. I'm at a state university and so we do introductory classes for large numbers of students. And so I thought about how can I create a philosophy class that I can present to students that probably won't become majors but can help them really understand how wonderful it is to do philosophy. Why should I do philosophy—you know, that dead stuff? If you don't show them how wonderful it is to do philosophy, they're going to be gone. So, what I do is, I help them to understand the values that we have in our culture and how our sexuality comes out of that. One of the values and one of the stories I tell—I talk a lot about stories because I don't think we can make a clear-cut distinction between myths and reality in many ways—is the belief that our sexuality is biological. If we're normal, we're heterosexual. If something goes wrong, then we're something else. But we all assume a story of heterosexuality. You can't have a story of heterosexuality unless you assume that there's a clear distinction between men and women. You can demark it carefully. There's nothing in between male and female, and also the belief that sexuality is primarily for reproduction. So one of the things I do in the classroom is try to show them that these are assumptions they carry by talking about other cultures in which those assumptions were not the case. So that we understand that our sexuality, as well as our beliefs about what constitutes a female, comes out of a particular culture. Then we have a chance to explore what we believe and to see whether or not we really want to continue believing that and practicing it and understanding it.

MM: Give me an example because I have this image of you saying this to Oregon farm kids who have spent their entire life out there in the barn looking at very distinct, you know, male, female, heterosexuality among farm animals. It seems to be that's pretty locked in at this point. How do you talk them out of that belief?

NT: Well, we begin, actually, by looking at Plato's *Symposium* and looking at the Greek view of love and the Greek views concerning sexuality. So, for example, [this is not unique to me, it comes out of Foucault and many other theorists] for Greeks, sex was something that was seen as a natural function. It wasn't seen as sinful or deviant. There wasn't a notion of sex as equated with sin. It was seen as a bodily function a lot like eating. You can't really live unless you eat, but you won't live well unless you eat well. They felt the same way about sexuality. You eat the wrong kind of foods, you're going to get ill. But you eat too little food, you're going to get ill, too. Same thing with sexuality. You have sex too much or in the wrong types of ways, you're going to get ill. But if you don't have sex enough, you're also going to get ill. So that brings a different perspective. But they added into that no conception of sex as linked with reproduction as its primary function. Sex was, rather, for them, a resource for education, for gaining knowledge, for conveying knowledge, and also for pleasure.

MM: How did they detach it from reproduction without an efficient birth control system?

NT: Well, for the Greeks—now we're talking about ancient and classical Greeks—there was no prohibition against same-sex sex. For example, the *Symposium* is about the love between men or, more accurately, the love between a youth and a more adult male and the way in which that's a very appropriate form of love and sexuality. I mean, clearly, if that's one of your forms of sexuality, there's going to be no connection between reproduction being a necessary function or a necessary component of sexuality. In our culture, we've come to assume that to be homosexual is to be deviant in some way, that you're either sinful or there's something wrong biologically. That's very much a belief of our culture and the various different views that we have.

Nancy Tuana

But there are many cultures in which same-sex sex is quite acceptable under certain circumstances. So, by beginning there, and by beginning with student reactions to these views—why is it that a student is so opposed to such a practice?—some of my students will start going, oh, homosexuality! One of the things that I'll say in class is, if you had been born in Athens in 500 B.C.E., and you were a male, imagine yourself a male at that time—you would have had male lovers and female lovers, depending on your age. And that's a very hard thing for us to imagine. But, it brings into relief all of the societal values that we have and all of the societal biases and values about sexuality and it then gives a person a chance to think about why. Well, why do I believe that and how would our culture be different if I didn't believe that?

MM: Now, if my memory serves me, some of this would have verged on violation of contemporary child molestation laws. How far do we want to press this?

NT: In Greece, it was believed that it was inappropriate to have sex with a youth who wasn't yet developed. But the reasons were very different from our reasons. For example, it was believed that when you have sex with a person, it's a very interesting conception—I wish we had more of this—that if you have sex with a person, it's not separated from coming to know that person, from spending time with them, from being influenced by them. So, if I had sex with a person who was not of good character, I would be harmed by that relationship. I would lose some of my good character. So if I have sex with someone who's so young their character isn't yet formed, I could do myself harm because I don't know whether or not I'm having a relationship with a good person.

MM: When did they consider the character gets formed?

NT: There were different ages, depending on different time periods, typically sixteen. Very much what we see in our culture. I mean, you may not want to permit your daughter to have sex at sixteen, but in reality, many of our daughters do; our sons, too.

MM: Not with a sixty year old.

NT: Well, what's wrong with that? It's okay if it's between two sixteen year olds, but not between a sixty year old and a sixteen year old? Because we have an assumption that there's something wrong.

149

MM: My socialized reaction to that is, yes.

NT: Why is it wrong?

MM: Because the older person is, in my mind, a predator on a young person who's still innocent.

NT: Okay. There, that shows you one of the values that you have from our particular culture. We see sex, especially if the sixty year old is a male versus a female in terms of a predation system. We think that people are—and a lot of our phrases tie into that—a male is often referred to as "hitting on" a female. In different cultures, sex isn't seen in that way at all. It's seen as a very consensual relationship. To have sex with someone who isn't interested in having sex with you or there isn't full consent or there isn't already a rich and mutual relationship would be seen as very odd. You know, why would one want to have that type of relationship?

MM: To say that there wasn't a predatory relationship and yet this was a society that a sixty year old is having sex with a sixteen year old and, in the next room, the slave is preparing dinner. There was a lot of predation in this society and not just sexual, but class, race, great pride in killing enemies.

NT: Of course, of course. But there wasn't a view of sex as being something that is sinful and harmful and that is corrupting. One of the things that bothers us about a sixty year old having sex with a sixteen year old is, we assume that the sixty year old has corruption in mind or harm in mind. If we had a culture that saw sex as something that was a joy to share between people, as something, as some cultures do, that had a sacred dimension to it, a way of invoking the gods, for example, we might not have a culture in which there is sexual predation. In fact, the anthropologist Peggy Reeves Sanday, in doing a study of various different tribal cultures, found that there were cultures that were rape free. We have what many anthropologists have called a "rape–prone" culture. We're a culture where rape is something that happens to men and women alike, but it's also something that we're very aware of. I live with the fear of rape. I'm very careful about where I walk on these streets here in the city of Boston—I don't walk the streets at night because I don't know which are the safe streets and which aren't. I live my life affected by the awareness that rape exists. There are cultures that are rape free. When you describe to such people our conception of rape, they act toward it very much like we respond to the conception of cannibalism. Uh, my God, how can anybody do that? I mean—why? That's so deviant, I can't imagine. It's a complete inability to

Nancy Tuana

understand that as a desire. We live in a culture where forcing someone to have sex, predating on people sexually is maybe not acceptable, but it's understandable. It's not seen as deviant.

MM: Rape isn't seen as deviant?

NT: Sexual predation is not seen as deviant. Compare the difference, for example, of how we treat what I call typical dating behavior, something which I'm sure you don't do, but, you know, typical dating behavior. When I was dating, and it's still happening today, males would be the aggressors. The thing we have to ask about: why is it always males who are the ones to ask to have sex and not females? Why isn't that changing? Why are there active and passive roles being scripted onto sex? A male who continues to try to have sex after a woman says no is not seen as someone who's exceptionally misbehaving in terrible ways. It's actually seen as part of normal dating behavior. Well, try a little harder; ask again. When you sit in the back seat of the car and the guy starts to rub along your arm and then he starts to rub along your breast and so the woman always puts her arm over her breast and he keeps pushing the arm away. Why is it that even when women say no, men don't always stop? What does that say? Part of what it says is a form of predation, not rape, but a form of aggression and predation, is built into even what we consider to be natural, normal sexual relationships between men and women.

MM: But you're not going so far as to say that other males don't consider this, after a certain point, to be wrong behavior. At a certain point, you go from being a jerk to being a bad guy, to going to jail. I mean, we do have these incremental punishments, social and legal punishments, depending upon how far you want to press this predation.

NT: Indeed. But think about that now. Imagine, now, we're a different culture. A rape-free culture. In a culture like that, you wouldn't have what you're talking about, a continuum of predation. Well, this guy's a jerk. This guy's getting to be really raunchy. This guy's a rapist. In a culture where sex was not seen as something where it was appropriate for it to be forced on another person, where it was very much like a conversation. You wouldn't have this continuum from "jerk" to "bad guy" to "a criminal." If I didn't want to talk to you right now, you wouldn't be sitting here insisting that I talk to you. A good conversation is a conversation where both parties are excited about being there, want to be there, are learning from one another. If we had a model like that of sexuality, you wouldn't have a predation model. People would be genuinely working to have a dialogue between themselves sexually, so that you wouldn't even have that in-between [of "jerk"]. What I'm trying to get my students to think about are the ways in which attitudes that are part of our culture are impacting our sexual lives. Something that when you're a freshman, a sophomore in college, you're very much thinking about. So it's a way to help them to see: *What is this thing philosophers do?*

MM: Let's go way out to the edge, then. Another taboo—incest—is that a conversation between, you know, a mature adult and a young person?

NT: We don't have it, we really don't have an incest taboo. The level of incest that happens in U. S. society is exceptionally high. If we truly had a taboo, it wouldn't be so high.

MM: No, wait, the fact that it's hidden and denied suggests that it is a great taboo.

NT: But, it's not a taboo in the way in which cannibalism is. We're so offended by cannibalism that we can't imagine anyone doing it. We think someone's sick if they do it.

MM: But we forgave those soccer players because of desperation. I can't imagine a scenario where incest is ever excused for any reason.

NT: Oh, but, we actually are a society that allows a lot of incest to happen, where we really don't believe the reports of incest. Where we have Lolita stories.

MM: Yes, but, that's because it's so taboo, we can't even bring ourselves to talk it.

NT: Of course we can talk about it. Feminists have been talking about it. It's not hard to talk about incest, to identify the experiences.

MM: The denial of reports comes from people saying that it is such a taboo subject that the situation just cannot be so bad.

NT: No, I'm actually suggesting something much more complex. It's actually not taboo *enough* because we live in a society in which incest happens regularly but it's not being identified as such, in which we're [culture at large] not aware of its existence. It's interesting because we had a similar type of society, until recently, about rape. We really didn't think that rape—or, at least, particular forms of rape—happened very often. We thought that when rape happened, it was a stranger, it was in the dark, it was at night. It was a crazy guy and it was also a class issue, it was also a race issue. Now, if you look at incest, we assume it doesn't happen very often, maybe happens among the really ignorant, poor, inbred types of societies. But the reality of it is, it happens often. It happens in so-called "normal" families and we're not talking about it. There's a whole debate going on right now about recovered memories and a lot of people are putting great effort into arguing that there is no such thing as recovered memories. Now, isn't that interesting that when the Vietnam veterans have recovered memories of the incredible trauma that they experienced in Vietnam, there's not as much controversy about this; is it a real memory— or is this implanted by some therapist who has a particular agenda in mind? But when women began to have recovered memories of incest, there is an incredible societal eruption of "what's going on here? This can't be possible. Surely no one would forget something like that. This must be therapists implanting memories." And we have to really think about what's going on here. Is this really so taboo?

MM: Let me tell you what's going on. Because one thing I've noticed is that when something gets exposed, a taboo subject gets brought out into the open, the punishment diminishes for the incest taboo as long as it remained under cover. When it was exposed, there was almost no punishment too great for the perpetrator.

NT: Which historical time are you talking about?

MM: Well up until TV movies started getting made on the subject, you arrest a man, arrest a father for incest, you know, the community consensus is, put him in the river, hang him. Now, when it's exposed, it's a dysfunctional family, therapy, and we'll keep the family together and will make a fix. So is it less taboo now?

NT: You know, I haven't heard too many people who really want to keep child molesters in with children. Most people want to remove child molesters from the situation. Any kind of sexual molester should be removed from settings in which they'll continue to molest.

MM: But the solution to incest seems to be therapy now, which, to my mind, is a less severe punishment than the older punishments were. Fifty or sixty years ago the gentleman would just disappear.

NT: Well, what punishment should there be to stop incest? Will punishment stop incest? Or will we, being more aware of what's going on and not hiding it, not covering it up . . .

MM: Well, I am just arguing that it's less taboo now than it was before and you're arguing that it's never been a real taboo.

NT: I don't think it is taboo. I mean, what's a taboo? We may be having what philosophers love to call a semantical argument at this point. "Taboo": I'm using that word to mean something that people find truly appalling, unintelligible, just beyond the pale of human activity. In this culture, we see cannibalism in that way. We can't imagine why someone would want to eat human flesh, except for very unusual circumstances.

MM: But, ironically, in a world of the media, in the world of the Internet where everything is accessible, that unintelligible part begins to disappear.

NT: Oh, I'm talking about moral unintelligibility. And I don't think that does disappear.

MM: I don't know. I think the more we hear about it, the more we talk about it, the less horrifying it becomes.

NT: If we don't talk about it and it's continuing to happen, it's more horrifying for the people who have been victimized in that way. So I think that we must begin to look at the ways in which this is a part of our society and not just think about individual solutions. Either we'll kill the jerk, or we'll put him or her, because women also commit (?) incest, in therapy. But, rather, what's going on in a society where one of the most basic bonds—think about parent–child incest—one of our most initial bonds for children who are raised primarily by their parents is severed in such a fundamental way it will be very difficult for that child to develop and experience the art of living. How do we restructure society to make it the case that that happens less often, in which it becomes so appalling that it does not happen as much?

MM: So the real paradox is, how do we gain full knowledge of it and expose it, while still keeping it as egregious?

NT: That's right. That's right, keep it morally unintelligible. I'm actually suggesting it's not morally unintelligible in our current society. It's not going to be in a society that includes Lolitas. If we continue in our pornography to depict young women as sexualized—*Vogue* magazine not that long ago had a whole run where they had little girls, five years old, just totally sexualized, all the makeup, all the hair, you know, the little gowns cut low. If we continue to sexualize children, if we continue to see sex as having certain meanings, we're going to live in a society where incest exists.

MM: Nancy, thank you very much for being on the show.

LEWIS GORDON
The Liberation of Identity

Lewis Gordon, Full Professor of Afro-American Studies, Religious Studies, and Modern Culture and Media, with affiliation in Latin-American Studies, Brown University, Executive Editor, *Radical Philosophy Review: A Journal of Progressive Thought.* Professor Gordon calmly and coolly discusses provocative issues related to his interest in Africana philosophy, racism, and liberation, raising black and white children, mixed-race identity, and urban violence.

MM: Michael Malone   **LG:** Lewis Gordon

LG: I grew up in South Bronx in a neighborhood that no longer stands.

MM: Was it the old rough Bronx that we think of?

LG: Well, when one is there it isn't that way, you know; for me it was just a lot of fun. Home is home. When I was little boy I was in a lot of fights, but almost everyone I had a fight with became a good friend afterward. So there was a way in which a certain sort of communion can emerge.

MM: Conflict resolution.

LG: Conflict resolution. But, today, one worries whether the other child has a weapon.

MM: So then you went to the City University of New York?

LG: Yeah, I was jazz musician in New York. I had a girlfriend at the college. I wanted to see her more so I decided, oh, you know, maybe I'll take some classes.

MM: It's amazing how many guys choose college that way.

LG: Yeah, church, too. But at college I found myself enjoying eight courses a semester and I was put into a special program called the Lehman Scholars Program and two and a half years later, I was a college graduate.

MM: You play jazz?

LG: Yeah.

MM: What instrument?

LG: Drums and piano.

MM: That's an interesting combination. Who were your heroes?

LG: Both percussive. I loved Tony Williams. He made the instruments pray. It was beautiful and spiritual, it was great. And I also liked Elvin Jones, with his polyrythmic beats. Max Roach is just pure art with drums, and then they're some of the older musicians like Papa Jo Jones, Eddie Gladden, Jack deJohnette. I could go on and on.

MM: Do you still play?

LG: Oh, yeah.

MM: So at what point did you realize that philosophy was what you wanted to do?

LG: The strange thing with philosophy is that when you reach a certain point in life, it seems as if everything you did before was leading up to it. A lot of people knew no philosophy, never planned to be philosophers. They had a certain set of problems that manifested themselves in such a way that these people turned out to be philosophers.

MM: Their problems led them to philosophy . . .

LG: Yes. Or in some cases a person was just concerned about a solution and, as it turns out, it was a philosophical solution. For Descartes and Bertrand Russell, it was mathematics. William James and Karl Jaspers were physicians. Alfred Schutz, a lawyer. In my case, it was a different story. I was actually born in Jamaica and I had uncles who were Rastafarians and loved books, although some of them didn't go beyond the fourth grade. But they had a wonderful collection of books, and the books they particularly liked were books by revolutionaries. I read them and had a sense that these people were not only saying something important, they also spoke to the reality in which I lived. When I was in the ninth grade, I had a social studies teacher, Mr. Cirqua, who required that we read the *New York Times* each day. But I couldn't afford the *New York Times,* so he said why don't you come in at 6:00 in the morning and you read my *New York Times.* So I showed up at 6:00 in the morning and read his *New York Times.* One day we were talking to each other, and he said, "You ever read Hegel?" I said, no. So he brought in Hegel and he and I each morning began to discuss Hegel, then Marx, and we went through various philosophies of history. And at that point, I knew I liked that. Jazz musicians were also philosophical; I was playing jazz at the time and we'd been through long discussions about art, about aesthetics. Yet even then I wasn't thinking that I would do philosophy. I thought I would write. But then I got into college, took a lot of courses I liked, and a lot of them turned out to be philosophy courses.

MM: You taught high school at one point, didn't you?

Lewis Gordon

LG: Yes, I taught social studies, criminology, American history, and global history. And then I coordinated a program for in-school truants called The Second Chance Program, at Lehman High School in the Bronx.

MM: What did you learn from teaching high school kids about philosophy?

LG: That philosophy can speak to people at almost any age. For instance, I had kids whom I was told were delinquent, incapable students. And I had students who at fourteen, fifteen years old loved Kant and Plato. These philosophers had a great impact on their lives. So one of the things I learned is that there's something that can occur when there's recognition of other people's humanity and I think what happened with the students I was working with was that they were recognized for having a certain level of curiosity, a certain potential for which they had never before received recognition. I just saw great growth in them and I began to think about these questions about what happens if human beings are treated humanely. At first it looked more like a sociological question and a psychological question. And then I noticed that there was a problem with the way we talk about human beings and humanity, generally. And the more I thought about that, the more I began to think about it in philosophical terms. And at that point I decided that maybe what I needed was a community with whom I could have some dialogue on such issues. So that's when I decided to go get my doctorate in philosophy.

MM: Now one of your great interests is existentialism.

LG: Yes.

MM: You talk about treating people humanely, but "warmth" is not something that's usually connected with existentialism, you know what I mean? Isn't it much more of a raging against fate and setting your own path?

LG: I look at other people's freedom. And part of recognizing other people's freedom is recognizing the complexity of responsibility. So, for instance, if one patronizes other people in this sort of warm, fuzzy way of treating them, I think that's dehumanizing. There's a certain way of recognizing people's ability to manifest their potential in certain ways and take responsibly for it. But a way in which I look at problems of the philosophy of existence is very different than some of my colleagues.

MM: How so?

LG: The standard pitch phrase is philosophy of existence is a European phenomenon, that it went out of date in the '40s. Whereas I look at the philosophy of existence as problems about our very humanity. Now in that regard, people have struggled around these issues worldwide for millennia. When I put together works, for instance, on black existentialism or African-American or African existential thought, what I noticed was that they made absolute sense. Why did existential questions matter to nineteenth-century black abolitionists, or why did they matter to Caribbean radical liberationists? It's simple. We're talking about people whose humanity was denied. There's a catch-22 in existence. On the one hand, it's not one's fault, of course, that one is oppressed. The catch-22 of oppression is that, although one is oppressed, one also experiences responsibility. And this is something that people struggled with in the nineteenth century and the twentieth century. In fact, something people struggled with for millennia.

MM: If you start with that premise then, is there a distinct black philosophy, a black existentialism?

LG: Yes, there is. But one of the things that's happened right now in contemporary thought is that there's a struggle against what's called essentialism, and that's where you can have absolute foreclosure regarding a particular identity of a certain group of people. This is where existential thought is interesting because it is hostile to the idea that there's an essence that precedes who we are. In many ways we are making who we are. If there's a group of people who are struggling against something like racism or colonialism, the idea that you don't have to be a fixed identity is important. One can transform one's situation. This does not mean, however, that there isn't an historical or sociological reality of one's life. Now, when I say a black existentialism, I simply mean this. That there is a history of the way problems of existence have been discussed within the context of a group of people or an identity called black. This means that people who do black existentialism could be black people, white people, Asian people, because all those people are dealing with those problems. Now in the history of dealing with such problems, the contributors to black existential thought have been across the board. But what they have in common is that they recognize that raising the question of blackness in existence also raises other questions: How we talk about humanity in the normative sense; how we study human beings; do we require some sort of essential definition that will precede what human beings are? And in addition to that, they are contributing to dialogue with other areas of philosophical thought. Alain Locke's discussion of values and experience, the way he talks about lived reality of values, is very similar to the way existential thinkers talk about them, and one of the interesting things about black existentialism is that some may have been very critical of black existential positions, but in their effort to dialogue with people taking that position, they contributed to the field.

MM: Is there an African-American philosophy distinct from simply black philosophy or black existentialism?

Lewis Gordon

LG: Sure.

MM: Defined by the American experience?

LG: Yes. There's Africana, which refers to the diasporic African group, Afro-Caribbeans, African Americans, each with specific cultural positions. The category black is broader than the category African. Black people are not necessarily African people, so, for instance, you can see and understand how blackness functions among Australian aboriginal people. There's a sense in which also blackness is not necessarily the category by which one refers to Negro. That is something that really has very important historical specificity for the U.S. context. We could also refer to it as the New World black experience. Those tend to be African American and those tend to be dealing specifically with problems that have been raised by the history of people of color in the United States—specifically, people of African descent. Now it doesn't mean that it has to be stuck in that historical moment. For instance, there are people who do African American philosophy who may be interested in one who engages in social change. How does one effect a situation of freedom? Those tend to be more revolutionary thinkers. Then there are those who are more focused on identity questions—what philosophers call ontological questions, questions about being. What are you? Who am I? What am I? Now the thing about ontological questions or definition questions is that often in finding out who you are, you have a sense of what you ought to do. So they tend to be related to what's called teleological or questions of purpose. Now those kinds of questions tend to manifest themselves in African American philosophy in very interesting ways. If we think about W.E.B. DuBois, for example. DuBois struggled through the question, What is Negro? But he also struggled with questions like, well, Why is it that the question "What is a Negro?" also means "What is it to be a problem?" In other words, what is it to go through the world with the sense that you are a problem, as if the world considers itself better without you? Now DuBois began to think about this in terms of what should people of African descent do if they're looked at as problems.

MM: He wrote from the 1890s to the 1950s?

LG: In fact, he died the night before the famous Civil Rights March on Washington in 1963. The thing about DuBois that's especially interesting is that in his time there was every reason to believe that the world was heading politically in a direction toward the extermination of black peoples. He saw in the nineteenth century that the Native American population was reduced to 4 percent by 1900. And there was public discussion on what to do with the blacks. DuBois's emancipation project not only questioned the preservation of the existence of black people, but also raised the issue of what would properly constitute the emancipation of humankind? Of course, DuBois isn't the only one who did that. There was Frederick Douglass.

It's not that Douglass was an existentialist in the way we use the word to apply to, say, someone like Heidegger—who by the way insisted he wasn't an existentialist in the way we might think of, say, Albert Camus, or Søren Kierkegaard, Karl Jaspers, or Martin Buber. None of these people called themselves existentialists, either. But we call them so because they, like Douglass, all struggled with problems of existence. In Douglass's case, it was a problem of freedom. And the way in which he struggled with the problem of freedom was in an existential, political way. One of the ironies for Frederick Douglass was is that when he wrote his first narrative, the copyright had greater protection under the laws of the United States and Congress than Frederick Douglass himself. I've been arguing in my writings that people who are seeking a greater value in a text than in people (what philosophers call textualism) have a perverse moral system. Frederick Douglass knew he would like to have more rights than his book. In discussing the slave master Edward Covey, Douglass said that, although he was a slave in law, he was no longer a slave in spirit. Slaves did this in many ways. There's a rich history of discussion; of discussions of freedom among slaves. Not only because of the rebellions in Haiti and in Jamaica and other places, but also just on the basic question we have to ask ourselves, I mean, when we think about slavery, for instance, in the nineteenth century, we have this image of simple plantations, whips, and so forth. But what we fail to realize is that under every condition of oppression, human beings have found a way to forge an everyday existence. Why don't we take Sarajevo? There, somebody will be having peanut butter and jelly, making love and, you know, thinking through life. Well, similarly, in the horrors of slavery there was still somehow this sort of human resilience where they would find a way to forge an everyday existence. They found a way to get married, although slave marriages were illegal. They found a way to read and write.

MM: That you have managed to find humanity inside of Auschwitz somehow.

LG: Somehow. But that's part of the human condition. We're always struggling for humanity and in many ways, if we're dealing with questions of oppression, we have to understand that struggling for that humanity is also struggling to forge an everyday existence. I've argued, for instance, that some revolutionary struggles fail to realize that at some point people have to be able to do things just because those things are fun. You have a beer on a hot summer afternoon because it's refreshing, you know—it doesn't have to have political content. Or what it is simply to be able to look at your kids play and enjoy that freely. So in many ways when we're trying to think about freedom and existence, we are connected to what constitutes everyday reality. And philosophers don't spend much time on what the everyday is, but that's something I like about existentialism.

MM: Now that part of existence, though, transcends identity, doesn't it? That goes beyond the common desire to have fun, have that beer on a hot afternoon, or watch your kids play, or struggle to create some sort of normalcy in the most horrifying conditions. That transcends categorization, by race, by culture, by anything. Isn't that the essence of humanity?

LG: One of the things that I have been arguing is that when we talk about human beings we need to have an understanding of what is relevant, a field of relevance, and relevance is connected to context. Now one of the things that we should understand about human beings is that no human being is complete. Human beings have this intrinsic incompleteness, right? Mathematical philosophers, like Kurt Gödel, proved that they could not have complete systems of logic that could explain reality and so forth.

MM: And Gödel blew it up.

LG: What Gödel showed was that if systems are sophisticated enough to refer to themselves, then they are intrinsically incomplete. And, as we know, human beings can refer to themselves; we're sophisticated systems. Now the thing about that incompleteness, then, is that effort constantly to forge a completeness of human reality creates a situation of limited options—a structural reality limiting the options through which we can live our humanity. So one of the things about the identity question . . .

MM: Sorry to interrupt, but does that bring in the idea of absurdity, of choosing an act that doesn't limit your options?

LG: All existentialist are anti-nihilists. So, for them, the question of absurdity is that if you really have faith in existence, you have to confront absurdity to understand that you have to play a role in the construction of meaning. Put differently, it's in human beings' hands to put meaning into our lives.

MM: And isn't one of those ways, if you're talking about the limiting of options—I mean, as I read Sartre or I read in Camus—is to choose to break out of those limited options? To define yourself by the fact that you're not going to be defined?

LG: It's partly so, but the problem with choice is the concept of bad faith. What I've argued is that bad faith is multitudinous—it takes many forms. Here are two forms that relate to this question. One form of bad faith is to deny one's social reality. Another form of bad faith is to transform one's social reality in such a way that it is no longer social; in other words, to explain everything in a form of social determinism. They're both forms of bad faith because both deny our freedom. If we do that, we're recognizing what our situation is and the extent to which identities, although relevant, are not complete. So—and we see this all the time—you know, if something were to happen to someone at one stage of his or her life, we'll have an explanation of all the events that preceded it. But what if that person lived a day longer and did something else? Then all those things that preceded it might be transformed. Well, that's part of social historical reality.

MM: So, in a sense, our duty, as with the slave in the nineteenth century, is to constantly choose freedom?

LG: It's a duty to choose freedom but in any . . .

MM: So if I understand you right, our duty, just as the slaves' responsibility, is to escape bad faith by always choosing freedom?

LG: The question of the relation of bad faith to duties is tricky, but in terms of the questions of freedom, here are some ways in which I find the question of the history of people of African descent interesting. One criticism that's often used against European existential thought is that it's ahistorical. But, in truth, it wasn't that it was ahistorical, it's just that Europeans talking about Europeans in the European context is normative, so the history is presumed. The thing I'm saying, which is very different, is that we can argue critically that in the nineteenth century there were problems of existence being discussed among people which were not merely "derivatives" of Europeans. There were people engaged in their own struggle with problems of existence that had a history all the way through to the present. Often they would have to think about the fact that prior to the modern slave trade, there wasn't any reason for pre-colonial Africans to think of themselves in racial terms. So the very fact that we're dealing with a racialized setting has a catch-22 relation to it. On the one hand, the very source of their oppression was the very way in which they came into being, socially and historically. As they struggle with this, this means when they raise problems of existence, it's always raising problems of society and history—what has been called ontogenic sociogenesis. There are many things that are very positive or beautiful about the people of African descent that come out in the literature. When we talked about obligation, you asked me about duty. Quite often when philosophers talk about duty, they talk about it in terms of things like maximizing universals—you know, Kantian norms, that sort of thing. But they often talk about their own struggle with the notion of ancestral obligation. The idea that you could be obligated to someone whom you have never met. Who maybe lived 500 years ago, but somehow has a bearing, a very real bearing, on your existence. Now it's one of those things that pops up not only in West African philosophical systems, but also in the Caribbean, and other black communities. But I argue it's not something uniquely black. In fact, what has happened is that the modern project of secularism in the West has been such that it has been dominated so much by a positivistic or ahistorical conception of science that there is a desire to treat people as if they emerge without a history. As a consequence, I argue, if one were to look through many white ethnic communities who have come over—you know, Portuguese, Italian, Irish—and then go and talk to those families, the notion of ancestral obligation is taken very seriously.

MM: Absolutely.

LG: So the more we begin to look at human beings in not only a literal way, but peripherally—to suspend this way of looking at the ideal as an ahistorical secularism, but rather take seriously the way people actually live—we may find more interesting philosophical questions and we may begin to discuss questions of more relevance to the lives of people in the world today. Ancestral obligation is one among them.

MM: Wouldn't that require philosophy to detach itself from Plato? Doesn't it go back that far in the Western tradition?

LG: Plato contributed to philosophy; Plato didn't create philosophy.

MM: Yes.

LG: One takes Plato very seriously. He had a great sense of how he connected to people who preceded him as well. He didn't live in a vacuum. He also understood what was happening elsewhere, as in Egypt. But one of the great paradoxes, of course, in morality, is that when one becomes an adult, one finds that one has to make uncomfortable moral decisions. And sometimes the paradoxes are the most painful decisions; they are the moral ones. Now that sort of a struggle in terms of what we're doing philosophically is something that needs to be considered more seriously today.

MM: People think of existentialism as a continental philosophy that took root in the post-colonial world but never really set down roots in the United States. You said earlier that a lot of people, your fellow philosophers, look at it as philosophical theory that had its day in the 1940s. Do you ever feel kind of isolated?

LG: Actually, no. I've had a great time. I've been doing philosophy. Why? Because when I look at the history of ideas or engage in a philosophical problem, I find myself seeing things that, as far as I'm concerned, are obvious, but some of my colleagues do not. I'll give you an example. Not only did I notice that there was a history of black existential and other communities of existential thought, but if we go on, if we were to deal with the problem of existentialism itself, I think it's bad reasoning that a philosophical movement should stay static. What philosophers of existence did was create a set of questions that other people took in different ways. Existentialism didn't have its head in the sky; it kept transforming itself into other contributions. If you look at post-structuralism, for instance, a lost of post-structuralism is existentialism without a subject.

MM: But hasn't existentialism been sullied a little bit by the fact that a lot of the people who founded it were amoral?

LG: Yes. But I'm interested in morality, not moralism, which is very different.

MM: Okay, but I mean Heidegger wearing the armband and . . .

LG: Actually, I'm very critical of Heidegger; I'm not pro-Heideggerian at all. But one of the things we have to bear in mind is that if one is doing a philosophy of freedom, some people use their freedom a certain way and it may not be the way we would like. On the other hand, I find Sartre to be a person with whom I'd love to have a cup of coffee. Sartre is a person who, for the most part, stood by what he believed and took the consequences for it. Sartre was a person who made decisions that many of the people I find who self-righteously condemned a person like him don't even have half the chutzpah to stand in his shoes. They are people who would bend, for instance, at the possibility of not getting tenure or promoted. The situation that he would face involved his apartment being bombed. Sartre sided with all of the people who were struggling for freedom, people suffering, the realities that connect to my own experience. A lot of individuals who in a very politically correct way dislike Sartre get their ideas from Sartre. I'm also doing work these days on human science, aesthetics and several other areas. What I've found is that there's a strange moment when people who are struggling for the liberation of humankind, who are willing to put their lives on the line, still are set up as bad guys in thought. The fact of the matter is that when we raise problems of humanism—problems of existence, problems of social transformation, problems of how we set up the relationship of ontology to history, problems of what's involved in education—when we look at problems that are connected to a revolutionary praxis, we see a certain line. It connects to people who are very popular today. I'm thinking not only in terms of African philosophy, but feminist thought or the relationship between philosophy and other disciplines. One intersecting thing about the existential period of writers was that they never looked at philosophy in a vacuum. For instance, if someone asked me what do I do, I don't say philosophy first. I say what I do is a radical struggle to understand reality. Now if one is going to struggle with that, it pushes you into philosophical questions. But it also pushes you into other kinds of questions. For instance, how do I communicate this to other fields of inquiry?

Lewis Gordon

MM: When we started this conversation, you talked about how you reached points in your life where you stopped and you looked back and everything seems to have dovetailed together to reach that point.

LG: Yes.

MM: It seems inevitable. Do you feel that way now about your life and these components, your activism, your philosophy, and jazz. Do they all seem to fit together now?

LG: Oh yes. But, you know, they never felt out of place; they never at all felt out of place. And when I think back, the one thing I loved doing all my life was writing. I loved writing so much that it didn't matter to me whether I got published or not. I didn't sit there with dreams of being a published writer. I just knew I loved writing and I began to notice that, at least in my professional life, that writing is an activity that seems to have an impact on this moment, historically. It's very different from the past. I've been surprised over the past five years how much a writer can accomplish, as if we can create magic with words. Yes, of late I've found myself reflecting on notions like magic. For instance, I find it disdainful that in the past 400 years there's been a concerted attack on magic and I don't mean by magic, you know, something supernatural, but real magic. I mean, think about the philosophy of language!

MM: Awe-inspiring.

LG: Well, one of the beautiful things about grammar, which a lot of people don't realize, that is as we create new meanings, we seem to create new forms of life, right? There's a time at which it didn't seem possible somehow, but imagination always held such possibilities. Right now I'm finding as we struggle through and try to understand the world, we seem to be creating new worlds, new ways of looking at things. And I take very seriously what was said at the end of *Wretched of the Earth,* by Frantz Fanon. He didn't always say that we need to struggle to make the world better for humankind. But he did say we need to create new concepts through which to create a new humanity, and I think creating a new humanity through new concepts is something that's not only a very special social calling, it's something wondrous and, as you know, some people look at philosophy as wondrous. But I think this wondrous dimension of philosophy needs to be reintroduced. So when I do philosophy, quite often I don't think first about whether I'm doing philosophy. I think about the problems I'm struggling with and I try to see if I can bring out a certain wonderment with them.

MM: Thanks, Lewis.

DAVID ROTHENBERG
Wild Thinking:
Philosophy, Ecology, and Technology

David Rothenberg is associate professor of philosophy at the New Jersey Institute of Technology, and the Editor of an award-winning journal, *Terra Nova: Nature and Culture*. He holds a Ph.D. in philosophy from Boston University, and is known as a writer, philosopher, ecologist, and musician, speaking out for nature in all aspects of his diverse work. Rothenberg is both a respected authority on deep ecology and a jazz clarinetist known for his integration of world music with improvisation and electronics.

MM: Michael Malone   **DR:** David Rothenberg

MM: What do technology and philosophy have to do with each other?

DR: You have to look at technology in its widest sense. What is technology? It's really the whole history of tools that human beings have used to live in the world. We as a species are nothing without our tools. This is how you make technology philosophical. It's not just computers, building bridges, or civil engineering. It's the whole history of what human beings have needed to invent to relate to the world and fit into the world and you have to look at what this has changed about the way we think. Engineers don't usually think that. They just say we've got to build this bridge. We've got to create this new piece of software, but they don't think about how in the long term it changes the way we think.

MM: Does new philosophy lead to new tools or do new tools, new technologies, promote new philosophies?

DR: I think it goes both ways. When you look at a technology like the telephone, you know, how did it come to be invented? Alexander Graham Bell was doing some experiment for the deaf to help them to communicate. He started thinking that we could communicate over long distances. The telegraph wasn't so great. What if we could really speak? This invention gradually came to be and politicians said things like, "Oh, this is a great invention. Every city should have one, you know." Nobody knew quite how much it would change the way we communicate. You think about how business is done today, how people get to know each other. It's completely different because of the telephone, a technology that was invented for a whole different purpose. It's changed what it means to talk to one another, what it means to pass information around, and it leads to other inventions: the fax machine, computers connecting to communication, and these really changed the way human beings think. And when you change the way we think, then you enter philosophy.

MM: So what do you tell your engineering students about all this?

DR: I tell them that you've got to think about why you're doing what you're doing. I want to evolve beyond the place where philosophy has usually been put into the technology and engineering curriculum. Once the *Challenger* exploded a few years back and the case was examined it turned out that there were really conceptual problems and communication problems that led to that disaster; it could have easily been prevented. Because of that, all over the country, engineering ethics developed as a subject; as something to put in the engineering curriculum, and engineering ethics is a lot about the same kind of conflicts. Between the engineer who's got to worry about safety all the time and building the best possible thing and his boss, her boss, who might say, you know, we can't afford to make it as safe as you want.

MM: Right.

DR: These stories completely scare the students because, you know, there's story after story of the engineer saying we can't do that, it's unsafe. And the boss says we have to, then it explodes and they fire the engineer.

MM: So ultimately you are teaching responsibility?

DR: I'm trying.

MM: Is that what these students are worried about?

DR: You can start with trivial examples. There's a course at NJIT where students design a voice messaging system. And they design the programming and the software and they send it off and it's made on a chip. Your chip comes back. If it works, then you pass the course. So I asked one of these students, well, did you ever talk about what it would mean to design a *good* voice messaging system? Because don't we all hate those things? I mean, don't we all complain about them and wish we could reach a real person? Aren't some better than others? They said, no, we never talk about that.

MM: So you distinguish between good and say, elegant, which is a principle every engineer would know?

DR: I think they probably need to know more about elegance. I rarely hear any of my students saying "we know about elegance."

MM: But they know about simplicity of design.

DR: They know about efficiency and safety. But I think that they're not en-

David Rothenberg

couraged to talk about elegance as a positive principle that might connect from a machine or a design into real life.

MM: So when you say the idea is to do good engineering, what constitutes good engineering?

DR: That's the big question. On the one hand solving the problem you've been given to. On the other hand, I think good engineering should have a philosophical component such that you are forced to consider whether this particular problem that you're solving is really worth solving and what solutions will it succeed at? What new problems will it create? Will it really make the world a better place? Do we need this new technology and can we think more about how this technology is going to change us. You know, there are plenty of ways where technology has seemed immediately positive and then it doesn't always seem so wonderful when you see it in hindsight.

MM: Seems like that's a course for R&D directors of large corporations rather than twenty-year-old undergraduates.

DR: But they want to be the R&D directors. You know, everyone wants to be in management. Nobody wants to really do the nitty-gritty work and, you know, I don't think everyone will make it into management. But if they do, the wider the background, the more reflective you are, the less you just follow orders, the better you will be.

MM: Now I'm curious. You have a very eclectic career—music, philosophy, ecology. How do all these things fit together?

DR: As an undergraduate I thought I was interested in philosophy because of these big questions, but I could never stand any of the courses I went to. I didn't understand the way they were looking at these questions. So I pretty much studied music and literature and anthropology. And all the while I was very concerned with the fate of the earth, the ecology, what our species was doing to this world, and I began to hear about philosophers who were working on this problem, particularly a Norwegian by the name of Arne Naess who invented the phrase 'deep ecology.' And when he invented that phrase in the '70s, he didn't claim to be discovering or pronouncing a new way of thinking, but identifying something that was already there. He was saying, look at the environmental problems that our world is facing: increased population and pollution and using up finite resources. And he said this is because our civilization has not thought enough about the deep effects of progress and our reliance on technology growth into the future. We haven't thought enough about the finitude of this planet and we haven't thought enough about other species on this planet. We've been very self-centered and sort of self-limiting. And he said, well, if we change the way we think about our relationship to nature, we will evolve into a species that just chooses to shepherd the rest of the world; taking care of the rest of world; fitting into the world and not being so arrogant to say that the world is just there for us to use and transform as we see fit.

MM: So this is, in many ways, a teaching principle.

DR: Yes, in some ways all applied philosophy is a teaching principle because you've got to believe that changing the way people think will change the world. It doesn't mean that actually doing things is any less important. But it's just some sort of faith in ideas and, you know, thinking makes a difference. There are a lot people who think thinking doesn't make a difference; all that matters is what you do.

MM: Well, that raises an interesting question. Can thinking change the nature of the human species?

DR: Well, it certainly has through time. I mean, changing the way we think has changed what we do, or what we want to do.

MM: Are we changing right now?

DR: Yes. I think we're always changing.

MM: Is the digital age changing the way we're thinking?

DR: Sure it is. I don't think we're in control of it. I'm not sure we should be in control of it. You get all these debates where someone is in favor of computers on the left; someone is smashing computers on the right and you don't have enough thought on just what is changing specifically—like the ease at which communication is sifting through digital media, between television, the Internet, computers, and everything else. Ideas can be moved back and forth. A digital copy is the same as the original. It's a whole way of transformation and I don't think we're examining just what it's doing to the value of, or how we value, information.

MM: Well, let me ask you: Is this transformation salutary for deep ecology or are we moving further away from it?

DR: I think that deep ecology has come to mean several different things. There are some people who say deep ecology is real radical ecology; they say, let's cut the population of the world to one million human beings, or something, and then we'll have the right ratio and let the rest of the natural world flourish. That's a fairly radical idea and most deep ecologists have no clear ideas on how we would get there. So that is one approach, but it is not the approach I would align myself with, although it may not be a bad idea to have so few people. I'm more interested in this idea that if we really think of what it would mean to conceive of and value nature in a new way, we could be a better species; using technology, using thinking, using senses of restraint and looking forward to the future. We can respect the world much more than we do now. It wasn't so long ago there was slavery. It wasn't so long ago that women had no right to vote, own property and such in many cultures and, you know, we may in a hundred years from now have the same sense of expansion, include other species, and to value nature in a human way that will just expand our ability to care about the world around us and we won't be able to wantonly destroy it as easily. I do believe that changes in human thought and morality do happen.

MM: So how do you begin this process with your students?

DR: You get them to ask questions and you get them to talk about what matters to them. A technological university in one sense is a very good place to teach philosophy because they have no set rules. They don't say you've got to teach it this way, the way we've done it for fifty years. It's wide open. You can make speculative thought and reflection, and the questioning of how we live relevant to what people are studying and not be afraid of breaking with tradition.

MM: Nobody gets fired for asking the wrong question.

DR: Not in my school, no, it's a very open atmosphere.

MM: Is this the students' last opportunity before they're out in the world to ask such questions?

DR: Well, hopefully it's their first opportunity. You know, a lot of them want to get a good job, earn money, or support their families, a very straight ahead view on what's in front of them, but they don't think as much about how what they're doing fits into the culture at large. How working for a company might compromise your sense of responsibility toward the natural world. Most of my students do care about the environment. New Jersey's a big state for the environment because it's pretty clear that the previous, recent industrial culture has messed it up. Nobody denies that. They have different ideas on how to progress, but the students pick up on that mood in the state and they really care about the environment. But they're not always sure how their work in technology might directly connect to that and so I just encourage them to think about the connection. You do this one kind of job, you can get a good job, earn a good living, take care of your family, but you also have a responsibility to think about your place in the world, whatever way you think is appropriate. Your life will be enriched and be made deeper if you look around and connect your present situation to the world around.

MM: Tell me about *Terra Nova*.

DR: *Terra Nova* is a journal, a magazine I started three years ago, and it has several aims. One aim is to make this environmental, philosophical culture, to make this deep ecology not overly ideological as much as cultural. Many people identify ecology as science and politics and they forget that it really is a cultural movement to look at how human beings live and express themselves and what we have to say about our relationship to the natural world. There's a lot of nature writing. There's a lot of environmental art. It's sort of considered or used as a kind of propaganda, but it's my view that this is one of the reasons why, in general, the cultural elite of this country does not take environmentalism seriously. They think it's a fringe movement. They think it's something they don't need to think about. They think it's something bothersome, troublesome.

MM: But if deep ecology has a goal, then ultimately it has to move into the marketplace of ideas. It has to back itself with science, and then it has to aggressively go out and pursue the political agenda.

DR: Right. What I'm trying to do with this publication is move into the marketplace of cultural ideas. I want people in the arts in America to take our relationship with nature seriously and realize that some of the best and most important works have to do with our relationship with the natural world.

MM: Well, what about music?

DR: Music is there in many different ways. In fact, we did a special issue, probably our most successful one, on the relationship between music and nature. I'm not speaking of soft, gentle new age music with waves and loons calling in the background where you can relax, as in nature. Nor was it the assaulting avant-garde noise that would scare off people, even though it might be kind of fun for those who like it. But in between there were all these possibilities where nature and music blend together. Our first piece on the CD is a recording of a

David Rothenberg

bird from Australia, the pied butcherbird, and you play this for people, they can't believe it's a bird because it really sounds like somebody sitting in a field with a flute trying to write a piece of music, trying to play a piece of music. You hear the intelligence. You hear an idea coming, you hear the bird stopping, developing it, trying it out, just like someone writing a jazz tune by playing along. This bird is making music, pure and simple, according to any human characteristics of what that would be.

MM: So you're talking about natural sounds.

DR: On the one hand, music made out of natural sounds. On the other hand, the way it's put together somehow seeks to emulate nature, perhaps in its manner of operation, which is an aesthetic idea that Aristotle talked about, John Cage talked about it in our century. This is the way for art to connect to nature. To work like nature, not to imitate and look like nature, but to fit together like nature and seem to have an organic unity such that when you've got it in front of you, you're listening to it, you're watching it, you're hearing it, you're experiencing it. You're saying this artist is alive and necessary and right here. And that principle always interested me and it always seemed to be something that could be easily abused, could easily be made too simple. But it's really a tough goal. It's easy for birds and plants and animals, other animals, to fit into nature, but human beings because of what we've become, because of our technologies and our history, it's really hard for us to fit into nature. And yet we must if we're going to survive and last into the coming millennia. We've got to fit into nature.

MM: Well, give me an example, can you do it?
  [He picks up an instrument—long, thin, wood]

DR: This instrument which I'm holding somehow combines music, nature, and technology and I'll see if I can explain why. It is an instrument coming originally from Norway called the *seljefløyte* or willow flute, even though this one is made out of pear wood. You notice it has no holes to play the notes of the tempered scale that Western music is based on. It just has a place you blow into and you can play on the end. So it plays on what's called the natural harmonic series, which is the same kind of thing you hear when you play harmonics on the guitar and some would say it's the different tones you hear as the wind is going through the trees. It's not the tempered scale; it's closer to a blues scale or kind of the scale of folk music that's sort of de-tuned. And so I hear in that scale something natural and visceral and immediate, and yet it's this technology we can use that can bring this out. Whereas other flutes may have holes that force you into a human-designed scale, this is something of a more natural

175

scale and so the music that you can play on it has a basis of rhythm and a kind of naturalness that I think points human arts toward the environment and the wider world around. So we'll hear a little bit.

(Flute music in background)

MM: I'm curious, what's the role of consciousness asserting itself through that music? You talked about the bird. But the bird is deeply enmeshed into the natural world. We're somewhat detached from it. How much do you have to leave yourself to play naturally and how much do you have to assert your own consciousness on top of it to structure it?

DR: I would say that you do not leave yourself, but you kind of expand what yourself is outward into the world and if you spend as much time trying to explain and think things out as I do working as a philosopher, for me music can sometimes solve these problems and answer these questions that philosophy can raise. You find out this answer of how to fit into this natural world that initially seems so far away. Though it's hard to explain, you can do it, and I think it's always important not to just think about the problems, but to act and to do something and for some philosophers it's writing, for some it's organizing institutions, and, you know, for me music is this sort of public side of philosophy. I do it less for myself and more to reach outward and find a place in the world. People always liked music more than philosophy because it's less disturbing.

MM: So when you're playing, are you playing notes in their relation to each other? How much of it is you trying to capture the sounds of the natural world?

DR: Obviously, one is music and the other is something more or less. Well, as I said, rather than capturing the sounds of the natural world, I'd like to ease into the natural world by working in some sort of natural way, by figuring out what nature means.

MM: So this is your ticket into the world?

DR: It's one of the ways in. It's an instrument that I see as part of the way in. It has certain limitations, but it's almost like a form of meditation. As I play it I wonder whether it makes sense this idea of using music to fit into nature or am I just coming up with some explanation and then part of me says, you know, stop worrying about it. Just do it. In music you get involved in the process. For me it's the easiest way to forget about all this confusion. Philosophy doesn't make you settled, you know. In that sense it's different than meditation; it makes you more and more confused and through that confusion you can be

David Rothenberg

much more alive and sort of wonder about the world. You know, wonder is the best thing philosophy has to offer. You have to wonder about how this amazing planet, this amazing place where we are, and not get bored and not think there are too easy answers. Just keep asking, keep exploring.

MM: As long as we're on the topic, what s the worst thing philosophy has to offer?

DR: So many bad things. I think it was Keats who said that philosophers are the kind of people who pull off angels' wings; who try to explain every mystery away. When philosophy tries to explain away wonder, it's in error, and this has happened throughout history. You can trace it all the way back, certainly at least to Plato who was really confused about what he thought about poetry—these poets who lie, as he put it. He was already trying to explain away wonder and the great mystery.

MM: In his republic, there wasn't a lot of room for the poets.

DR: But the thing that saved Plato was his literary quality. He was so poetic himself, and beautiful and confusing.

MM: So, ironically, he was a poet who didn't quite make it as a poet.

DR: Absolutely. He was a philosophical poet or a poetic philosopher and I think that's the way for philosophy to improve and or develop in a better way is to have an artistry about it, have a poetry to it, and not try and explain too much away. And that's one of the reasons I started *Terra Nova* because I want to change academic culture as we know it and get academics who are well-meaning people, who are interested in thinking and working and writing, to have the luxury of time to think and write, to not just communicate to a specialized audience. particularly in the humanities. To not make the humanities like science, which is a specialized field, or a collection of specialized fields, but to really reach outward and think deeply and widely to the general public. Take the public seriously. Television often doesn't take the public seriously, they dumb down too many of the programs. But, you know, philosophy and academia can take the public seriously and say, "Let me discuss some ideas in that area a little bit hard to grasp onto, but they're worth thinking about and we'll lead you into it, but we'll take you seriously. We want to interact with you." Forget interactive machinery. Ideas can be the most interactive things and you get people thinking once you show that you respect them. And, you know, philosophy has not done this because it's shied away, it's hidden away in its little corners, but it's starting to change. I think in this television series you're doing you'll find numerous philosophers who really are trying to reach out and change this field which, you know, started out by asking the big questions everyone's interested in. For years philosophy has been diverted into using the wrong methods for answering them and I think we're going to see philosophy becoming more and more relevant in the next century.

MM: I'm intrigued that your students are at the age when people ask big questions, but then the majority of folks don't enter into a contemplative, academic life. They go out there into the reality of commerce and careers and they don't really get a chance. I mean those questions emerge from the subconscious every once in a while, but usually there's not enough time to think about it. You've got to get back to work until, you know, in your later years you finally get a chance to return to them. How do you fill that gap in the middle?

DR: In the middle? People have time. This idea that people have less time than ever before is a myth. I think people believe that they're busier than ever before, but you can make time to think.

MM: How do you get them to make time to think about philosophy?

DR: Well, you just don't say it's thinking about philosophy. You say it's thinking about what's most important in life. And you move people away from the self-centeredness of modern psychology, which is booming, by the way. Everyone wants to figure it out themselves. A lot of this urge to figure out oneself is a little misguided. People really want to figure out bigger questions: What are we here for, not what am I going to do with my life, but what does it mean to be a human on this earth? What is a good life? How can I live the best life that satisfies my role in the world? How can I define myself, not around my own problems, but in relation to the world around me? I think that people really are interested in philosophy, but, you know, rarely are they asked to talk about it.

MM: You've spent your life so far as a philosopher. You watch those people out there on the sidewalk, people like me racing around to and from, you know our business and our jobs and those things. Do you ever wish you were out there running around with us or do you wish that more of us were in the tower there with you?

DR: I don't think I'm in a tower. I've spent a lot of time running around and my interests cross over from teaching into the world of the general public so I'm a person who will probably always go back and forth between these worlds. I value the time that I have to think and the fact that all this thinking, the work I do, is not dependent entirely on the market. I don't have to decide I'm going to write a book that's going to sell a lot of copies because I need the money because I have a job that pretty much pays me to think, which is nice. But, on the other hand, I do want to influence people. And I would like to have a wider public for my work. So I think more than a lot of my colleagues about how to reach the wider public. I'm sort of in between, you know. I've spent years and years in school. I never liked school that much, and I'm still there, whereas all my friends have graduated. I'm still there; teaching, and so I think that I'm interested in taking philosophy from the schools outward.

MM: One last question.

DR: Yes.

MM: You play a lot of jazz; you compose jazz. Where does jazz fit into this spectrum of things you're doing?

DR: Well, jazz is the most philosophical kind of music because that's where you sit and think as you play. You hear the musicians thinking, you know, so it's a complete laboratory of thought. I think there's no surprise that many philosophers are jazz musicians. Many jazz musicians are philosophers. Actually, I think my first exposure to philosophy was in a jazz workshop taught by the trombonist, George Lewis, who has a philosophy degree from Yale. You know, he got me interested in philosophy and showed me the connection. I certainly do some of my best thinking while playing and not even knowing what it's about until afterwards and I think it's important not to get bogged down in words if you're a philosopher. To think through music is a wonderful, wonderful thing.

JOHN STUHR
Prospects for Democracy

John Stuhr, Professor and Head of the Department of Philosophy at Penn State University, and Founding Co-Editor of *Studies in American and European Philosophy* and Co-Editor of *The Journal of Speculative Philosophy*. A highly regarded John Dewey and American philosophy scholar, John Stuhr focused on a variety of topics, including democracy and education, bioethics and public policy, and the cultural roles of philosophy—a clear precise dialogue resulting in fruitful insights.

MM: Michael Malone   **JS:** John Stuhr

MM: Is there such a thing as an American philosophy?

JS: Pragmatism is a distinctly American philosophy. And all that pragmatism means is that you're going to test theory by practice; you're not going to believe something just because somebody says it's so in theory. It has to be borne out in experience.

MM: So the Missouri rule, eh?

JS: Pragmatism is a kind of *show me* philosophy and it says if you don't find this to be so in your experience, if its not confirmed in your life, it's not so.

MM: Okay. Give me the leading American philosophers.

JS: Leading American philosophers? People like Charles Peirce and William James and John Dewey.

MM: What happened before? What happened since?

JS: What happened before was that the university system in America wasn't established and a lot of important thinkers didn't think of themselves as philosophers. So, Thomas Jefferson, Emerson, Thoreau, Fuller, DuBois. They were philosophers but they would not have said that they were philosophers.

MM: Because they weren't professors of philosophy in a university?

JS: Right. But those people would not have identified themselves as philosophers. In fact, I think that's one of the problems with the field in the United States today. People restrict it to philosophy professors when some of the people who really, I think, are writing some of the most philosophically important stuff may or may not be credential-carrying philosophers.

MM: Could you give me one person in modern American life who's not an academic philosopher that you consider a philosopher?

JS: Lester Thurow is an economist, but I consider what he does to be philosophical. I think that lots of writers like the poet Wallace Stevens—I think that he's a philosopher. People like Wendell Berry who are writing about agrarianism and so on. That's philosophy. Lots of fiction writers, I think, are raising the same kinds of themes that philosophers deal with: questions about the meaning of life. How one ought to live. Those are philosophical issues.

MM: Do we Americans just have a natural resistance to talking about philosophy as philosophy even though we're doing it?

JS: It's partly that philosophers haven't done a good job of explaining to the general public what they do. I mean, they haven't gone public in a good way.

MM: So how does American philosophy manifest the American character? How much does it have to do with the frontier, with the new world?

JS: I think a lot of it does, not just with the frontier, but basically what you have is Europeans arriving in the new world. And carrying with them, besides whatever stuff they have, a whole set of concepts and beliefs, many of which are absolutely unsuited to the new environment that they find themselves in.

MM: They're sitting there hanging on the beach looking at 2,000 miles of woods.

JS: So under the pressure of this new environment, I think a new outlook is formed. And I would say, in kind of a simple way, it was much less important who you were and it was much more important what you could do. Pragmatism is just the kind of theoretical expression of that aspect of the American character.

MM: Okay, so give me some of the characteristics, the deep characteristics, of this philosophy, this culture.

JS: There is a real practicalism and individualism—a kind of pluralism. Your life may be different from mine in significant ways, and the values that I hold may not have to be the ones that you hold. Now there's also concern on the other side of that with community. So at the same time that there's all this

John Stuhr

concern with individualism, people are concerned about community and the kinds of ties that bind people together.

MM: So how do we Americans resolve this tension between individuals and community?

JS: It's not a tension. It's not something that's resolved. The two interpenetrate one another. It's difficult to be a real individual unless you're supported by a community. It's difficult to have a real community unless you have real individuals in it. Otherwise you just have groups of conformists.

MM: But now you're talking about a different kind of community than the sort of political return to community that we see on the conservative side of the political spectrum.

JS: Right. A lot of that rhetoric is bound up with a certain kind of conservative political agenda, a kind of family-values agenda. These are all good words but in a way these words have been kidnapped, I think. Family values, it's like motherhood and apple pie—how can you be against that? Community—how can you be against that? I think the question to ask in some of these cases is who's being excluded? What's being left out? And I think that from the standpoint of some groups of people in the United States and certainly from the standpoint of some other people around the world, some of this rhetoric looks very exclusionary.

MM: Today the American character must be changing some. Turner declared the frontier dead 110 years ago. Now we're sitting on the Pacific rim, we have hundreds of different ethnic groups merging together and at this nexus we're also meeting with technology. Then there is the global business community. What happens now to the American character? What kind of philosophy comes next?

JS: I think that it becomes increasingly less valuable to talk about the American character. In other words, there are multiple American characters. It's not that there's one American culture; there are lots of American cultures.

MM: But it's never going to be monolithic again.

JS: Well, I'm not sure it ever was. But there may have been a story told that it was. It's certainly an experiment, the world's leading experiment in pluralism.

183

MM: Okay, so what happens when this crazy quilt runs into the Internet and the microprocessor? What happens then?

JS: Well, you tell me. I mean one of the things that happens is it becomes globalized, right, so that you see aspects of American culture in other parts of the world and you see the United States inviting in aspects of other people's culture. So I think that the Internet is simply another kind of mass communication tool that breaks down conditions that used to allow ways of thinking to survive in isolation from one another. I mean, now we're aware of some of these things and they push and press and they have to responded to and so on. So it's so potentially a very good educational thing.

MM: So can American philosophy emerge from all this? Or, can it continue from its history as it moves forward or does it just begin to break up into dozens of different American philosophies?

JS: I think that one of the most important aspects of American philosophy is *a commitment to pluralism.* There's a way in which American philosophy is kind of in the avant garde of these kinds of changes around the world where it's a spirit that's much less fundamentalist, much less absolutist, than lots of other ways of thinking around the world.

MM: So if I were to look for examples of this emerging new philosophy, where would I see it? Popular culture?

JS: Yes, in part.

MM: I was flipping through one of your books, and all of a sudden there's lyrics from Neil Young's " My My Hey Hey."

JS: Right. I use a lot of pop culture references, a lot of poetry references, too. I think that one of the reasons why I do that is to try to break down these supposed barriers between high culture and low culture. Philosophy looks like high culture, as though it doesn't have connections with these other things that we see on a day-to-day basis.

MM: One of your duties as a philosopher is to try to get philosophy out there?

JS: Well, I think so. It's one that *I* feel, anyway. I don't want to report it as though everyone feels this—I think they don't. But it seems to me that the

John Stuhr

question here is not if it is a good thing for philosophy to be more practical. That doesn't matter. Or maybe it matters for a few philosophers in their careers or something, but it doesn't *really* matter. What matters is, is there a kind of practical intelligence that people can bring to bear on social problems? Right. And if they don't connect, then it's like what everyone experienced at least a couple times unless they've been incredibly lucky, a very bright scholar who's a terrible teacher, who knows his or her stuff and doesn't connect with you. So you can't follow a *Field of Dreams* strategy; if you build it, they won't come. You have to go to where they are.

MM: Is it really there in popular culture?

JS: The things that I'm trying to pull out in the book that you're mentioning, it's not just a random assortment of popular culture. I'm trying to pick out lyrics that I think are brilliant and they're very moving and I think they're very revealing and they're illuminating.

MM: What do they reveal?

JS: Well, I think that they seem immediate to people and I think that what they reveal is a quality of experience. Philosophy historically means love of wisdom. It's not just a field that asks what's true, what do I know? It asks you what sort of person should you be and many of these poems, songs, films in popular culture are dealing with just those issues. The ones that I'm trying to pick out, I think, are ones that highlight certain themes. I mean, I think that they're ones that highlight issues like the meaning of death for human life, the meaning of finite existence. They're talking about the importance of interpersonal relations in one's life. They're talking about the kinds of principles that might guide choices. They're talking about the things that we learn ideally as we grow older in age. So, those are the kinds of things that I think are important. Now whether those are called high culture philosophy or popular culture, it doesn't matter, but they're there. And I think that many of these things are much more effective in reaching most people, students, and even professional philosophers.

MM: Are the messages they're sending about what's valuable in life, how should you live your life, what is death—different from what you read when you read Thoreau and Emerson?

JS: Sure, sometimes they're different and sometimes they're similar, and one would hope that philosophers in trying to think through these issues more

185

systematically have gone into more depth on them. But I don't think that they're different in the sense that—let me put it this way—*I don't think that philosophy is optional.* I don't think that people have a choice between whether they engage in philosophy or not. You can engage in it more or less consciously, you can engage in it more or less successfully, but it's not an option because every single day as you go about making choices, you're giving voice to a certain kind of life. That's what philosophy is about.

MM: But implicit in that is you can become better at making those decisions.

JS: That's right.

MM: Can you be trained or is it part of your upbringing?

JS: You can't be trained, I think, in the sense that you can't be given a formula, which is often what students want in beginning philosophy classes. Please give me the answer, show me a moral dilemma. Give me the three right steps I go through—there it is: boom. That's obviously what irritates a lot of people about philosophy classes; they're not quite sure which one of my notes here is going to be on the final. Okay, the answer is sort of all of it. There's no formulaic answer like that, but, yes, you can be given certain principles for clear thinking. You can be given certain analytical tools. You can be given exposure to what other smart people have said, right? In other words, the reason why anybody should read Plato or Aristotle or any other great dead philosopher isn't so you can pass a final exam and say, I know what Plato said. It's because maybe Plato said something that'll be useful to you.

MM: Now we do have a formal method of conveying a lot of this called education.

JS: Well, I think that education, higher education, public education in America, is in a problem, it's in trouble in a lot of ways in the United States today. One of the few things that I think that the right and the left in this country agree on is that the public schools aren't working very well. And, at the level of higher education, it seems to me and one of the things that I've written about is that there are certain structures of the business world that are entering into education.

MM: You've written that education shouldn't be business. Hasn't it always been business? The public school system that we all grew up in was basically

John Stuhr

the legacy of the factory model of production from the 1850s, you know, we all went through. We go through this step process: first grade, second grade.

JS: You went to a different kind of school than I did.

MM: Well, yes, but Eli Whitney and I went together. No, you know, but it's first grade, second grade, it's a step function, just like traditional factories were and then you test at the end.

JS: Right.

MM: That came from the factory model.

JS: Right. I don't know what school you went to, but most of the schools didn't have as their goal sort of fitting you into some particular slot. It was rather developing certain kinds of abilities in you, which is why reading, writing, and arithmetic were taught. I think that today there's some structures that are present in higher education that are producing certain kinds of not fodder for a military, but fodder for industry, for business.

MM: But business isn't happy with what's being produced by the educational system. I hear business people say, look, schools are still operating under a model that's been obsolete since 1970. The factories now, for example. Factories now produce six signal production, they produce total quality, and they test continuously. And they're saying, why don't schools do that? Why aren't kids, every kid, guaranteed, you know, that he or she comes out with a full and complete education no matter how long it takes or how short it takes. This sort of notion of creating total quality—why aren't schools doing that now?

JS: Well, there's probably no university that doesn't have total quality management in place. But what is the product that you're testing for? I mean, if you're building a car, we have some sense of what this thing should look like when you're done and presumably the engineers and the factory workers and so on have the same view, okay. The curriculum is more contested and so there's a question of what exactly should people know.

MM: Okay, what should people know?

JS: That's the kind of question that a certain mind-set wants to ask. Give me the content! I think that the more important question is what kinds of *skills* should people have. I don't think that it matters much whether people take philosophy classes; they can get the same things that philosophy provides in a whole host of other classes as well: history classes and literature classes and so on. I think they often don't get it as much or as carefully and so on. But, it doesn't matter and the student who thinks that everything depends upon what major do I pick, that's just not the case. The question is, do you come away with certain kinds of analytical skills? Do you come away with certain kinds of historical knowledge? Do you come away with certain communication abilities? That's what matters.

MM: How can we possibly educate children for a world that we can't imagine?

JS: That's why the liberal arts and the humanities are so important because what you're getting there is not simply a body of information that you know and can always use and will stay the same. You're getting certain kinds of skills.

MM: You're preparing for the future by not taking computer sciences, but by taking humanities?

JS: It's not so. It's not a question about one or the other—I mean it's not, it doesn't have to be that you take only one or only the other. It's that I think there's a real difference between education understood as a kind of learning of information to be put to use in a certain place and the kind of education that liberal arts gives you. And I think philosophy is kind of quintessentially so, that gives you a kind of skill that basically allows you to keep growing. So the real question is educating for conditions of indeterminacy. We don't know exactly what it's going to be like. So the answer is, we can't answer that question. We better have the skills to answer those questions as we go along.

MM: So at the moment what you're saying is the education system is doing a worse job than, say, popular music to prepare young people for the indeterminacy of the future?

JS: Well, there's certainly a lot of popular music that's pretty terrible as well. But the best of it I think is very good and I think that, you know, is it having that effect on people or not? It depends on what use they make of it. It may or it may not. It depends upon how it's hitting the audience and so on. But it might. It could and it may be just as important and so, yes, it may be that these song lyrics are more significant and more meaningful than this dusty old book of philosophy. That may be so in lots of cases and it may be the reverse as well.

John Stuhr

Again, it seems to me it, it is counterintuitive because I would argue that the only really practical subject matter is philosophy. It's the only really practical subject matter. Other ones give you information.

MM: Right.

JS: But then there's a question. I mean, so you can study the guns and butter curve in economics, but when the question comes, so what should we do? More of one, more of the other; they say, wait, we're a value-neutral social science. We don't answer that question.

MM: So this is humanities reductionism, just like over in the science department they'll tell you all you need to know is physics.

JS: It's not reductionism, but you can know all there is to know in physics and it won't tell you how to lead your life.

MM: But the humanities departments are blowing it. I mean, you have a pretty, devastating chapter title in one of your books. It says Humanities, Inc.

JS: I think that humanities departments are blowing it by retreating into a kind of specialized jargon that's distant from the experience of most of the students.

MM: And nowhere more than philosophy.

JS: Right, and nobody more than philosophers.

MM: So how do you break philosophy out of its jargon-laden, analytical world and get it back out there.

JS: The way to do that is by starting out with the so-called problems of philosophers by connecting with the experiences of students and other people. I think that's the way the best teachers in all fields work. They don't start with their theories; they start with the experiences and the problems of the people that they're trying to teach. One of the problems that lots of philosophers have, I think, is in introductory classes, informing students that these are the problems of philosophy and the students think, I didn't know these were problems and they don't seem like problems to me and okay, if you say so, and this will be on the final so we'll pretend to. But what you need to do is be able to reach the experience of the students.

189

MM: I mean, as an outsider looking in, it seems as if the twentieth century has been the story of philosophy moving from what's the meaning of life to symbolic logic.

JS: Yes, I think there's more to it than that, but it's certainly a century in which philosophy moved from figures like Emerson and Thoreau, who were public intellectuals, into the Academy and then, essentially, quarantined itself in the academy. So I would say that philosophy is, largely in this country, suffering a kind of self-imposed quarantine.

MM: Okay, so where does the Inc. part come in Humanities, Inc.?

JS: The Inc. part comes because several things are happening in higher education that are intertwining business and universities in ways that they haven't been intertwined before. One is that businesses are simply providing more education than they ever did before. There are lots of businesses that run training and education programs.

MM: We're getting eighteen year olds who read at the third grade level and we've got to bring them up to snuff before we can even get them started on the assembly line.

JS: Yes, right. No question about that. I don't disagree. And the other thing that's happening is that universities are taking on more and more of the structures of business because universities, historically, they're this old, medieval institution. And here it's almost the next millennium, right, and they're still around. But what's happening now is that the image of a university as a community of scholars is being replaced by something that looks more like corporate board room and decisions are being made in different ways, and philosophy and the humanities in general haven't done well in that environment. They haven't showed themselves to be cost effective. I think that there are kind of two things you can do when you're attacked that way. You can either say this: these are the barbarians and I choose not to respond. In which case you suffer certain kinds of consequences, or you can say, no, I need to be able to make the case and show you why this is important.

MM: So you have to show humanities to be cost effective?

JS: Yes. I think you have to show that philosophy is important.

MM: Okay, and how do you do that on the bottom line?

JS: Not by saying, "Have I got a theory for you!" because persons are saying I don't need this stuff; these aren't my problems. I think that lots of people have gone into philosophy because of events in the world around them that demanded reflection. There was a war going on or—what about the environment?

MM: What got you in?

JS: I was in college at a time that the Vietnam War was ending, the first Earth Day, the women's movement—lots of things to think about that needed some reflection. It wasn't clear that the right answers had been given before.

MM: So when you go out there to make this case with humanities, do you go first to the humanities departments or do you go first to the corporations?

JS: You go first to all those places. And you go first to the students. And you go to the corporations and you go, I mean, you have to, you have to go everywhere all at once. I realize that may seem like, okay, that's a non-answer, but it's not that one of these segments is more important then the other. You have to be able to reach out in all these ways.

MM: College campuses believe that the corporate world is, you know, the very embodiment of human evil.

JS: That's right. So you need to show up and so you need to talk to these people where they are and you need to not say things like, geez, philosophy is just so much better than this. You need to say, this is interesting. The people who score the lowest on the MBA exam to get into business school are undergraduate business majors. Why is that? Why do philosophy majors outscore these people by a mile?

MM: Is that true?

JS: Yes. Why do philosophy majors have the highest score on the LSAT to go to law school? That might get the attention of somebody who's in law. Why do they have the highest MCAT exams to go to medical school, okay? That's something that they can understand.

MM: Good case, I'm sold.

JS: So there're some skills. It's not because the business exam says name four of Plato's works, right? It's because that in reading Plato or reading James or reading Dewey or somebody, certain kinds of skills have been developed. That's what's important and I think that, more than anything else, what it is is a kind of sophistication about values and about reasoning about values.

MM: A lot of those CEOs were actually philosophy majors at one point.

JS: That's right, and these other people are working for them. But, no, I think that you have to explain to them that here's an opportunity in which they can have a big impact in a way that will really matter. If you don't believe in what you're doing, and I think this is true in philosophy in other ways, if you don't believe in this, go into any other walk of life, it's not going to be convincing to anybody else. Right? But you need to be able to explain to them, here's an opportunity that you . . . where you can do something. These are resources that you have. You can put this to use. Here's why this is so important. It may not seem at first like it's a good connection. Why would this individual or this business have some interest in philosophy? But here's what it is. Okay.

MM: And it works?

JS: Yes, I would say that, again, this is not an either-or situation either, but if were just to say which does the society suffer from? A lack of data or a lack of wisdom about how to use it? It's the latter by far. We have an information glut. We have, you know, a poverty of wisdom about how to deal with it. So those kinds of fields that deal with those issues are really important.

MM: Let's go past higher education. Let's look at the baseline, K–12. Everybody goes to K–12. If you're going to turn a culture, you work on K–12. You're now the czar. Well, let's make you the czar of education, public education in America, public and private education in America.

JS: Okay.

MM: What would you do?

JS: The political landscape is littered with people offering too easy solutions: "All we need is to privatize the schools, all we need is vouchers, all we need is charter schools, all we need is more money, all we need is a computer in every classroom." None of those things is *all* that we need. We know that a lot of people want privatization and vouchers mainly because that the public school system is the juggernaut.

John Stuhr

MM: And so what do good American citizens do? They put their kids in private school, but they vote for school bond issues, too, to assuage their guilt.

JS: That's right, but again, in different school districts, voucher systems or charter schools are going to work out in different ways. If you talk about certain populations, there's going to be a group of people who, even if given the voucher, aren't free to take their kids elsewhere. So it seems to me again that this a kind of artificial either-or question. Do we have sort of more private incentives or do we give more resources? It's going to require some of both. Is there something that the schools can do in lots of specific cases that will benefit by having the injection of competition? Yeah, without question. Is that a kind of overall answer to all the problems? No, I don't think so at all. One of the other reasons that I think schools have a lot of problems here is that, so you'll have to make me czar of even more, because they are handed a lot of problems historically in the past . . .

MM: Done by families.

JS: Yeah, or not done. But now there's a lot of demands that are made on the schools and so, if you have a child there with certain kinds of home problems, if you have people there with certain kinds of drug problems, if you have certain violence problems, these aren't problems, historically, that schools have had to face.

We say we want our kids to learn the basic curriculum, but, by the way, we also want you to teach them computer literacy and a couple of languages and blah, blah, blah, and etc.

MM: So, okay, Mr. Czar, what are you going to do with the curriculum?

JS: Well, I think, you've got to try to do two things. You're going to have to have a conversation that we haven't had in this country about what kinds of subjects, what kinds of experiences we think are so important that they need to constitute a kind of core of education. One of the things that's happened is not only did we not have that conversation, we're not even exactly sure how that would take place. In other words, these are conversations that generate a lot more heat than they do light. Schools don't teach logic, which is basically how to think properly. They think, well, we can teach speaking or writing, but many speaking and writing problems are problems of thinking. It would be important to introduce more students at an earlier age to logic. That's not a solution or anything, but it seems to me that's something that's important no matter what one's interests are, no matter what one goes on to do. Now, historically, the schools have had certain goals for higher education. Those have kind of fallen apart and I think that that's a kind of parallel to the unraveling of issues of value in our culture more generally. In other words, it's not surprising that the public schools don't agree on just exactly what they ought to teach, what the curriculum ought to be, because the parents that are sending their kids there don't agree.

MM: Okay, now you're no longer czar, you're no longer philosopher king—we're going to strip the monarchy away from you. You're back to being a philosopher.

JS: Okay.

MM: This isn't going to happen, is it?

JS: Well, I think that's a prediction question: will it happen, right? That doesn't interest me in the least. One of the other themes that is dominant in a lot of the American philosophers that I think are most important, people like Peirce and James and Dewey, is a view that's called *meliorism*, which is a word that no one's ever heard of. But it's a very simple idea. We understand pessimism and optimism. The pessimist thinks things are going to be bad, the optimist thinks it's going to be good. A meliorist says, I don't know how it's going to be, but it's only going to be better if I work toward it, if I act toward it, if I make an effort.

MM: If we can start the virtuous cycle.

JS: Well, if we work *hard*. In other words, pragmatism is, to some extent, puritanism without the puritanism. It's just the work ethic. It says, I don't know whether we're going to solve this problem or not, but we're certainly not going to solve it unless we put a lot of hard work into it. We may, but there's no guarantees. So pragmatism is not a philosophy like fundamentalism. It doesn't tell you everything's going to be okay in the end.

MM: And a meliorist says, let's give it a shot.

JS: Right and that seems to me to be important. So different people will be in different positions and can make that shot in different ways. One of the things that I think that philosophers can do, for instance, is they can volunteer and do work in public schools, elementary schools. I do that. I teach logic. I get more from it probably than the kids. But I do that in elementary schools. It's amazing what the students are able to do. They're able to think very clearly. It's like mathematics; it's formal, they're great. I think that almost everybody who teaches at the university level has at some point experienced the kind of student who thinks I'm really not very interested in this. I'm just here to pass through—is this going to be on the exam? When you teach people who are in third grade, they're interested in everything. Everything is interesting. So one question to ask is, what happened between elementary school and the university that this kind of curiosity and interest got killed off? Something very bad is happening.

MM: If you can answer that, you may have the beginning of your solution.

PETER CAWS
The Passing of Philosophical Fads

Peter Caws, University Professor of Philosophy at the George Washington University and organizer of the Bicentennial Symposium of American Philosophy. Peter Caws speaks with complete confidence and he believes that philosophy is much too slow to react to historical events. In the mode of constructive criticism, he suggests numerous ways philosophy can contribute to the human predicament related to such issues as the causes of quarrels, war and peace, philosophy and literature, and artificial intelligence.

MM: Michael Malone   **PC:** Peter Caws

MM: Peter, we live in an age where everyone is obsessed by change, by progress. We're obsessed with time and its passage. It seems to be accelerating. The world seems to be undergoing this perpetual recreation of itself. Is philosophy doing the same thing?

PC: The great thing about philosophy is that it has a really long history, but it moves very slowly.

MM: How slowly?

PC: Well, it appears to move fast. Let me give you something I just came across the other day. In 1965, a big encyclopedia of philosophy was published by Macmillan, and I had a piece in it on scientific method. In 1995, they published a supplement. Now, in the meantime, I had been working on something called structuralism. There was no entry on structuralism in the 1965 encyclopedia. In the 1995 supplement, look up structuralism. It says, "see post-structuralism." So, it was just elided—thirty years had just gone by. But my view of the matter is that, actually, we've just got to the point of being able to understand there is a new way [namely, structuralism] of looking at objects, literary objects and political objects and things like that. I think there's a new entry [in the history of philosophy], but it's a couple hundred years since the last entry. Really, the whole thing is moving very slowly. There's this passion for thinking in a historicist way. Everything's got to be before or after something else. But when you get back to the books and [the business of] thinking, it's a much slower process.

MM: Why does philosophy seem to move so much slower than everything else?

PC: Well, the question is, why is everything else moving so fast?

197

MM: Okay, let's ask it that way.

PC: Because human beings, I think, are very much what they were 2,500 years ago, when philosophy started. The theme of the Congress we're at right now is "philosophy educating humanity." What kind of job has it done? Because what we're learning now, we could have learned pretty much in the fourth century B.C. if we'd really been paying attention.

MM: They were pretty smart guys. How come we weren't paying attention then? We had other things to worry about?

PC: The question is, who pays attention now? We've got a few thousand people here, maybe less than that, a few hundred people at this Congress. How many philosophers are there compared to all the rest of the world? And who's listening to them?

MM: But, why aren't we listening? Especially in the twentieth century. It would seem that in this century, of all centuries, there has been an awful lot of bloodletting. We need a philosophy, perhaps more in ethics, one of your great interests, than at any other time in recent history. Why haven't we been listening to philosophy?

PC: I think one of the reasons is, it's harder to listen to anything in a sound-bite culture, when you're expecting speed, when you don't really have time for reflection. I'll tell you one other little story. I gave a talk at a congressional breakfast a while ago and I asked around: how much time do people in Congress have for reflective thinking? And somebody, naturally, had done a study and they said they have seventeen minutes a week for reflective thinking. Which, when you're directing the fortunes of the world, that's not a whole lot. I was talking to Senator Robb from Virginia shortly after that, and I mentioned this to him, and he said, "What seventeen minutes? I want my seventeen minutes." Now, to do philosophy, you've really got to do the work yourself. You've got to do it in an interior kind of way. You've got to do it reflectively, and you've got to take time for it.

MM: Yes, philosophers I've talked to, almost to a person, have said that the centerpiece of philosophy is reflection and meditation on these important questions. There aren't that many questions, but you've got to devote the time to them. In the modern world, in the 24–7 world where we're working sixteen hours a day, outside of perhaps a professor of philosophy, who has time for this? Not just in Congress, but in industry and everywhere else?

PC: Right. Why don't they have time? That's the question. I mean, why don't they take the time? Is it really so necessary to do all this stuff?

MM: Well, we seem to think so—the demand, the external demands placed upon us.

PC: So now we're in a kind of bind and I want so say to people, "Lighten up, slow down, think." And people don't even have the time to hear that.

MM: Right.

PC: So that's the challenge, I think, for philosophy.

MM: Well, so, philosophy, if it hasn't really been heard in the twentieth century, how do you make yourself heard in the twenty-first century?

PC: Well, on programs like yours.

MM: Okay, take a program like this. A program like this, now, will function in a medium that isn't five television channels, but 500 digital cable channels, combined with an Internet that within the next ten years will have one billion people using it on a daily basis. The sheer amount of noise is going to increase exponentially every couple of years. Just like the power of the integrated circuits doubling every couple of years, the amount of noise coming off the various forms of media is going to double every couple of years, well into the next century. The lonely voice of a philosopher, no matter how brilliant, is going to be drowned in all that.

PC: You know, people can, if they like, recognizing just what you said, decide to back off for a bit and decide to go looking. One of the great things about the Web is that people are beginning to look. There are individual people—and it all happens with individual people. Nothing happens of any importance in this world that doesn't happen inside one person's head. It could be a lot of people's heads, but decisions are made by individuals and it all adds up. You have to understand something I call secondary accumulation: if I do something, it has an effect. It may not [have much of an effect] now, but if a lot of us do it, it comes to matter much more. And more people have got to come to understand that. They've got individual roles to play and that's really all that matters at one level. Do you see what I'm saying?

MM: Sure. What if I reply to you that, okay, let's say I want to listen to philosophy. But philosophy right now seems to be in some sort of crisis. It's divided against itself. It seems to have split into two armed camps that don't talk to one another. There's not even a monolithic voice from philosophy. So if I want to listen, who do I listen to?

PC: Well, you listen to the next person who comes along. It's a good thing there's not a monolithic voice. It is true that there has been a pattern over the last decades of opposing continental philosophy, phenomenology, existentialism, and all that, to analytic philosophy and the philosophy of science.

MM: I asked you in particular because you're known for being able to straddle this divide, unlike an awful lot of your peers.

PC: Well, it's a problem for me too, because you get kind of invisible. To be a player on one side or the other is, in a way, a much better game than standing back a bit and seeing what they're both doing. And, frankly, I don't know how to answer the big question, except to keep saying that I don't really think this is the opposition people think it is. Again, to be anecdotal about the way I came [to be where I am]: I started out in physics and then I did philosophy of science. And I was out in a midwestern university, many years ago, and some students came to me and said, "We want to read existentialism." So I said, "Why are you asking me? I do philosophy of science," and they said, "No, we'll buy the beer—we'll have a seminar, we'll read the available stuff." And we did that, and I came to see that the whole existential side has to do with the fact that we are individual subjects living individual lives, and the whole science side has to do with the fact there's a world out there that we can describe, but that you need both of these. If you get preoccupied with the world and its structure and forget that we're all existing individuals—that's a line from Kierkegaard—then you're going to lose in one way, and if you're so preoccupied with what's inside and forget that there's a world out there, then you're going to lose in another way. So that's a balance that has to be struck.

MM: Let's talk about the balance, then. Is there some sort of synthesis, a hybridization, of these two camps?

PC: No, I don't think that's the way to put it. I think the synthesis only happens person by person. That's always been true. This may lead to another bit of the conversation: I remember that in school we used to have little services—I grew up in an English school and we had what we called assemblies—and there was a hymn we used to sing about the domain of Christianity:

> And soul by soul and silently
> Her shining bounds increase—

that comes back to me. And, I didn't realize then, but that's actually something Socrates says in *The Republic*. It's in Book IX; there's a conversation going on and somebody says to Socrates, "Well, I guess this ideal state of yours will never come into being." And Socrates replies, "Well, on the other hand, you could be a citizen of it, if you wanted. You can live by its laws whether anybody else does

Peter Caws

or not." That's just exactly the same idea you get in Christianity later. It's my view that Christianity hijacked the history of philosophy for a long time.

MM: Well, I wanted to get into that. Getting back to this issue of taking time for reflection, it seems as if for many people, especially in the United States, the one time for reflection each week might be sitting in that pew. What role is religion playing in this reflection process?:

PC: Well, that's a really interesting question. You're right and that's valuable— if people can be persuaded to sit back and think even in that way. But the trouble is there are two components to religion. We're jumping from one thing to another, but let me tell you something that really struck me a little while ago. I read an article about what was called "faith-based social programs." There are some around Boston here. These ministers go out into the community and show people a lot of love. But they call it "faith-based." They should have called it "love-based"—that's what's really going on. The difficulty with religion is that you don't just get the meditation, you don't just get the affection and all that— you also get the doctrine, and it's the doctrine that trips you up. So yes, if you could have a church where people have this reflective possibility without attaching the doctrine, that would be terrific.

MM: So is that how Christianity has hijacked philosophy, Western philosophy, in the last 2,000 years?

PC: Well, I think that it claimed that people had to believe all this stuff. And philosophy is really not very comfortable believing something without good reasons.

MM: How does that resolve itself in the future?

PC: It's very hard to tell. I don't know, because there's been this resurgence of fundamentalism and superstition. All we can do is keep saying, Look it's possible to lead a good life without being religious. It's possible to understand the world without thinking it had some superstitious or mystical origin. And just keep saying that. But philosophers—you're right—are better at living in their own heads and not so good at talking to the rest of the world.

MM: Now one thing that religion offers is a morality. Philosophy offers an ethics. Do they collide? Do they overlap one another? Is that the common ground between the two?

PC: Well, I think that it's possible to have a really quite tight philosophical account of what it means to lead a moral life, which comes down for me to thinking about the effect of what you do on other people. And that doesn't need a religious basis at all. So I'm not sure it's a question of joining—there's another way of thinking about all this. If I can be personal about that: I grew up in a fundamentalist household where belief was everything, and it took me a long time to get rid of that. But I came to see that a lot of what Christianity was offering had actually been in Greek philosophy 400 years earlier—with better reasons.

MM: Well, let's get to ethics. I mean, that's one of your great interests. It seems that we live in an unethical age. Perhaps that's just a narrow perspective of someone living in this time. But ethics almost seems to be in disrepute. Why is that happening now? And what does philosophy do about that?

PC: I think one of the reasons that kind of thing happens is that we forget that all these social institutions and practices and cultural objects and so on aren't out there, as objects having their own [independent existence]—they are sustained by people like us, and if we don't communicate them to other people, they'll just fall away.

MM: It's been suggested that civilization can disappear in a single generation . . .

PC: Absolutely.

MM: . . . and we have to convey . . .

PC: I've done a lot of work on something called structuralism. We don't have time to get into the technicalities here . . .

MM: I'd love to have a brief explanation of structuralism, because we hear it all the time, we hear about post-structuralism—

PC: Yes, that was the little story I told you a while ago.

MM: But we never see a good definition of it.

PC: Oh, I've written a good definition. Structuralism looks at the objects of what I call the human sciences, which are everything from literature to philosophy theories themselves to legal institutions, everything cultural, and says: What's the nature of these objects? And the quick answer is: these objects are relational objects, they aren't substantial objects. The objects of the natural sciences are there, but they're substantial; the objects of the human sciences are sustained by individuals who see them in a particular way. Take money, for example. You've got a piece of green paper, but it's the relations of that piece of green paper to other pieces, and to other objects, and to banks, and to commerce, and so on [that constitute it as money].

Peter Caws

MM: The value we invest it with.

PC: Yes, that constitutes it as an object of culture rather than an object of nature. For me, there are [four] important terms connected with the concept of structuralism. "Structuralism" itself is one, "structure," which, as I've been saying, is relations is another, and then there are "in-struction" and "de-construction." Instruction is how we acquire the mental structures that we have, that really populate the world of culture, and de-construction is how we take them apart when we find they're not working. It's the instruction component that we're talking about now. Unless in each head—and I mean in each, all the billions of people, it has to happen in each head—unless you manage to get those objects, as it were, replicated, so that people understand them in common, in my language, "co-intend" them—I work with the concept of co-intentionality, which would take a seminar—[they won't survive]. You have to get people to co-intend these objects of culture; then they'll be able to get along with each other. But unless you do the work of instruction, it won't happen.

MM: So absolutely central, then, to culture is education.

PC: Yes, but one doesn't have to be talking here about formal education, because when I use the word "instruction," I mean any way that the structure gets built. Some of it's genetic—some of it comes hardwired. Some of it is, as they say, epigenetic—that is, it's developmental. Some of it is just experiential—the child burns its finger, that sort of thing. A lot of it is cultural, and some of that is formal education. But even more of it, and this is really the crucial point, is [or could be] what I can autonomic. By that I mean that people are thinking about these things and continually engaging in this process of reflection. I'm glad everybody has been telling you that's necessary. I think it's the first thing that should be taught in schools—how to work on the contents of your own head.

MM: We don't teach that at school at all, do we?

PC: I don't think so, no.

MM: And that should be the first thing? The first grade?

PC: Well, absolutely.

MM: How would you teach a first grader that?

PC: Well, you have to . . . you have to be gentle about it.

MM: I'm a parent of a first grader, so I'm a little curious.

PC: I am too, as it happens.

MM: I'm real curious how you would do that.

PC: Well, you know, I talk to my daughter as though she were a grown-up. I don't use long words and that kind of thing, but I don't talk down to her. And I try to get her to understand that she has a head, that she knows something, she's learning, she's learned to talk. She has these brilliant insights sometimes. I'll tell you one family story. She was disobedient one day and I said to her, "Why did you disobey Mummy?" And she said, "My brain told me to do what Mummy said, but it was so far inside my head, I couldn't hear it." That struck me as wonderfully reflective for—as she was then—a four year old. But if you start thinking in these terms, you just point out that you've got a body, that your body is partly driven by your brain, and you can point out the difference between objects like plants and flowers and objects like birthday cards and money and so on. And it's not a big deal—you teach the principles of structuralism kind of easily. One of the basic ideas is the idea of a structural transformation. Just get a kid to understand that clean water + dirty clothes = dirty water + clean clothes. And start thinking in these terms—I mean, kids are capable of doing that.

MM: Sure.

PC: We don't ask them to most of the time. I don't know why.

MM: Now how do you instruct ethics? Do you teach it in theory?

PC: No—you just say, what you do has consequences, and these consequences affect other people.

MM: But we're told that all of our lives—and I'd get back to what I said a minute ago: We seem to live in an increasingly unethical age. Why isn't the instruction taking?

PC: Partly because culture has a terrible uphill battle against nature, against greed, against lust. It's a perpetual battle.

MM: So culture's inadequately armed at the moment?

PC: It always has been.

MM: But it's been better—

PC: Has it?

MM: I don't know. Has it?

PC: I don't really think it's ever been better. I think there have always been rebellious kids, there have always been social inequalities, and so on. I think one of the things about the current age is just the technological point. People are always talking about technology and values. My take on this is that technology doesn't involve any new values, but it puts strain on the old values. Now if the old values haven't been taught, so that somebody feels like popping a schoolmate, put technology into the hands of that kid, like an AK-47 or something, and you wind up with the Jonesboro case.

MM: And, furthermore, with the power of technology to disseminate information about that event, kids all over the United States can see that on television.

PC: But, you see, what we've got to do is to harness that power for disseminating this other stuff I'm talking about.

MM: Well, then, let's get back to instructing ethics. Give me a methodology for instructing ethics at the end of the twentieth century, using all this technology and all that we know.

PC: Well, start young.

MM: Do you use case studies?

PC: Sometimes.

MM: You don't use theory in ethics.

PC: Actually I do use a lot of theory because I think it's quite possible for people to understand these things in abstract terms and make the application themselves. But the abstract terms aren't very complicated.

MM: Give me an example.

PC: Well, everything you do, like—you're talking to me now, and you've probably thought through, some, what the possible effects of this conversation are, but it may be that under some other circumstances, like, I don't know—I don't know how you drive . . .

MM: Like I just robbed a bank . . .

PC: . . . maniac behind the wheel, you know. And you don't think of the possible long-range ramifications of that. If I had anything to do with radio, I would want radio stations that are listened to by people in cars to keep on repeating, "Remember that what you do has consequences for other people." I mean, it's a simple message—and it's not a theological message. It's a very practical message that everybody is capable of understanding. It just has to be said again and again and again.

MM: So you convey the theoretical message, the underlying point you want to make. How about examples in teaching ethics? Do you use examples?

PC: Yes, but not as much as other people do. I did a book recently that had a whole bunch of little case studies at the end . . .

MM: You wrote a book called *Ethics from Experience*. That's case studies, isn't it?

PC: Well, I saw an old friend last night who'd been a student of mine and she told me that I put her in a very bad situation once. I gave her an exam to do, in her office, and all her notes were there. And the question was, should she look at those notes? And she was very uncertain about the exam. And she didn't. Well, I raise questions like—suppose, for example, here's somebody who is late with a term paper and goes home for his mother's birthday and doesn't know what to do. And he's got an older brother who went to another college who wrote a paper on this topic some years ago, and says, well, you could have my paper. Now I don't tell people how to answer the moral dilemma. But I do say a couple of things. I mean, it's not just the consequences, as I say, of individual acts, but it's the secondary accumulation (which is an oblique reference to Kant's notion of generalization in ethics): Suppose this were the way people always wrote their term papers. What would happen to the value of diplomas and things of that kind? So these aren't just simple one–two things. I mean, you have to understand the culture in which you are embedded. And this gets back to the question of how that gets instructed and how we teach people about the culture in which they're embedded.

MM: Now, in a sense, we used to treat ethics as part of the curriculum. You look at an old reader from 1890 and the writing exercises, the reading exercises, were also moral lessons. And, somehow, it was supposed to inculcate into the children, even as they were doing their penmanship. We don't do that now. Do we need to re-embed ethics into learning?

PC: Well, I don't think you have to call it that, you see. I think if you stress what we know about the nature of the human being . . .

MM: But you're saying on a car radio, say, remember there are consequences of

Peter Caws

speeding or, you know, changing lanes without signaling. You're saying, we do this enough it'll constantly remind people and they will internalize it. Should we be doing that with kids?

PC: Sure.

MM: All the time?

PC: Philosophy is an all-the-time kind of activity, and if you can get people to take thinking and reflecting as an all-the-time kind of activity . . . it doesn't mean you have to do it all the time, but, in idle moments, the thought comes back. I mean, let's check up—where we are now. And I think that can be taught.

MM: Now I want to go back to technology again and the pace of change. You said philosophy changes slowly. It hasn't changed that much since the fourth century B.C. Yet society and technology are accelerating because of Moore's Law and Metcalfe's Law and all of these things. Does there come a point where philosophy just can't keep up?

PC: I don't think so. Because, well, who's all this happening to? It's happening to individuals who have their own agendas. You have a very crowded agenda, you've been rushing about, but it's you, and you've got to make sense of your own life. And you could back off if you wanted. Right now it looks as if you're enjoying it. But nothing is happening to society that isn't happening to individuals. And philosophy always speaks to the individual and always will. There's no collective solution. All the collectivity is a lot of people co-intending the culture in which they live. There's a lot of alternative stuff—you find bookstores are full of self-help things . . .

MM: Bookstores are full of philosophy, but not being written by philosophers.

PC: Right—full of philosophy often resting on not very good arguments. So that's a challenge we have.

MM: Well, you're one of the individuals noted for, as I've said, crossing the divide. How does philosophy get back into the conversation to all of those billions of individuals?

PC: One of the things it needs to do is to bring itself down a bit. Not in-house, as it were, but in relation to the outside world. Philosophy has always been associated with great ideas. I'm working on a project right now in which I'm thinking about good ideas, not great ideas. I think there are some good ideas in philosophy and the history of philosophy, some of which you would recognize and some you might not. I mean, Jefferson had a good idea: You can teach people, it will improve democracy. Jesus had a good idea: You can base a social system on love. Get the good ideas and get rid of some of the mysticism and you can start saying, look, remember? In a way, we've learned this over the last 2,500 years. We want to remind you.

MM: Don't sweat the great ideas right now; just focus on the good ideas and you'll have a good life?

PC: I think so. I mean, I think that's one of the ways to it. You also need some affection, and you need some satisfaction of other kinds, of course.

MM: What about writing? Philosophy is becoming increasingly undecipherable to the average person.

PC: So is physics.

MM: Yes.

PC: One of the things that I remember with gratitude from my training in physics in England was that, on the final exams, there was always a question like, "Explain the blueness of the sky to a lay person." And that was a bit of a challenge—you had to learn to speak another language. Some physicists are pretty good at this, although there they get off on philosophical tangents that even they don't understand too well, but I think philosophy has to learn to translate itself into the idiom of the more popular culture.

MM: Let's talk about your career for a minute. What did your father do?

PC: My father worked in an insurance company, but he was a member of a very strict fundamentalist sect that meant you couldn't associate with people in the world too much. So he never rose. He was a scholar in his way. He'd gone to a good school and he knew some Greek and he taught me a lot. But he was very, very narrow, religiously speaking. That's why I'm in America. I left to get away from my family.

MM: So you began in this fundamentalist household. Why physics first?

PC: Well, I suppose I was good at it in school and it was an okay thing to do. I was good at history and things like that, too, but that was too secular. Physics is, you know, the heavens declare the glory of God. So you're working on the natural world . . .

Peter Caws

MM: Sufficiently rarefied.

PC: Right. But the only thing you could do with it was teach. You couldn't make bombs. So I am a qualified physics teacher in the secondary schools of the United Kingdom.

MM: You are? Did you become a working physicist in a corporation?

PC: No.

MM: Academic?

PC: No. I mean, I saw ads for the Fulbright Program, and I applied all over America, and Yale gave me a fellowship, and I hightailed it out of there when I was twenty-two and never went back, except for visits.

MM: Why the switch from physics to philosophy?

PC: Probably several reasons. One is, Yale was very generous to me. They gave me this fellowship. I was this person from abroad, and they didn't tell me I had to do anything special, and when I got here I thought, well, I'll read philosophy. I'd already been reading some Whitehead and the old philosophers of science. And I guess I had a four-pronged interest in philosophy. One was, there were these neat analytic questions like, If I see blue, do you see blue? And I started with those when I was thirteen or fourteen. And then, actually, my headmaster at school—a man called Vernon, I'm always grateful to him—he used to teach Scripture, which was in the curriculum then. But he taught us philosophy instead; he read us some Kant and Locke, things like that. And then there was physics itself, space, time, causality, what's the world made of and that kind of thing. And there was religion. Why do people believe these things? So all of those things drove me toward philosophy.

MM: It intrigues me that in a sense you've gone toward fundamentalist points of view inside the fields—inside science, physics, the reductionist part of science, in philosophy the philosophy of science, which is sort of the fundamentalism of science. Is there a fundamentalist impulse in you?

PC: No. I want to absolutely reject the notion that any of these things are fundamentalisms in the sense that religious fundamentalism is. The characteristic of religious fundamentalism is that you've got a rock bottom you cannot question. In all these other respects you go to the bottom—you keep going. I mean, you may get to the point where you can't go any further, you can't [practically]

209

question any more. But it's open, and the thing about fundamentalism is that it's closed, and that's a world of difference.

MM: Now from philosophy of science to suddenly go sideways into issues like existentialism?

PC: I had been taught at Yale that nothing on the continent had been worth anything since Kant. We didn't read Hegel except as an illustration of what not to do.

MM: What do you put in its place? There's not a huge American tradition.

PC: Well, there's Peirce, there's pragmatism, and all the analytic philosophy that American departments have been so fond of . . .

MM: A continental tradition too, right?

PC: Now, not so much then. I realized that there was this rich domain of inquiry having to do with the nature of the knowing subject. If you ask about scientific theory—theory's not in the world. I have a little tag for that: The stars are indifferent to astronomy. They do what they do, the world does what it does. The theory is something we invent. How do we manage to sustain that? Well, there have to be physicists for there to be physics—physics doesn't just exist by itself—and they pass that on to one another. And there are criteria: This is a better or worse account. But that's also true in other domains, like the human sciences—there are criteria.

MM: You wrote once that "the stars don't provide much illumination, but they do provide direction."

PC: You read that? I like that. Yes.

MM: Is philosophy at this moment one of the stars in the firmament that we're using for direction? Or we don't guide ourselves by it, we don't really see it much any more?

PC: Well, it's up there. But I'm not sure I want to push that analogy too much. There's a task for philosophy which is a bit more than just twinkling and expecting people to invent the instruments, you know. I think we could speak much more directly.

MM: Are we navigating by philosophy right now?

Peter Caws

PC: We could.

MM: There's that chasm again, we've got to get over.

PC: There are some wonderful passages in Plato about ships and what people seem to do—shoot the navigator—after all that's what happened to Socrates. And we're still in that kind of mode. People don't want to go necessarily where philosophy says they should go. But it's a better world.

MM: Haven't we punished the navigator even more? Instead of shooting him, instead of giving him hemlock, we just ignore him.

PC: Well, the navigator needn't just sit there and be ignored. He has to speak out. And people like you are helping.

MM: Well, I'm intrigued. Given all that you know, given the state of the profession, given the state of the world, would you want your child to grow up to be a philosopher at this time in history?

PC: My child, or my three children . . .

MM: You have three children?

PC: Yes. One's a librarian, one's a rock star, and one's in first grade.

MM: How about your first grader?

PC: My first grader? I'd be delighted if she grew up to be in philosophy. But, there again, one distinction that we ought to pay a little attention to is the distinction between professional philosophy and the thing we're talking to one another about here—namely, philosophy as a guide to life. You know the motto of Phi Beta Kappa? "Philosophy is the steersman of life." Well, it isn't, of course, for many people. But, again, it's available. I mean, there's almost no problem you can think of, if you have it as a problem for yourself, for which you couldn't find rich resources, even in contemporary philosophy, let alone in the more ancient material. You have to look for it.

MM: Peter, thank you.

YOKO ARISAKA
Crashing the Tea Party

Yoko Arisaka, a native of Japan, Assistant Professor of Philosophy, University of San Francisco. As a Japanese woman, Yoko Arisaka offers a unique perspective to bridging the gap between Eastern and Western thought. Shortly after coming to America, following severe injuries from a pedestrian accident, she discovered a passion for philosophy and has since struggled with attempting to reconcile her Western academic pursuits with her Japanese heritage.

MM: Michael Malone   **YA:** Yoko Arisaka

MM: Yoko, you came to the United States in 1980 as an exchange student, and you'd told me you had always wanted to come to America. Why?

YA: When I was growing up, my mother kept telling me, hey, you know if you stay in Japan, you're just going to pour tea for the rest of your life. That's what it means to be a woman in Japan and my mother kept saying that I should really think about going somewhere else. I just watched a lot of movies and it seemed like the United States was a place where you can be who you are.

MM: Was it hard to leave your home, your country of birth?

YA: No, no. I was really so thrilled about coming to the United States. I enjoyed every minute of it, but at the same time I realized how heavily coded with Japan I was.

MM: How did you de-code yourself?

YA: Just by living in a different culture. On a daily basis you go through this realization that you are really more than just your cultural person. I then went back to Japan, and then again returned to the United States, and, within a few weeks, was nearly killed in an auto accident. I was riding a bike on my way to the beach, wearing my bathing suit, and was run over by a Jaguar. I had a crushed pelvis, crushed knee, and I was dragged for about fifty feet. My skin was all lost. I required six surgeries and was completely bedridden for more than three months. Three months to just sit there and think. My body was in bad shape, but I was fine in the sense that I could think. It's not me, right? It is me, but I am an "I" thinking that my body was in pain.

MM: You were engaging in philosophy?

YA: But without knowing it. Actually I had a prejudice against philosophers.

MM: How so?

YA: I just thought that they were weird people. Too much free time on their hands: "How many angels are on the head of pin?" Well, it's kind of a pinhead question, that's the way I used to think. But it was during my recovery that I first realized how fragile we are. No one is eternal. But is that correct? You can suffer for a long time, you can come out of it, your body can go through all these changes. But is it really you? I still didn't connect it to philosophy because I refused to think of myself as a philosopher.

MM: So when did you change your mind about philosophy?

YA: At the end of my junior year I realized I should "fess up" to the fact that I was actually one of those weird people who think about questions of life. What it means to be a human being.

MM: Does philosophy arise from some essential person underneath?

YA: From a rich human concern. It's about life, about having a history, and what it means to be a person that's not bound to culture. In every culture, every setting people wonder about that and have a picture, a story, which details out what it means to live.

MM: Now Western philosophy is obviously heavily bound up with the Judeo-Christian tradition. Is Japanese philosophy bound up with Buddhism and Shintoism?

YA: You can't deny that those elements are there to the extent that they are in the culture. In the West, for example, the person or the concept of personhood is strongly connected with ideas of autonomy, individuality. But in Japan that's not really an obvious idea.

MM: As we move to a more global society, are those differences reconcilable?

YA: To the extent that human beings are capable of communication. It's incorrect to divide philosophy into Western and Eastern that way. If you define philosophy narrowly, that might be true. People sometimes say, well, is that really philosophy, or is it religion? But philosophy is a rich activity that is not simply bound to a certain narrow set of defining cultural confines or characteristics.

MM: Is there a universal?

Yoko Arisaka

YA: Probably, although the way in which the concept is understood may vary.

MM: How so?

YA: For instance, is a truth just one thing? That's a big philosophical question. And then I suppose you might say, yes, because if it isn't, then it's not the truth. That's one way in which it has been understood. But if you decide that only one reality is the truth, you narrow the richer concept. What might be considered real in one culture may differ from another. So you have to be open, I think, to the different approaches to truth, ideas of truth.

MM: You're currently a professor at the University of San Francisco.

YA: It's very exciting.

MM: What do you see emerging from your students?

YA: Students come up with certain ideas of truth, but they have to be exposed to the way the idea of truth is discussed in different ways and cultures.

MM: For example, in the work of the philosopher Nishida. I gather you've focused on him. Tell me about him.

YA: He's a Japanese philosopher who died in 1945. He lived in the period when Japan opened up to the rest of the world. That was 1868, when the Japanese endured much change, especially trying to incorporate the Western modern culture. Nishida was a philosopher who thought that philosophy spoke a language of thought that was universal. Hence, ideas that reflected Japanese tradition should be understandable in other languages and foreign contexts, right? So I was interested in Nishida to the extent that he was the first Japanese philosopher who thought about these things. Many philosophers at the time, not just Nishida, were struggling with this question: If Japan can say something unique, universal, then the world, will have to recognize it as being true. But, first, Japan must have something unique to say. In claiming such things, these people were swayed by a nationalistic tradition which declared, Well, maybe it's now time for Japan to have a voice to counter Western imperialist thought.

MM: How far did Nishida go?

YA: He never endorsed the imperialist government. But neither did he oppose what the military was doing. He wrote about Japan's role in the world and his tone was, in that context, nationalistic.

MM: I'm intrigued by your interest in him because here's a man who wrote about Japan truly from the inside out. And when you're looking at Japanese philosophy, you're obviously looking from the outside in.

YA: Right.

MM: Are you interested in him because he is the opposite of you?

YA: I think my interest in Nishida operates at many levels. He deals with experience. What does it mean to have experience? So that's a big topic in philosophy. Neither inside out or outside in. Experience that's beyond personal experience. It's more a question of what is the idea of experience? What is the mechanism? What's going on? Is it just a subjective idea? What does it mean?

MM: He also addressed what it means to be unique, what is it to be uniquely Japanese.

YA: Yes, but that's a trickier question. When I was recuperating from that auto accident, I certainly gave much thought to being Japanese. But many of the things I was thinking about myself turned out not to be true. Obviously I'm Japanese, but it's also equally true that I am not. That was a strange discovery.

MM: What's the reaction to you back in Japan? I mean, you're almost unique in terms of being a female Japanese philosopher, I would imagine. You lived up to your mom's prediction that you were too wild for Japan.

YA: Well, there are more and more women in Japan who are speaking out about the situation.

MM: OK. As an active, working philosopher, what issues intrigue you the most? What are the burning issues?

YA: Philosophy is really a human activity; to use our understanding to address what it means for people to live in a culture, live in a political climate. What does it mean to be a woman? What does it mean to be somebody who comes from a certain environment, disadvantaged or privileged? You can use philosophy as an activity to understand and to improve conditions of injustice. For instance, I really think of philosophy as a way of addressing, and hopefully overcoming some of the difficulties in life. Philosophy is the only discipline I have found that really touches on the deepest questions. For example, what does it mean to think? How should we live? It's true, of course, that everybody wonders about these questions—just simply wondering about life and wondering about the universe. Philosophy is a path that I have taken. I had this passion for it, a passion so strong that I had to do it as my life. But you can be philosophical, of course, without becoming a professional philosopher.

MM: Having lived in two cultures, do you have a better sense of what a good life is and is a good life different in those two cultures?

YA: I think that the ultimate good life transcends cultures because to me a good life is a life of reflection.

MM: The essential person.

YA: Yes. And I think that's not bound to culture. Deep down, everybody would like to have a personally enriching life and I think philosophy is integral to that.

MM: You were lying in a hospital bed with all that time to think. Now you're a teacher. Is it possible to help people get to where you got to without having to go through trauma?

YA: Oh, I would hope so. All they have to do is allow some time to think. Make the time. Just to ask, what am I thinking? That's already a first step.

MM: I think that happens a lot at stoplights.

YA: That's true. Well, then, maybe stoplights are not so bad.

MM: I guess not.

MM: Do people have more time to think philosophical questions in Japan or here?

YA: I would think here.

MM: We have more time here to think about it?

YA: Yes, because in Japan you have to always think about other people and society first.

MM: And philosophy in a sense comes first of all from self. You have to take that time for yourself before you can start the process?

YA: You could, I suppose, think in social terms or interpersonal terms. It's just my personal experience that to gain this idea about life requires reflection on a personal level. You have to somehow be personal.

MM: What about your students?

YA: Well, it's interesting because they come with that kind of attitude which says, "God, why do I have to take a philosophy class?" But then they really enjoy the class because they see that they are not just listening to me for fifty minutes——they're thinking.

MM: So the kid daydreaming in class is actually doing good work?

YA: Well, I don't know if they're daydreaming, but it's true. I mean, I like to talk about the activity of thinking and not just abstract thinking or the big obvious philosophical questions, but just the ongoing activity itself of thought.

MM: Is thinking a skill that you develop? I mean, is that what you're saying—that you can become better at thinking?

YA: That's certainly true. You can have a confused way of thinking about things or you can confuse personal opinion with clear thinking. So those are the skill aspects. An educator should expose students to the difference between good reflection, good thinking, and clear thinking versus confused and opinionated thought. Such things are all vague in the beginning, but you can tease them apart in the purposes of clarity and fairness, while always keeping an openness. That's important. To have a certain disposition or orientation that is open to thinking. I think that's what it is and I think that's where philosophy is. It's not closed, it's open.

MM: So we can all become philosophers?

YA: Absolutely. And I think that philosophy should be something quite exciting. I'm always excited. Philosophy is really about an ongoing involvement with life. Philosophy has a particular way of facilitating reflection in the immediate here and now. It allows you to analyze problems that are relevant.

MM: But what about yourself? I sense that you're trying to achieve, in your mind, a synthesis, somewhere out there in the years to come, between these two cultures, Japan and America.

YA: Well, yes. It's a personal journey, of course. I've now lived half of my life here, so I'm bicultural. Each culture has a rich tradition, different structures, revealing deep voices. And wonderment about human beings. Whether it's a synthesis or whether it's a hybrid. I'm trying to talk about this activity of thinking, this negotiation between cultures.

MM: Do you think you'll find that common ground?

YA: I think so. I don't even think of it as two different worlds anymore. Not that I think it's the same thing; it's definitely not. There are certain things I still find confining in Japan. People may perceive me as somehow not fitting in to Japan anymore. I speak out too much, or I don't look authentic when I'm pouring tea for others—that sort of thing.

MM: We're back to that pouring tea thing.

YA: Yes, I'm traumatized about this pouring tea activity. It's like all my life, for eighteen years I had to pour tea just right. And I'm left-handed so I can never do it right, the right-handed way. So my father would say, you look clumsy. Well, okay. Let them kick me out forever. But then I go back to Japan, I think, okay, I'll try one last time. I'm trying to pour my tea just right. But here I'm not traumatized by pouring tea. I don't have to get it right. So there are a lot of internal things going on and philosophy is part of my activity of relating to these, looking from different angles. It's very exciting for me.

MM: It's how you puzzle it all together.

YA: Yes. To see that it is a puzzle, a story we have, both at the personal level and the collective level. Ultimately it is about the human condition.

ESA SAARINEN
All We Need Is Love

Esa Saarinen, a Finnish philosopher at the University of Helsinki, is flamboyant and daring in his efforts to commercialize philosophy for the corporate world. A highly sought-after speaker, he conducts seminars for many major corporations in Europe. The interview encompasses such topics as happiness and the good life, consumerism, business ethics, and self-fulfillment.

MM: Michael Malone   **ES:** Esa Saarinen

MM: I'm curious about something. You're known for not allowing yourself to be called professor. You call yourself a philosopher, even though you are a college professor. Now why is that?

ES: That's because I like to think about my activities and I also describe them to others through the process of what I'm doing rather than through the position. And I'm not that excited about an academic connection anyway. Academic life doesn't really excite me so much.

MM: So you are a working philosopher, a philosopher of the streets.

ES: A philosopher of the streets, yes. That's a great way to put it. That's the way I want to present myself. If you look at the whole history of philosophy, most of the best of philosophy has been conducted totally outside the system ...

MM: By non-academics?

ES: I want to try to keep up that tradition.

MM: So do you think philosophy went in the wrong direction when it went inside the ivory tower?

ES: Definitely.

MM: Really?

ES: Of course. Much of the energy that there was originally in philosophy has been essentially lost.

MM: Well, it sure got hard to read fast.

ES: That's one thing. But another thing is that it's become too technical. It's not accessible to laymen or to people who don't have the background. But if you look at philosophy as an enterprise that tries to give people a more reflective mode, surely you want them to put your things in such words that people can understand, but this academic trend essentially has destroyed this possibility. There are some exceptions, but the overall trend is . . .

MM: Now from what I hear, you scare the hell out of academic philosophers. You don't dress like an academic philosopher; you hold lectures to large crowds in public places. You're on television a lot in Finland. Is this a conscious choice?

ES: I don't particularly try to be provocative. Ah, earlier I perhaps tried to do it because, in the media especially, it's a strategy that works to some extent. But now I think the key point is that I simply try to live up to a style of making philosophy which many people outside academia expect of philosophy. I mean, philosophy is something that picks up any theme and comments . . . and then tries to find fresh perspective on that theme without doing it in a technical way or without demanding that you show that you are "good enough" to hear those words or take them seriously.

MM: What do you have to compromise to make philosophy comprehensible to millions of people?

ES: When people are starting to stare at you on the street and they have strong views of you before you arrive, it also has its drawbacks and sometimes it can happen that you're not taken seriously because of the way you look, let's say. This is what happens in my case. So many of my academic colleagues don't take me seriously at all because of these media appearances. So if you want to do philosophy through the media, you're going to pay quite a high price, academically, because you lose your respectability. But at the same time, I think you gain a new type of crown because you gain access to people who otherwise wouldn't have picked up your books or read your articles or come to your lectures.

MM: So you have thousands of people gathering and listening to you give a talk as opposed to a handful of other academics.

ES: Yes, that's right. But what's astonishing is that most academics don't face this feature of their activity, which I think is so scandalous. That is, nobody understands what they are up to. And it might be okay in some other fields, for some other disciplines, to go very, very narrowly into some particular millimeter . . . It could be okay in physics or computer science or some such field, but, in philosophy, I think this tradition, of being a generalist, somebody who addresses issues of life that's on everybody's mind, is something we ought to live up to and, in my humble way, that is what I try to do. But there's a price to pay and the price is in losing a certain amount of academic respectability.

MM: Now you've written "philosophy is performance." What do you mean by that?

ES: Well, one way of looking at the figure of Socrates is to look at Socrates as doing philosophy in a performer theme style. He doesn't present any discipline or any content that somebody should agree with or disagree with, but rather he performs philosophy.

MM: He's a character in a play that is his dialogue.

ES: Well, he's a character, for sure. But, at the same time, he's also somebody who challenges the thinking of the people who he encounters irrespective of their background. And asks questions; he tries to point in new directions, new type of perspective. And that's the kind of tradition which I think is great.

MM: Let's talk a little bit about your work. What do you mean by communicative intellect? IQ?

ES: No, no, cognitive intellect. I mean that you try to think in such a way that it's not only inside your head, whatever your thought is, but you try to complicate it and it's of course in the process of communication, it's not only your words and the order in which you say things that come out, but also the whole of the theater in which the thing takes place as it were. So it's your credibility, your eyes, ultimately, what people experience as your life, what you are serious about, and so on. So cognitive intellect is intellect in the service of communication—in other words, in the service of others. So it's not only your own thoughts that you love, but you want to push the thinking of other people into new dimensions.

MM: So it's an interactive intelligence?

ES: Interactive. Yes, I would say it's also heavily visual and this is something new and this is something that the academic philosophers, as a rule, despise, this visual element, because academic philosophers like to think that thought ought to be pure if it's really to be good. So the ideal type of thinking is completely pure thought which is abstracted away from emotions, from personality.

MM: And in the best model, absolutely symbolic.

ES: That's right. In the best possible world for the academic, thought would be not only totally abstract, pure, but also expressed in some technical analysis. But this is not the way I think.

MM: No, in fact, your books, I've noticed, are heavy with aphorisms. You play around with fonts and typefaces and pica size and things are going different ways on a page.

ES: That's right, and that reflects the conviction I have, which is that in philosophy, as opposed to some other disciplines, it's not an increase in knowledge which is essential, but rather a movement of thought. Movement of thought may occur, even if the person doesn't really know anything new after that moment of thought. Still, his or her perspective has changed, so, in my writing, I try to produce movement of thought in the reader irrespective of his or her background. And the same goes, of course, for the lectures I give or the media appearances I give.

MM: So philosophy becomes bandwidth?

ES: In a sense. At least philosophy becomes something that takes a certain distance from key academic traditions of only concerning itself with pure content and with abstraction, with argument, with analysis.

MM: Now I live in Silicon Valley where terabits of information are racing back and forth all the time and you begin to see that you've become awash in information, but without a whole heck of a lot of content. I mean, isn't the danger of speeding up and essentially becoming a node in a network that you lose the content? That all just becomes shallow and fast?

ES: That is a danger, definitely. But that only points, I think, toward the kinds of themes which I am trying to address in my philosophy. Orientation in life, and leadership of one's own life become more and more critical in the kind of age in which we live where where you have this overload of information.

MM: But you're the guy, though, that wrote: "Can you dare to be naive and superficial and still be deep and profound?"

ES: Actually, I think it is quite a good line.

MM: It is a good line.

ES: To me, it's critically exciting to try to combine the so-called profound elements that relate to contents and thoughts with a history of philosophy with so-called superficial elements. The way things look or the way things appear— the kind of dress one wears for a lecture for example.

MM: And that brings us to media because in a world of television and computer screens, of pixels, everything is two-dimensional. And yet it represents depth of one degree or another.

ES: That's right. Many academics don't want to have anything to do with television because they can't really get understood properly; they can't explain their tremendous and profound ideas. But, to me, it is simply a different type of medium. It's a theater which has its own laws and it's exciting because of that. You can contribute to the lives of people using the possibilities of that particular medium.

MM: But the danger, of course, as you know as well as I do, is that you can become trapped in a persona and end up playing the same part over and over again. You become typecast and do the same role and you never personally grow. Television can just turn you into a two-dimensional figure.

ES: That's right. But that is probably worse in the United States which is so much bigger than it is in a smaller country like Finland, in my case. Because in the United States, excuse me for saying this, there is such a pressure for stereotypes; it is such a huge culture.

MM: When you're surfing 500 channels, you've only got about a half a second to figure out what's there.

ES: So there's the danger for somebody who is here to become entrapped in the role or the person that he or she is presenting. When you are in a smaller country, you really have the possibility of having such a tremendous access to people. Like in my country, almost everybody knows me. I go in an elevator in a department store and everybody knows me. So high school kids, retired people, professionals, whatever. So if I'm then having open lectures or public lectures and people hear about those, they come to hear those lectures because they know me. So the person there is kind of an anchor.

MM: Don't you ever crave anonymity?

ES: Certainly, but that's also part of the energy. When I have a big lecture—let's say I have 1,000 people and it's a varied group of people. There are different types of emotions in the air and that's something to play with, that's an instrument.

MM: But from what I hear, it's almost like performance art, it's not a dialogue. You're not interacting with the audience verbally; you don't take questions from them.

ES: That's right.

MM: You're doing a performance for them.

ES: That's right, I'm doing a performance, but what I'm also doing there is that I'm doing what I call 'energy discussions.' These energy discussions are something I said that, okay, now for twenty seconds, think about what I've said so far. And I look at the watch. Okay, twenty seconds. And now let's have a discussion of two minutes with four or five people in your neighborhood. Two minutes. So you better find those people pretty fast and the time is starting now. Okay, so when you have hundreds of people, you know, a tremendous discussion is going on. So it is, in a sense, interactive, but it's not interactive in the U.S. style, you know in that I open the discussion.

MM: You're not doing Oprah out there in the crowd with a microphone.

ES: I'm not doing Oprah there, no, no. I have my doubts regarding these 'questions and answers.'

MM: Wait, wait, it worked for Socrates.

ES: That's true, that's true. I . . . but still, when you want to build an atmosphere and when you want to make people address themselves, you need to have the right atmosphere. Now for that, for you to build, you need to have all the strings in your hands. But if you open the floor for open discussion, the atmosphere is typically destroyed. It becomes automatically, almost immediately, too rational. And also the persons making the questions think that, you know, I'm quite a guy putting forth this question, although there's 1,000 people and this is such a brilliant question. So the aim of the lecture, which is that the person would go into his or her own thoughts in a fresh way, is destroyed.

MM: Let's talk about another part of your life. One of the things you do is talk to corporations. Now there's not a whole lot of philosophers out there in the world consulting for the corporate world. What do you tell these guys? You go to Nokia, you go to Finnish Telecom—what are you saying to them?

ES: I'm giving lectures and seminars on the theme of magnificent life.

MM: Magnificent life?

ES: Magnificent life.

MM: Not just a good life?

ES: Not just a good life.

MM: Magnificent life!

ES: That's right. It's a philosophy of life brought to the company environment. The philosophical challenge is to just try to think differently.

MM: Is that audience different from your public audiences?

ES: No.

MM: The same desires, same needs?

ES: Same desires, but I'll give you an example. One of Nokia's managers wanted me to come to their annual meeting of the managers in the Asian Pacific area. The program looks great, two-day seminar, this is great. But I have a better idea. So the manager says, well, what's the better idea? The better idea is that firstly, we'll cut your business things to a minimum, step one. Step two, everything else on the program is thrown out except Esa Saarinen. That's step two. Step three is that we'll make this a seminar with spouses coming with their husbands all over to this seminar in Singapore and step four is that the seminar will have just one theme on which I'll speak. That's love.

MM: Not the usual corporate event.

ES: This is exactly what he said.

MM: They must trust you a lot.

ES: Ah, well, it came off beautifully. But this is the kind of work that I do, so bring me the kind of things that actually affect people everywhere and also in the work context.

MM: So if you live a good life, if you're happier, you live a rich life, you become a better employee, you become a better manager?

2

All We Need Is Love

ES: Exactly.

MM: Is that what you're saying?

ES: Exactly. And the more pressure there is to innovate, the more pressure there is to network and to get along with all kinds of people. The more pressure I think there is and this kind of leadership of self skills, understanding oneself and understanding also those forces in oneself which are in the realm of beliefs, attitudes, emotions, one's loves, that type of thing. So it's that realm that I try to bring to the attention of company managers. But not only managers, but also anybody else in the more popular lectures there.

MM: Okay, well, let's talk about a magnificent life. What makes up a magnificent life? What are the parts?

ES: Well, one, that you are serving something of value. If you are doing things for somebody else.

MM: Not just yourself.

ES: That's right. So that's why I don't personally endorse this "success evangelist" type, you know, how you become a billionaire in two weeks by saying I can do it. They may have their value, but, to me, just producing wealth isn't really that great a value. So having in mind, and inside, genuine values is I think one of the ingredients of magnificent life. But another thing is that you actually also have it inside yourself. So implement it in your own being and that's, of course, a constant struggle. I would say these are the two key elements. And the third one is understanding better and better and refreshing one's understanding of the mystery that the human being is. So, bringing that to the forefront is what I'm trying to do within this company context.

MM: Now within that company context, people are working sixteen hours a day. They're working hard, they're on the Net, they go home at night and they read their e-mails and they, you know, they teleconference at 5:00 in the morning with Japan. When do they have time for the introspection required to think about the great mysteries of being?

ES: Well, for one thing, I say, don't work so much.

MM: I bet that makes you real popular with the firm.

ES: Yeah, well, but this is true. This is what I say. It's don't work so much, spend

228

more time with your family. Think about values, what really matters to you. I mean, look at your children as they are sleeping and, ah, also realize the fragility of life. So this kind of indirect route to productivity is one that I'm endorsing. But the indirect truth is true happiness through a more balanced life . . . embracing the grand way of life *with others*.

MM: Is there a process for this? I mean, you said one thing—spend some time at home with your family, watch your children sleep. Anything else you tell people to do? Anything they can do at the office while they're sitting there?

ES: Well, of course, these are just very small examples. It's not that I say to do a list of twenty things. It's much more a frame of mind.

MM: Now, despite the fact you don't call yourself professor, you *are* in academia. Is there a philosophical grounding for all the things you're saying? Are there particular teachers you had?

ES: There's a philosophical grounding. I try to combine from Western traditions, from Eastern traditions, from other disciplines—psychology, sociology, all kinds of human studies. So, ah, making a, you know, tremendous mixture basically. Also, I'm excited about popular films, especially James Bond.

MM: James Bond movies?

ES: James Bond, that's right, James Bond movies. Something to draw key lessons from. Like, for instance, key lesson number one in 007 philosophy.

MM: Yes?

ES: As I see it, you don't get irritated, no matter what happens.

MM: Stay cool, number one?

ES: I don't like to put it that way.

MM: Don't get irritated?

ES: I mean, it's the kind of attitude that 007 demonstrates most forcefully in the beginning of *Moonraker* where he falls out of the airplane without a parachute. I mean, if you ask is 007 now irritated? The answer is, he isn't. Instead he just goes in to investigate his situation. And observes a guy with a parachute half a kilometer down, so, I mean, the key point here is that he, 007, doesn't approach the world as predictable.

MM: Don't get irritated, get used to an unpredictable world. One might respond that it also helps to have a license to kill and a Walter PPK in your jacket pocket.

ES: That's right, but that's something I don't go into because I like to use this metaphor, you see. The point here is that we ought to have metaphors that actually go deep into ourselves as, how would I say it, five year olds, as opposed to ...

MM: And this is that naive element you were talking about?

ES: There's a naive element, that's right. In order for somebody to orient himself in a fresh way it's, of course, not sufficient to know that things ought to be in such a way because the five year old in him may not believe that. I mean, he knows it, but he doesn't believe it. So therefore it's essential that we find concepts and words and metaphors and images which go deep into the subconscious, into the attitudinal world where the five year old is ready to be excited, ready to love, and also expecting to be loved. So it ... this is the kind of frame here which I try to explore.

MM: Now a five year old also lives very much in the present.

ES: That's right.

MM: In the sense that the world's constantly providing unexpected things.

ES: Exciting things, yes.

MM: You're suggesting that we need to be much more present? Engaged?

ES: I'm suggesting that we ought to give the world more broadcasting time. We already believe that we know what's out there. So this is not the attitude of the five year old. The five year old gives the world broadcasting time; I think it's great. And that's something I encourage in my lectures, and in these company seminars.

MM: Now one of the burdens of being a philosopher is that people ask you if you are living your own philosophy? Are you living magnificently?

ES: Yes, I'm living pretty magnificently . . .

MM: I have a business card that has you and your wife's name and then it says, "a crazy couple in love."

ES: That's right, in Finnish. You know, actually it's better than in English, but, well, I think love is the most important thing, the single most important thing. But also love is not just a state of mind or kind of emotion, but something that you constantly struggle to create.

MM: So love's a creative act?

ES: That's right. Love is a creative act and love . . . love is something that must be demonstrated.

MM: So, once again, it's communicative intelligence?

ES: It's communicative intelligence, that's right.

MM: Bingo, done. Whew, that was fun. That was good.

ES: Very fun, excellent. This was remarkable. Thank you so much.

TOM HUHN
The Anatomy of Beauty

Tom Huhn, Assistant Professor of Philosophy and Letters at Wesleyan University in Middletown, Connecticut, draws on his expertise in aesthetics to discuss the role of the arts in culture with examples from the visual arts, music, film, and literature. Some of the more interesting topics covered include beauty and the sublime, the irrational in culture, art criticism, and the end of taste.

MM: Michael Malone   **TH:** Tom Huhn

MM: Let's start with some definitions. I'm really curious. Most people have a pretty good sense of what aesthetics is.

TH: They do?

MM: I think. Is there a formal definition of aesthetics?

TH: I'll tell you a big problem I've run into with the word aesthetics. Twice in my life, I've met people at parties, on two separate occasions. And each of them, before they knew what I did, each of them introduced themselves to me and said that they were aestheticians. I thought, oh, that's wonderful. How rare. They do the same thing I do, so I was like rubbing my hands. This is great. We can start talking about Kant and Schiller. But it turns out these two aestheticians wanted to talk about hair conditioners and nail extensions. So aesthetician also means beautician.

MM: So you have kind of a fallback career if this philosophy thing doesn't work out.

TH: Well, what I'd like to do—I mean, when language plays a trick like that on you, the best thing to do is just sort of reverse it. So what I like, the way I like to describe myself now is to say that I'm a beautician and not an aesthetician. But the difference between the kind of beautician I am and these other aestheticians is that I can't make anything prettier. I can't make anything more attractive. They're better at that than I am. But what I attempt to do as a beautician is to try to understand what kind of experience it is that people are having. What happens to us when we have an experience of something that, in the eighteenth and nineteenth century people would call beauty. In the twentieth century, it doesn't matter so much what term you use. You might just say, oh, cool. But the term doesn't matter because it's a moment in which there's a rare experience that occurs unlike any other kind of experience. What I want to try to understand is what happens in that moment.

MM: Is there a boundary line between being an aesthete and being an aesthetician? We think of Oscar Wilde as an aesthete. But he obviously had an underlying aesthetic he was working from was, didn't he?

TH: Yes he did. And there is some similarity. I mean as an aesthete, think about the kind of dynamic that is going on in someone like Wilde. And Warhol's another example of a great aesthete. What is the dynamic that Wilde and Warhol are cultivating?

MM: Are they manifesting their aesthetics in their persona?

TH: I think they are because they take any experience from the world and try to actually distance themselves from it. This is Warhol's great trick. This is why he wanted people afterwards, after a party or after seeing a painting, to call him on the phone and describe it. He didn't want the immediacy of experience. I mean, we talk so much these days about, oh, isn't experience wonderful? I had a great experience and all that. The aesthete has the opposite reaction to experience. The aesthete wants more distance between him or herself and experience and there is a continuity between that aesthete's desire and a certain tradition in aesthetics. The continuity is trying to disavow or distance oneself from certain kinds of experiences. From the immediacy of, if you will, sensuous experience. What the aesthete and, you might say, the aesthetician have in common is they don't want *just* sensation. They want a kind of reflection upon sensation.

MM: Is there a value judgment involved in the study of aesthetics? Are you just studying the process of aesthetics or are you actually rendering value judgments yourself? Can you say, this is good versus this is bad in the 1990s?

TH: Well, I'm like you probably. I make all sorts of judgments of taste. I do it all the time. We almost can't avoid doing it.

MM: Can you say this is good art?

TH: I can say it. It doesn't mean it has any validity. Anyone can say it. It's curious how few people actually listen to anyone who says that.

MM: But your judgment has no more weight than mine does as, you know, the man on the street?

TH: Certainly it doesn't.

MM: But this is your profession!

TH: But I'm not interested in designating certain objects as art or non-art. What I'm interested in as an aesthetician/beautician is trying to understand what happens during the moment when someone judges something to be art or to be beautiful. What happens then?

MM: It seems to me the line has disappeared between what is art and what is non-art. You're suggesting that that line still exists somewhere out there?

TH: No, I don't want to suggest that because this is the great thought that Kant comes to at the end of the eighteenth century. I mean, from a Kantian position you can never decide what objects ought to go into a museum because, although you may judge a painting or found object today to be beautiful, there's no guarantee that tomorrow even the same person will find it beautiful. Therefore, how could you ever collect certain objects, put them in museums, and say not just the same person will find them beautiful, but everyone ought to find them beautiful?

MM: But what about reversing the process where I declare it a work of art? I take the urinal in 1927 or whenever it was and stick it in a museum and I say this is now art. Is that a permissible act? Is that an aesthetically proper move?

TH: It's not aesthetically proper at all. That's a kind of ontological claim. It's a claim about the status of an object.

MM: Okay.

TH: Whereas aesthetics is much more concerned not with adjudicating, not with saying these are artworks and these are not. Aesthetics is much more concerned with what *happens* in aesthetic experience. I think you want to talk about the object and aestheticians for the most part, want to talk about the subject who makes the judgments, regardless of the object. I mean, the great counterexample to "this is an art object or this is not an art object" is that the great experience of beauty in the seventeenth and eighteenth century is not artworks at all, it's nature. So which parts of nature do you get to decree beautiful or not?

MM: Well, once again, take the point of view of the average guy walking into a museum. I expect a professor of aesthetics to say that aesthetics is value laden, that this is a good work of art, this is intrinsically good, this is intrinsically beautiful, this is intrinsically sublime, and that somehow it's invested with these characteristics. And this work of art over here is not beautiful. It is not sublime and it does not somehow render the world a better place.

TH: Right. This is the great mistake that I think is the founding moment of aesthetics as a discipline. The great mistake is the mistake that we all make every time we make an aesthetic judgment. When I say "that thing is beautiful" or, "oh, wow, isn't it wonderful," I'm making the mistake of thinking that the object or feeling or believing that the object has certain characteristics that give rise to that feeling in me.

MM: So, in a sense, an aesthetician is not a critic.

TH: Not at all.

MM: They have distinct roles.

TH: They do. A critic is interested in talking about the qualities of the object that perhaps elicit certain responses in the viewer. The aesthetician is much more interested in, again, not the object, but the subject. But the really curious and I think wonderful thing about all aesthetic judgments is that we always believe that the object really has the qualities that give rise to certain feelings in us.

MM: Let's get on then to the subject of beauty. First of all, are Kant's aesthetics more valuable today than ever before? You've certainly written that way . . .

TH: I didn't think I would ever call myself a Kantian, but I think Kant really founds the modern discipline of aesthetics, and the great moment in the *Critique of Judgment,* which he writes in the 1790s, is the recognition of the difference between saying, "I like this" and the judgment, "it's beautiful." We all have likes and dislikes. For example, Kant's example, you take a sip from a glass of wine and you say, "I like it." Pretty straightforward. But think about it for a minute—who's speaking, "I like it?" In a funny way, you're giving a report of a certain affect on your palette. You're kind of literally the mouthpiece for your tongue, having gotten a very favorable sensation. You could think about that in terms of your five senses. The distinction Kant makes is between saying "I like it," "this feels good," "that looks pretty"—in other words, the distinction between pleasant stimulation and aesthetic judgment. When you say, according to Kant, "something is beautiful," you're not saying "my palette finds it agreeable" or, "oh, that's really pleasant to look at." You're making a judgment from a wholly different part of yourself than from one of your five senses. For Kant, any animal—a dog has likes and dislikes.

MM: Sure.

TH: It licks certain things and likes them or doesn't like them. But, for Kant, it's only human beings who make aesthetic judgments and that means that we all recognize this. If you and I go into an art gallery together and I know that yellow is your favorite color and you point out this large painting to me full of yellow and you say to me, "oh, that is a beautiful painting," I say to you, "you just like yellow. Yellow is pleasing to you. That's not beautiful. You just like that color." The distinction for Kant, when you say "something's beautiful," you're not saying "my senses like it." You're not saying that I, as the repository of the sensations from these five capacities, like it. You are liking it in a total way. Your whole being likes something. That's why for Kant we make the distinction in language between "I like something" and "it's beautiful."

MM: Is it possible to stand in front of a Gilbert and George excrement painting and say "that's beautiful"? Or can we only say "that's important" or "that's a major work of art" or "that eparte la bourgeoisie" or something like that. Can we say "that's beautiful"?

TH: Of course, why can't we? And on Kantian grounds it's a wonderful capacity we have because it means that I'm not subject to just the sensations I get. I can step back. This brings us back to the question about the aesthete and aestheticians. I can step back from the immediacy of sensation and this is why the term reflection is so important in aesthetics and reflective judgment. I can reflect, distanced from my sensations, and make a judgment based on some wholly other grounds than sensory input. For Kant, that's the moment we actually raise ourselves above nature. This is why being an aesthete is sort of pushing that dynamic to an extreme. Because what the aesthete does is to say, "oh, I can transform any unpleasant experience into a moment of beauty." That's a great capacity to distanciate all sensation and transform it into something pleasurable. I mean, for Kant that's one of the great achievements of civilization. You have a lousy experience, but, guess what—you take that as an opportunity to have a wonderful experience.

MM: But can't you take being an aesthete too far? I mean, we sort of look upon the dandy as somebody who is so detached from the vagaries and the ugliness and the sordidness of getting through life that they're almost inhuman, they're almost hothouse flowers.

TH: This is why I think so often people bring in ideas like the innocent eye. We want to believe that what we find beautiful is natural to find beautiful. This is why we are so often in our culture of people want to assert things like, well, why would I need any special education to appreciate the beauty of that work of art? If it is really beautiful, I don't have to cultivate its beauty; it ought to be present to me as a sensuous being.

The Anatomy of Beauty

MM: What's the difference between beautiful and sublime?

TH: For whom?

MM: For Kant. Let's start with Kant and then Adorno, who I guess you see as sort of a spiritual, intellectual descendant of Kant.

TH: I do.

MM: What does sublime mean?

TH: Well, in the tradition of Burke and Kant, sublime . . . it's a moment when . . . well, think about how Burke puts it, just a few years before Kant was writing. Kant read Burke, Burke writes his inquiry in 1757. For Burke, the sublime—and Kant takes much from him—the sublime is, I mean he's an empiricist. There's this really interesting question for empiricists. Empiricists believe that all of our ideas are copies of our impressions, okay? Now someone says, gee whiz, I have certain ideas in my head that I can't find the impression from which it supposedly arose. The sublime is an example of that. What is the experience of the sublime? It's a moment of great fear usually and recovery from fear. So the examples of the sublime are raging seas, overwhelming cliffs, storms, and so on. The distinction that Burke and Kant want to make between beauty and the sublime is to say that the sublime is when we come to a kind of precipice in ourselves. You get a sensation, this is how Burke puts it, your mind races ahead. What does your mind race ahead toward if you can't see something, you can't discern it clearly? What's the thing our mind's always raced toward? Fear of death, right?

MM: So this is that moment when the earth seems to give way beneath you? This is that scene in Proust where the painter is looking at the little square of yellow in a painting and the natural world seems to melt away around him. It's Vermeer's view of death and he sees it and he dies looking at . . .

TH: Yes, it's sublime because there's a kind of losing of oneself. And you lose yourself . . .

MM: With a transcendental moment?

TH: Yes, because you transcend your capacity as a natural being and you become, for Kant anyway, a different sort of being at that moment. I mean, Burke has these wonderful examples of the sublime. He says at one point in the *Inquiry,* a clear idea is a very small idea. What are the really inspiring experiences?

The things that we see that are obscure. Look into a dark cave. What happens? Oh, my God. Your mind is filled, not with darkness, but with all the portents of fear and so on. So the sublime is, you have an initial sensation that makes your mind race forward and then when you are nonetheless safe, there's a feeling of relief and, hence, pleasure.

MM: Was romanticism kind of a cult of the sublime then?

TH: It was indeed, yes.

MM: You have a wonderful line in something you wrote that "the sublime, like natural beauty, is hope." Hope's a little different from fear.

TH: Yes. I think it's connected to that moment of recovery, that what happens in the sublime is you actually return to yourself. But the self you return to you is not the return to that sensuous self who can have impressions of the world. The self you would turn to, for Kant actually, the self that you make in that moment of a sublime experience is a moral being, is a being above nature, a being who can make judgments based not solely upon sensuous impressions.

MM: Does the hope derive from the fact that you survived that fear? That you made it through to the other side?

TH: Yes.

MM: And, therefore, you're hopeful that you can survive.

TH: It's not just survival because you survive as a sensuous being. What's important for Kant—he even uses those terms in the passage—is not just survival as a sensuous being. It's rising up and surviving—you would survive even if your sensuous self was destroyed because your true self is generated in that momentary experience of the sublime. Your true self is not the one that's locked in to these five senses. Not even locked into nature. Your true self rises above that.

MM: Now tell me about Adorno—where has he taken aesthetics?

TH: That's a big question.

MM: Demanding a very simple answer.

TH: How does Adorno take aesthetics? The short answer to that would be something like, there is no short answer to that. Let me try anyway. He's a Kantian; what he wants to understand is the way in which Kant formulated judgment at the end of the eighteenth century, aesthetic judgment, as a capacity for human subjects. Adorno sees—he follows Hegel to some extent in this—the whole history of art after the end of the eighteenth century as a kind of making art objects into something like kinds of human subjectivity. That the capacity to rise above nature is one that human beings lose because it wasn't realized. The French Revolution didn't provide freedom for everyone and so on and so there's a kind of hibernation of that possibility. The hibernation occurs within artworks. So for Adorno, as a twentieth century aesthetician, the place to look for the possibility of human freedom, or sublime hope, is *within* those artworks. So you asked earlier about the relationship between art critics and aestheticians. Here there is a moment of overlap between the two. That there's a certain kind of aesthetics that might be done in the twentieth century in which what one tries to do—this is Adorno's idea—is to read off from the artwork the embedded possibilities for human freedom and what social fulfillment there is exists not so much in the subjects any more, but in these hibernating objects. I mean, this is, I think, the great message modernism.

MM: You've written that Adorno believes that "nature should free itself from imperious subjectivity by an art aligned in opposition to us."

TH: Yes.

MM: Art and nature conspire? Modern art is nature's revenge?

TH: It is, it is indeed. I think, I mean, gee whiz, think about our relationship to nature in general. It's not a very friendly one. We dominate it. Right. The possibility of an aesthetic relationship to nature which Kant first discerns is the possibility of extracting some pleasure from nature without having to dominate nature. In Kant's description of the sublime, this is his great example of the difference between the supposedly savage person and the supposedly civilized person. The savage person is in the midst of a huge storm. What does the savage person do? Well, just like all those old movies that we've seen, the savage person hurls his spear at the heavens, or something like that. It's a relationship, you know, that's based on mastery and domination. What does the civilized person do in the midst of a storm? Oh, the civilized person doesn't need to conquer the storm externally. The civilized person conquers the storm internally. What's the internal storm? My fear of the storm. The great moment of civilization is not only do I no longer need to conquer nature externally, I conquer it internally. And, guess what, I get pleasure from it.

MM: It's when that sense of the sublime arises within us.

TH: That is his description of the sublime, exactly. Which means I no longer need to dominate nature externally. I dominate it internally. Now you could take that argument a step further and ask, well, why don't we go beyond domination altogether? For Adorno, I think the artwork, at least in the twentieth century, is an attempt to give an inkling of what it would be like to have a non-dominating relationship, not just between oneself and nature, but between oneself and other people or, even better, between part of oneself and some other part of oneself. Why do I need to control, why is one part of me waging war with another part of me? In some regard, the artwork as the place where aesthetic experience occurs might be the possibility of having a kind of non-dominating relationship.

MM: Let's talk about a moment in your life, of when the sublime appears, full of fear, and the ground giving way in which nature asserts its dominance over everything. You just became a dad.

TH: I did.

MM: What does that do to a man who studies aesthetics?

TH: I don't think there's anything special about studying aesthetics that makes it happen, but I would be happy to share with you what the moment was like and I think it's a somewhat philosophical reflection, but I think it's also a fairly common one given the anecdotes I've heard.

MM: I think we all get philosophical at that moment.

TH: We do. It's just the funniest thing. Because you go into a room, you have a kind of project. You go in with the doctor and the nurse and the pregnant woman and, in effect, the principle is, you're not coming out of here until there's one more of you. It's this mad kind of math. Well, how do you get one extra person? So, I mean obviously, I know where children come from. I've read about it, I've seen films about it, and so on; it's pretty obvious.

MM: Not until you're there.

TH: Not until you're there because this is, I mean, my wife Nancy said it so wonderfully. She said "I knew we were pushing something out of me. I didn't know it was a person." And for me watching the person come out, the thing that shocked me so much was the moment the baby was halfway out. The doctor turned it and it had a face. It's the last thing in the world I expected: a face? I mean, I didn't know. A person emerges from another person. It's astounding.

MM: Both of whom you have an infinite stake in, unlike watching a movie or a filmstrip or . . .

TH: I don't know. I mean, it's such a foreign thing. And I'm not sure I had a stake in it. I'll see.

MM: You do now, dad.

TH: I suppose so. I suppose so.

MM: You quoted Stendahl as saying "beauty is the promise of happiness."

TH: Yes.

MM: What do you mean by that? What does he mean by that?

TH: It's a line that Adorno was very fond of as well. I think it's a wonderful expression because it means that the great moment of pleasure that we have in beauty, which is better than any sensuous pleasure, is still itself not happiness. It's the *promise* of happiness—it's the vision of what happiness would be like. The beautiful painting, let's say, is a picture of happiness.

MM: So it's a map to happiness.

TH: It is. It is not happiness itself, and I think this is one of the reasons why people sometimes get turned off by contemporary art is that they see the promise and then they realize, damn it, it doesn't cash out. It doesn't deliver the happiness. That's the really crucial moment for reflection for an aesthetician. Why is there promise which is then withdrawn?

MM: Now, I'll take an entirely different tactic. I look out there and I see ugly, ugly art—art of cruelty, art of eviscerated animals.

TH: Damien Hurst, for example.

MM: Exactly. Art of violence, bloodletting, self-mutilation. And I think—this doesn't seem to me to be a path to happiness. I look at popular culture. Now I'm as good a consumer of pop culture as anybody else. I go to all the big budget action films in the multiplex with everybody else and eat my popcorn and enjoy the cheap thrills. I don't see a lot of beauty there.

TH: I think we have to go back to the distinction we made a little while ago of the difference between stimulation and an aesthetic experience in which there's the possibility of being freed, of freeing oneself from pure stimulation. A Hollywood film is, for the most part—and I like stimulation myself, I'm a sensuous being, I love that stuff sometimes—but the problem is, does that entertainment, does that stimulation ever allow you the space to withdraw from it in order to have a different sort of experience, a nonmanipulated experience?

MM: So it's sort of a nickel-and-dime sublime.

TH: It is. The roller coaster is a great, sublime-like experience.

MM: But not the sublime itself. It gives us only the *sensation* of being sublime.

TH: Hurtling your body through space—it's thrilling. So is the blockbuster Hollywood film thrilling. The difference between those experiences, on the one hand, and the way aesthetic experience has been theorized is that aesthetic experience or the true sublime allows you to recover yourself, gives you an occasion, an opportunity, to make yourself other than just this sensuously stimulated being. I don't want in any way to discredit stimulation. It's wonderful.

MM: But it's addictive.

TH: It may be; it depends on your personality.

MM: But is it sufficiently addictive that it supplants the desire for the sublime? You're the monkey that keeps hitting that lever to get that stimulation.

TH: I think this is one of the best explanations of how television works. I mean, television is just a certain low level of stimulation that we all get used to. I mean, this is, for me I turn the television on at a certain hour in the evening and turn it off an hour or two later and inevitably there's less of me and I feel worse at the end of it. And I ask myself, why? It's because it's a kind of stimulation that didn't allow me the space to recollect myself.

MM: And you're not left with any map to happiness.

TH: No. I mean, this is what's so fascinating. Television and Hollywood entertainment don't even strive to promise happiness. It's as if we've become satisfied with the promise of stimulation. Oh, do you want, you know, a bloody horror movie or do you want to be stimulated by a romance comedy? The promise has been withdrawn by the 'culture industry' as it's been termed. But I think that's related to your question about contemporary art and about how ugly it is. That's another way to withdraw the promise. If art can't fulfill that promised happiness, one of the strategies that artists might then employ is, let's make art that itself denies making any promise whatsoever. But that still is an aesthetic mood because it's still hopeful that space must be created for human freedom apart from stimulation and manipulation.

MM: Or is it just surrender from responsibility? You became an artist and in a sense your responsibility as an artist is to help provide that road map and now you're saying, "I don't want that job. I'm going to do artwork that talks about the lack of a pathway to happiness." Isn't that abandoning your responsibilities?

TH: What responsibilities should artists have?

MM: I don't know—you're the aesthetician.

TH: I'm not sure they should have any responsibilities except to work on whatever they find most engaging. Just as I think our responsibility as human beings is to try to have an experience *other* than the one that's programmed for us.

MM: The sublime does appear in popular culture though, doesn't it?

TH: I would say that the effects of the sublime appear in popular culture.

MM: Okay.

TH: The film *Godzilla,* for example. The kind of decibel level in that film—I mean, we're sensuous creatures.

MM: Sure.

TH: So if you give us a certain level, literally, of stimulation, we're going to respond. There's a wonderful line of Adorno about film where he says, no matter how vigilant I am, when I leave the movie theater, I find myself stupider. What happens in the cinema is that we are, in effect, defenseless from that kind of barrage.

MM: But even going to see *Rules of the Game* or *Seven Samurai,* you still come out of the movie stupid—or do those things cross over into something that approaches beauty in the sublime?

TH: That's a good question. I think one might want to then say, those art films are closer to intellectual stimulation.

MM: Okay.

TH: I don't want to describe any object.

MM: Can we learn how to distinguish between the cheap thrills and the real sublime?

TH: I don't think it's so much a matter of learning how to discern them. I think it's what things in this world we now occupy, this cultural world we now occupy, which things provide an opportunity for us to not be manipulated. You might have a wonderful way of going to a film like *Godzilla* and in the midst of the film doing a brilliant critique of it. Of finding the space for reflection, having great thoughts in the midst of it. You might do that. I think it's hard to do it. But there's nothing saying that you absolutely can't do it. So it's nothing against stimulation at all. It's that I'm against . . . I don't want be against anything. I want to be *for* something. I want to be for more possibilities; this is what I take culture to be. For the production of more possibilities for opportunities to create and find human freedom. I think artworks should be an attempt to do that.

MM: Thank you.

TH: Thank you.

K. ANTHONY APPIAH
Global Culture and Its Discontents

K. Anthony Appiah, Professor of Afro-American Studies and Philosophy at Harvard University, is related by marriage to the royal family in Ghana, Cambridge educated, and an accomplished writer of both fiction and nonfiction. Professor Appiah brings a unique global perspective to his discussion of issues related to multiculturalism, race, African literature, and much more.

MM: Michael Malone   **AA:** K. Anthony Appiah

MM: Here at the end of this race-obsessed century, you have stated that "nobody has a race." That's an extraordinary remark, especially now. What exactly did you mean by that?

AA: Well, when I said it, actually, I didn't think it was extraordinary. I thought it was obviously true and the only thing to do was to remind people of it, and I have spent twenty years learning how to respond to people who find it puzzling. In the late nineteenth century, biologists, anthropologists, and others began to try and explain why people are different in the world in terms of this concept of race. They started from the assumption that there were a few races—blacks, whites, yellow, red, brown, and so on—and that they had certain characteristics and that those characteristics explained many important things about them. This was a research program. It was a perfectly plausible research program and it has turned out to be a mistake. You can't very satisfactorily classify people for biological purposes into a small number of groups: They haven't explained culture, or religion, or behavior, or the difference between imperial cultures and those other cultures that they conquered. They just haven't explained anything.

MM: It's not even really apparent at a genetic level either . . .

AA: No. Most of the genetic variety in the human species is in Zaire. That is to say, there's a little more variety if you take the whole human species. But take [just] two people at random in Zaire and they are about as genetically different as if you were to take a Swede and Zairian. So, it turns out that these superficial differences—and there are obvious superficial differences in skin color and how your eyes look and your hair, if you have any hair—but those superficial differences turn out not to correlate very well with anything else.

MM: So why are we so obsessed with race? And why has it taken you twenty years to figure out how to respond?

AA: I was young and I was a medical student before I was a philosopher and

I just thought that everybody knew this and the question was to think through the consequences and, you know, biologists and physical anthropologists don't much use the concept of race and those who do don't use it in the way that ordinary people think that they're using it. I would now like to say, look, it's not a biological concept. If you want to understand what divides people along racial lines in modern societies, let's just put the biology aside. Let's forget about the biology. Let's think about the social processes by way of which people come to count as black people, white people, Asian, Hispanics, Native Americans. Let's think about those categories and let's accept that whatever the differences are—and there are going to be some statistical differences between different populations—they're explained by the social things, the things we do to and with each other in virtue of classifying each other in these ways.

MM: And one of the things we do is to classify ourselves as a member of some group.

AA: Yes. People classify you. They put the label on you. Then they do things with the label. Not everybody does the same. Some people are nice to you because of the label. Some people are less nice to you. Some people studiously attempt to avoid the consequences of the label, and so on. But it's hard to ignore it once you've thought about people as white and black in our society. You do things as a black person sometimes, or you respond as a white person. We act out roles that are tied to our notions about race.

MM: So, even though we can despise a stereotype, we find ourselves performing the stereotype.

AA: Absolutely. You can't ignore it. Whatever we do, we've got the stereotype in the back of our minds. We've got, as it were, the agenda of our supposed race there. We can work with it or we can go against it. But what we can't do is ignore it.

MM: Do you think of yourself as Ghanaian or do you think of yourself as Ghanaian-English-American?

AA: I'm a citizen of the United States. I'm tied to Britain by ancestry and by education and I'm tied to my home in Ghana where I grew up, where my mother is, and where my younger sister still lives, and where I spent those formative years of one's early life that makes one think of a place as home.

K. Anthony Appiah

MM: And, I would think, you're also tied in an even deeper way because of your bloodline in Ghana. Aren't you part of an old royal family?

AA: Well, both my uncle who is still alive and my great uncle who's no longer alive, they are the last two kings of the place that I grew up in, but that's by marriage. It's just that my family has provided wives for the royal family, as it happens, for the last two generations, not because it's a custom, but just because, I guess, I have wonderful aunts and great aunts and the kings wanted to marry them.

MM: Now you were born in London.

AA: Yes. My father was a law student when I was born.

MM: How old were you when you went back to Africa?

AA: Less than one.

MM: You wrote that wonderful book, *In My Father's House,* about that world. I'm interested in the roots of your philosophical views. Is there an African philosophy?

AA: Well, certainly not a *single* African philosophy. I think there are ways in which African experience can shape what you do in philosophy. And, obviously, when you have an African experience, you don't have a generalized African experience, you have a particular experience of, in my case, Asaute, which is a region of Ghana which is in West Africa. Trying to explain how I was led to philosophy, I'd say it wasn't so much Ghana by itself as living between; growing up with an English family on my mother's side and the Ghanaian family on my father's side and going back and forth between them, visiting my grandmother when I was a child and then going to school in England. And having a sense of living in places which had very different assumptions about certain things. I don't like to do this because this sort of example is exactly the sort of thing people expect you to say about Africa. But the fact is, I grew up around people who believed in witchcraft. My father was a Methodist, an elder in his church and my mother is British. She's an Episcopalian or an Anglican originally. But our relationship to the church was very different in the two places. I mean, the church in my hometown in Ghana is just an everyday, taken-for-granted kind of presence. And people didn't argue. I mean, smart kids in school didn't argue about whether there was a place for it; they argued within the framework of those assumptions.

Whereas in England, you could have arguments about whether there was any-thing to be said for religion at all. That wasn't a question when I was growing up in Ghana. So, I think that now the obvious question is, who's right? And then: How are you to decide? How are you to decide in a way that doesn't beg the question against one side or the other in these disputes? And I don't want to exaggerate the ways in which these are associated with Africa or Ghana or Asaute, in particular, or Europe and England and the part of England I grew up in when I was there, in particular. It's everywhere once you start looking. You discover that people look at the world in different ways. They start from different assumptions.

MM: So it's not the two places that define you—it's being *between* the two places that defines you.

AA: Yes. I do think that it helps in disentangling yourself from the particular kind of assumptions and commitments and presuppositions of one place to have a place that's real for you where different assumptions and presuppositions are active. And to have it be a real choice in your life, not a merely hypo-thetical question. If I talk about witchcraft with my students at Harvard, I mean, they know that there are people who believe in that, but it isn't some-thing that they're tempted to believe in themselves.

MM: You don't think they'll go out and practice it after class?

AA: Right. Whereas I grew up with people for whom a lot of things we can put under the broad rubric of witchcraft were real. I have to decide for myself about these things. I don't believe in witchcraft but actually I don't believe in Christianity either anymore. I mean, I have a sort of rather boring standard Anglo-American philosopher's metaphysics. I think that, you know, I believe in the natural world. I think we evolved out of it and I think that as far as con-sciousness goes, we're probably it.

MM: Well, let's talk about the between-ness again. Your first published writ-ing is poetry. You write mystery novels. But your dissertation was on probab-ilistic semantics. Now, if ever there were different worlds one inhabits as a writer, this has got to be it.

AA: Yeah. Well, I must say, I like that. I like living between different kinds of philosophy. I do a sort of social philosophy, philosophy that's about what I think of as real, real serious problems that we have to think about in our society. I did this work in probabilistic semantics which is not a problem that we *have* to think about in our society, though I think it's very interesting.

MM: But I mean, there is that schism right now in philosophy—You can see it here. The analytical side versus this sort of traditional classical philosophy out in the world. And, once again, here you are in the middle.

AA: I think that this schism shouldn't be taken too seriously and shouldn't be worried about too much. I believe that the training I got when I was thinking about these questions in logic and philosophy and language helped me to think carefully, to make distinctions and that thinking carefully and making distinctions, which is sort of the baseline thing that philosophers perhaps do professionally with the most attention, is useful in thinking about lots of things. There are things that I think philosophy of that sort doesn't train you very well to think about and which I've had to learn since my undergraduate and graduate education. For example, I think that in order to think about race, you do have to think a lot more about history and social facts and everyday life and you have to learn how to think about those things with, as Aristotle said, the degree of precision that's appropriate to the subject matter. You want to be careful in your thinking. Sometimes it helps to make conceptual distinctions; to say, wait a minute, when you take me to be disagreeing with you, in fact, you're misunderstanding me. Let's invent some words that will take the heat out of this and maybe shed a bit more light. And all those tools and techniques are something that philosophers are trained in. We're not the only people who train in them. But we have a particular way of arguing which I think can be applied to almost any question productively.

MM: I'm struck by this image of you as the man in-between.

AA: Um-hmm?

MM: Between cultures, between natures, and here you are, in philosophy, between two great schools of thought. In one respect, it's an interesting place because you have the detachment. It's also a kind of a safe place because it's not committing deeply to one or the other. But it's also a lonely place, I would imagine.

AA: I think it's less lonely than it was. More and more people in philosophy, at least in this country, are willing to draw from whatever they need to draw from in order to think about a question.

MM: But as you were growing up, didn't you feel like a man without a place?

AA: No. I felt that I was a man with two places. I have a deep-rooted attachment to two places. I mean, I think of the west of England, my grandmother's part of the world. It's deep in my imagination if I think about poetry, if I think about imaginary landscapes and so on. But when I'm thinking about my childhood I feel deeply rooted in the Asaute Ghanaian landscape.

MM: But, isn't there a natural human desire to resolve divisions in one's life?

AA: Yes, there is. And it should be resisted.

MM: Really? Why?

AA: Because I think human life is more interesting if we accept that there are many ways of living. And that while you can only live one life, it's not true that you can only participate in one community or only take part in one experience. The problem is, you have to give stuff up.

MM: But you're the mystery novelist. We try to write our lives as a narrative.

AA: Yes, we do.

MM: And, we want the narrative to have some sort of internal coherence and have a plot.

AA: Yes.

MM: When you're writing your mystery novels, you're not running two plots simultaneously that never, ever come together. The whole point of a mystery novel is everything comes together at the end.

AA: Yes.

MM: Does your life come together at the end?

AA: Yes. I don't want to claim that the mystery novels have any philosophical significance. I mean, I enjoy reading them, I enjoy writing them, and they do have a kind of rigor and clarity which real life doesn't have and maybe that's part of the attraction. I mean, real life doesn't finish . . .

K. Anthony Appiah

MM: It's messy.

AA: It's messy. And, I don't mind that. I like living in the mess. I'm not the kind of person who wants to simplify life. If people ask me what I do and I reply, "I'm a philosopher," there are two responses. One is, "you must be very clever," which is a complete conversation stopper. What are you supposed to say to someone who has just told you, "you must be very clever?" Or they say, "what's your philosophy?" And that's not a question that many contemporary philosophers find it easy to answer.

MM: I would think saying probabilistic semantics ought to end the conversation pretty fast, too.

AA: But I do have a philosophy. My philosophy is, everything's more complicated than you thought. It's sort of what I believe. And that means human life.

MM: And, at that moment, people realize that they're philosophers, too.

AA: Yes. And if I've learned anything in my life as a philosopher, I think it's that you build pictures of a certain set of answers to a certain range of questions and those pictures illuminate some aspect of the question, but usually you discover after a while that you've either obscured or even misrepresented some other question and so you move along.

MM: That sounds like science. You come up with a hypothesis. It doesn't quite fit the data, but it's good enough for now.

AA: Right. However, unlike many people of a scientific disposition, I'm happy to work with many different pictures at once. That is, I don't think that it's desirable to try and resolve all the tensions. I'm not attracted by the positivist project of the unification of the sciences. I think it's good that we have lots of different sciences, because each of them illuminates the world from a certain angle and the trying constantly to build only one picture simply means that you stop attending to certain important things. I'm happy to live knowing that I can't give you a simple explanation.

MM: In the middle again.

AA: Yes.

MM: With all these plot threads going by.

AA: Yes. But that's fine. Why can't we live with many pictures? People want to try and force you to say that the only intellectually coherent position is one in which you have one picture. I want to say we are fallible, finite creatures and that, for fallible, finite creatures, the best way of giving yourself a chance of having a grip on the full range of the things that concern you is to make sure that you have a lot of pictures and to see which ones help you in which circumstances. Now this is one way of formulating what I take to be a sort of pragmatist thought.

MM: The reference is to America.

AA: Yes. Absolutely.

MM: We've talked about Ghana. We've talked about England. Let's talk about America. What are your experiences in America?

AA: When I first arrived in this country, my best friend, my colleague, Skip Gates, drove me straight from Kennedy Airport to Washington Square in New York City and this was in the late '70s and there were people smoking dope all over the place, as Washington Square hadn't been cleaned up. And I thought, this is absolutely not the country that I had imagined. This is completely not what I expected.

MM: It didn't look like Hollywood.

AA: Didn't look like Hollywood. Then we drove up to New Haven, Connecticut, to Yale. It was a beautiful fall day. And the master of one of the colleges, who turned out to be the Chairman of the Afro-American Studies Department, was walking across the lawn in front of the great library there with his dogs, in his tweed suit, in his tweed jacket, and I thought, okay, this is a very complicated place because I'd just gone from, you know, one thing that I didn't expect to another thing I wasn't really expecting either and, basically, being delighted all the time to find new strangenesses. I've now lived here full time, more or less, since the early '80s and I've lived in New Haven, I've lived in Ithaca, New York, at Cornell, I've lived at Duke in North Carolina, and now I live mostly in Boston and sometimes in New York.

MM: So this is a country composed of people in the middle.

K. Anthony Appiah

AA: Yes. And I like that.

MM: Do you feel a fraternity with these people?

AA: I do.

MM: So you're teaching in the Afro-American Studies Department, you are from Africa, and you are talking to students who are seven, eight, nine generations removed from Africa who have this tremendous craving to know about the place. What do you tell them?

AA: I can say, look, what a place looks like from far away is different from what it looks like from close up. I know that from my experience in this country and let me tell you a little bit more about what Africa might look like from close up. Africa is incredibly complicated and diverse which, of course, fits with my general philosophy. We're talking about a continent which has, depending on how you count, up to 1,500 languages, more than fifty countries in the Organization of African Units. Most countries have many, many languages within their borders. I grew up in a country where there were Muslims and Christians and people who were neither. I grew up in a country where some people traced their families through their mothers and some through their fathers. I grew up in a continent where some people liked bland food and some people liked spicy food. I start with that. And I start with my own experience of moving out of Ghana into other parts of Africa for mostly family reasons. My sister now lives in southern Africa. And discovering for myself that—in a new part of Africa—all my Ghanaian assumptions didn't work.

MM: So—is the notion of Africa itself an artificial construct?

AA: For Africans, the interesting thing about the concept of Africa is it's older outside Africa really than it is inside. I mean, it comes from an Arabic word. And most Africans, until this century, didn't think of themselves as inhabiting a continent, they thought of themselves as inhabiting a particular society. It was other people who thought of them all as this homogenous thing, in racial terms. We speak of sub-Saharan Africa, which is really a euphemism for the Africa of the Negro, because we don't count North Africa because they're not Negroes, right? Africa is a continent as far as I'm concerned and has people of all shades and colors in it and it always has had.

MM: Are your students disappointed when you tell them all this stuff? Don't

255

they imagine a single, monolithic Africa that is this sort of homeland? As mythical as, say, Ireland to fifth generation of Irish Americans?

AA: Yes.

MM: As you talk to these students at Harvard, in the African-American Studies Department, you must feel a certain amount of anger and resentment about American society and racism and yet you haven't been part of that conversation. You're not in the midst of it. Do you feel left out? How do you deal with it, what do you tell your students?

AA: Well, I think you have to begin by respecting the experiences that they've had in trying to provide a context for thought.

MM: Can you commiserate? Do you understand what they've been through?

AA: Oh, sure. I mean, if you've lived in this country with a nonwhite skin, you've had experiences of being treated badly because of that. But you can't make the comparison between that and growing up here, and I grew up in a biracial family in a society where that was an easy thing to do. So I don't have that as a childhood experience, but I have certainly seen and, of course, American racism is very famous around the world. When I was growing up in the '60s, we knew about the civil rights movement.

MM: You read James Baldwin and you saw these things on television. Were you nervous about coming to the United States because of all this?

AA: No. My nervousness about the United States wasn't actually race. It should have been, actually, but it wasn't. I was more nervous about just getting shot on the street. I don't want to place myself as the kind of African coming and saying, "I'm the real black person and why don't you guys get your act together," and so on, which is a position that some African scholars and visitors take. I think that's not a good idea. One thing that I want to insist upon always in my teaching is that it's not a matter of who you are or where you come from or even any kind of privilege of certain experiences. I don't claim authority in virtue of my race, I claim authority in virtue of my work.

MM: So what do you tell them?

AA: I tell them that whatever they think, they've got to take into account the truth. And the truth is that a lot of what they think about Africa, about race, and about ethics is wrong. And they've got to figure out a better picture.

MM: At that point, do you step forward as the philosopher?

AA: I'm always using tools. If philosophy has a distinctive contribution to make to these debates, it is by being careful about the language, by saying, you know, you use this word very freely, this word *race*. What do you mean by it? And realizing how complex a set of ideas it is and how easily we can be led astray by thinking we know where we are intellectually, when in fact we don't. I have political/philosophical views. I think that we should be a liberal society. I think in a liberal society (because "liberal" as a word is about freedom), people are entitled to construct their own identities. And even if you think they're mistaken, they have the right—it's up to them. It's not the business of the government to tell you who you are or who you should be. Nor is it my business to tell anybody else who they should be. My business is to provide my students and anybody who is willing to read me and listen to me with tools for thinking about who they want to be. But I think that you can only make a sensible life for yourself if you take account of the facts.

MM: What does your friend Henry Louis Gates say to you about all this?

AA: He tells me, correctly, that it's all very well to say these abstract things and to get it all clear in a kind of neat way. But, the fact is, in the everyday world of people's lives, racial identities matter. They're powerful and they're not negative for everybody. When Skip walks down a street in a black community, he says hello to strangers on a sort of black-to-black to basis. And that kind of racial solidarity seems to me a positive thing and I'm not with those who say that the mere fact of noticing race and using it in those sort of positive ways, in your everyday life, is a bad thing. I'm not against that. Racial solidarity has led to good things as well as bad things. And so we have to constantly negotiate between what's good and what's bad in this area. It's not simple. You can't just say throw it out because in throwing it out, you'd be throwing out the bad with the good. What I think you have to do is to reformulate, rethink, and also change social relations. It's not enough just to change our ideas. We have to change the way we behave.

MM: Now, at a certain point, you became an American citizen.

AA: Yes.

MM: That implies a major choice for a man who's been in-between.

AA: Yes.

MM: What happened? What made you make that decision?

AA: I became an American citizen because I wanted to vote, because I believe that once you've decided that you're living in a place, you have political obligations to be a citizen, to be an active member of the community, and I think voting is an important way of being an active member of the community, though it's, of course, not the only way. I guess also I wanted to be able to sit on those juries that I had to keep sending the note back saying, I can't sit on your jury . . .

MM: Well, your dad was a lawyer.

AA: My father was a lawyer. And a politician, and when he died he actually left us a sort of testament of things he believed in and one of them was, wherever you want to live (and you can live anywhere you like) you have to make that place better. Remember, you're citizens of the world, but you have to also be a citizen in a particular place. My sisters and I have done that. We live in four different countries. I'm happy to boast about my sisters that they are good citizens in the three countries that they live in.

MM: I've got to know. There have to be some mornings . . . the car is broken down, you're riding the subway, you got soaking wet in the rain, the gas bill's arrived, and you're thinking to yourself as you're hanging from the strap on that subway, I could have been a king in Ghana.

AA: (Laughter). Well, knowing what it's like for my uncle, I have to say that that isn't a very appetizing prospect. Actually, I think that one of the things that's nice about coming to America and being an American is to be free of those hereditary expectations. I grew up in Ghana at a time when my father was relatively well known in the country and so everybody thought of me as his son. My mother's father was in the British government. And so, everybody in England, when I went to university, thought of me as his grandson. I like being in a place where I'm just me and where I can construct a self that draws on all that I'm free to draw on but is also my own. So, actually, I've never regretted coming here, not for an instant, and I think, in part, that's because it's now—in my view—the best place in the world to do philosophy.

K. Anthony Appiah

MM: Okay. I want to explore how your theories of philosophy have changed as you've gone through all these changes in your life. You start out with probabilistic semantics in England and you end up in the African-American Studies Department at Harvard. What happened in between, intellectually?

AA: I don't want to create a kind of artificial unity to it. I mean, there are lots of things that can't be fitted into a simple story.

MM: That's life.

AA: Life's a mess. But, if I want to sort of follow one's plan through, I'd say it's this: My work in the theory of meaning and semantics, whatever you want to call it, was really driven by a concern to understand questions about the concepts of truth and how language relates to reality and whether the best way to understand how language works is in terms of the concept of truth, the idea of language fitting reality, a correspondence between language in the world or some other way of thinking about it. Now I actually ended up being pretty much convinced of what is called a realist position, a position in which language and the world fit each other in a certain way. But the question about the relationship between language and the world is not something that we can talk about without taking account of the contribution that the mind makes, that language makes, that society makes to the language we use in order to talk about this really existing independent world. So when I started to think about race, I used the same tools that I had used to think about philosophical questions before. I used the philosophy of language tools and I started asking: How does this concept work? How does this word work? What do we do with it in the world? And I came to the conclusion that, in the case of race, the best account of it wasn't that it fitted the world. It was that it didn't fit the world, but is still there. So that it turns out that simply deciding whether something's true or adequate to reality—or not—isn't the only question. There are other questions. This is the pragmatist's view: that it isn't enough to say something's true. You have to ask: How do we think with this concept and what does it make us *do*? How does it make us behave so as to think in this way?

MM: It may not be true, but it *is*.

AA: We have this concept. Once you start thinking about it as a concept, not as a thing—once you start thinking about the way the concept works, you can then explore how people use it without committing yourself to the existence

259

of anything in the world that they're talking about. That there are many ways of referring to, or denoting, whatever word you want to use. And that's, I think, very freeing because it allows you to take the thing seriously—race as a concept—without committing yourself to the existence of an object. Now that's part of what I think is powerful about all of these social constructionist views. They allow you to say, yes, the concepts of gender and race and ethnicity and sexual orientation and so on, do powerful work in the world, but they do it in a way that involves assumptions that turn out upon inspection to be false. My initial response, when I was a young guy, was, if the ideas behind it are false, if the presuppositions are false, you just have to throw it away. Now my inclination is to say, we have to understand how it's related to falsehood and then think about whether revision is possible; whether we can, as it were, disconnect it from the false presuppositions and still find something useful to live with that the concept is doing and I think that that's the question about gender. It's the question about sexual orientation, gay and straight, and it's the question about race. It's not a matter of just throwing it out because we can demonstrate that the people who use the concept may have false assumptions when they use it. We have, rather, to think about how to refine, reform, develop our understanding and that's what philosophical training very much helps you to do. To think about those questions. But it isn't just a philosophical question. It's not just an intellectual question. The world has to change. Not just the way we think about it.

MM: At that moment, you've got to go out into the world.

AA: You've got to out into the world. And my view is, here the philosopher is in dialogue with his or her fellow citizens. We can't decide these things by ourselves. I don't, by myself, know what the right solution is to the reforming our conceptions of gender and race and sexual orientation.

MM: That's a very unphilosophic remark in itself.

AA: Maybe. But I think the truth is that philosophers should go out into the world because it's only in dialogue with other citizens that we can actually make that change. I can't tell you how we should reform or I can't tell you, by myself, how we should reform our understanding of race. Because reforming our understanding of race is not just changing the way people think—it's changing the world. It's changing how people act, it's maybe changing how we do things, changing how we organize the physical space of our cities. Do we want to go on having highly segregated cities? Do we want to go on having segregated school districts? These are practical questions which are relevant to the reform that the philosophical understanding of the concept makes it possible to imagine. But actually carrying it out is something where the philosopher counts for one, because the philosopher counts for one as a citizen.

MM: What about the philosopher as a teacher?

AA: I think that opening up your students and your readers who are not your students, anybody who has access to what you do, these possibilities are an important contribution. This is part of the citizen's task as a philosopher.

MICHAEL HALBERSTAM
Politics without Reason?

Michael Halberstam, Assistant Professor of Philosophy at the University of South Carolina. Born in Germany of Jewish descent, Michael Halberstam has focused his academic career on the meaning of totalitarianism. The discussion explores the relationship between rationalism and modern politics, with special emphasis placed on how totalitarianism arises in response to remaking society according to a rational plan—the modern experience of the freedom of will.

MM: Michael Malone   **MH:** Michael Halberstam

MM: Michael, I've been talking to a lot of philosophers here, looking at the history of philosophy and at the various crises that philosophy is in right now. Let me give you the way I see it, and you tell me what I've got wrong, or what I've got right, and what the solutions are. Philosophy starts out as this great, noble project twenty-four centuries ago, a conversation about life's great questions, trying to gain wisdom about how to live a good life, how to deal with questions of good and evil, and of meaning and existence. This conversation goes on for twenty-three centuries, as if in preparation for some sort of test. We hit the twentieth century, the test arrives: Auschwitz, the Gulag Archipelago, the killing fields in Cambodia, forced starvation in the Ukraine, the cultural revolution in China. This is when we need philosophy. This is presumably what it's all been preparing for. And where is philosophy? We end up, for example, with one of the greatest minds philosophy has ever produced at the culmination of twenty-four centuries of philosophical conversation: Martin Heidegger, with a Nazi armband on. What happened? Why did it go bad?

MH: Well, these are very difficult questions, and they're very good questions. I don't think that philosophy proposes solutions so much as being part of our culture and being on both sides of the fence.

MM: Wait, wait. I go down to a cab driver down there on the street and I say "what's philosophy for?" I suspect he or she is going to say "it's about wisdom, it's about a better life, it's about living life properly." Isn't that philosophy's job?

MH: Well, yes, you're also speaking to a philosopher, however. So, of course, I have my own views about what philosophy is and what it arose out of. I think that most philosophers in the twentieth century would agree that philosophy has changed a lot, but also that philosophy really *was* identical to thinking about things in a systematic way, in general. So, with the Greeks, it included scientific thought, it included mathematics, questions of practical wisdom, politics, astronomy, and so forth. So what has happened throughout the centuries is that philosophy has generated all of these different scientific disciplines—or has at least been part of the generation of these different scientific disciplines—and they have slowly split off from philosophy proper as they have generated their own methodologies. As a result of this development, philosophy now has a different kind of place in relation to politics or science than it had in the beginning with the Greeks.

MM: But now, you're Jewish, you were born in Germany, and you're a philosopher. The question of somebody like Heidegger has to haunt you to a degree. You have to be thinking about this, I'm sure.

MH: The question of totalitarianism, as you know, is a concern in my work and specifically the question you have asked—how many intellectuals, some of the leading figures of their time, not just on the radical right, but on the left as well, could follow? There is the Stalinist philosopher Georg Lukacs on the left, for example, who was called by Max Weber the genius of his time. How could intellectuals have participated in movements that have had such devastating effect? This is the question we intellectuals have to contend with today.

MM: Now we have to qualify things a little bit. I threw out Heidegger because he's such an extreme case. But we could also look at somebody like Hannah Arendt who, in many ways, is just like Heidegger in terms of philosophical background, but who comes out on the absolutely opposite side, becomes a conscience of the twentieth century. What's the difference between the two? How come philosophy produced both?

MH: Well, clearly Hannah Arendt, a student of Heidegger's, was very much influenced by him, as were many other very prominent thinkers. But I would not go so far as to call Heidegger a major political figure in the National Socialist movement. He, like many other intellectuals in Germany, was caught up in a kind of exhilaration of the time that had its very dark sides, and that had consequences many of them didn't foresee. Some of them did and willingly participated. Heidegger, as is now well known after the long discussion that's occurred about his involvement with National Socialism in 1933 as the rector of the University of Freiburg, had this period in which he took on a task for himself of trying to participate in the transformation of the German higher education system. And he thought somehow he could guide the National Socialist education policy.

MM: Change the system from within?

MH: I think he must have had those ideas to some degree. Although, on the

Michael Halberstam

other hand, one has to say that he was also very much caught up in the movement for a total transformation of German society that had very strong nationalistic elements.

MM: See, I'm very intrigued by that. You used the word *exhilaration*. And yet I
keep hearing from philosophers over and over that philosophy is about *reflection*. How come nobody was doing any reflection on manifest human evil during this period? Why were people caught up in these great totalitarian movements in the twentieth century, people of wisdom?

MH: Well, first of all I would say, yes, reflection distances us from our immediate experiences and from certain subjective ways of looking at things, and also
sometimes from our emotions. But reflection is also an emotional experience.
And a certain kind of reflectivity can become very emotional. So, for example,
what sociologists of religion have—excuse me, sociologists of science—are
well aware of and have worked on for a long time, is the way in which the scientists of the seventeenth and eighteenth centuries . . . the birth of the New Science went together with a very strong sort of religious experience. Rationalism
itself is a very emotional experience.

MM: It has a religious structure to it. Revelation.

MH: Yes. A kind of revelatory structure: opening the book of nature with the
key of mathematics. Newton, for example, was a very religious man. I'm not
sure that many scientists are aware of this, but Newton also had a theory about
religious matters and tried to write a book about what went wrong with Christianity to produce the great religious divisions during his time. He and Locke
got together for Bible readings.

MM: So this spiritual desire, then, seems to be buried deep in human nature
and even philosophers can't escape it—no matter how hard they try?

MH: Yes, I would say that is very true.

MM: So, are the two great totalitarian movements of the twentieth century—
Fascism/Nazism and Communism—are they spiritual movements? Is modern
totalitarianism a movement like that?

MH: I would say, yes, there's a very strong spiritual element in totalitarian
movements. And, of course, the distinction between left and right, which is so
much part of our own political consciousness and which puts these two

265

movements at such a distance, is undercut by the concept of totalitarianism, which brings these two very distinct movements together with the help of a theory, which is part historical, part philosophical, part sociological.

MM: We know that Hitler and Stalin watched each other's moves, adopting techniques of social control from one another.

MH: Yes, that's certainly true. Certainly, Hitler learned a lot from Stalin.

MM: Hitler even expressed his admiration for Stalin's techniques at various times.

MH: Yes. Of course, I'm not a historian. What philosophy can do—the kind of philosophy I'm interested in—is look at the history of ideas and at the connections between different ideologies, if you will. But what I'm also interested in is looking at the way in which ideas are connected to an emotional, felt stance or attitude toward the world, which these ideas imply and which these ideas are at the same time influenced by. So, for example, in the case of totalitarian movements, Hannah Arendt, who I admire very much and who, as we have mentioned, was a student of Heidegger's, has put forward the thesis, which many others thinkers have put forth as well, that totalitarianism is a modern phenomenon . . .

MM: Distinctly twentieth century, industrial?

MH: Well, let me tell you what I mean by *modernity* or what I mean by *modern.* One of the fundamental ideas of modernity in opposition to, let's say, a traditional or religious society and conception of the self, is that we can make and fashion ourselves and also that we can make and fashion our society according to a plan. The idea of society as artifact is a fundamentally modern idea, which is very different from traditional conceptions of the self and of the relationship between individual and society.

MM: Does technology give us the tools to do this fashioning?

MH: Sure. Technology does not just give us the tools to do this fashioning, but the technological attitude is itself all about making things. That we can make . . .

MM: You can make society, but you can also, then, make the 'New Man?'

MH: Yes. You're referring, of course, to the Soviet project to make the New Man. The National Socialists tried very much to do the same. They tried not

Michael Halberstam

only to reform society, but to create a whole new culture. And that is very much a modern project. What I think philosophy can do is to help rethink the whole idea of modernity, in light of the devastation wrought by totalitarian regimes, and in light of the fundamental difficulties that certain aspects of the modern project have led us into.

MM: I'm curious about something. As a journalist, when you're reporting on a story, it can be very hard to stay out of the story. You get emotionally involved with the events that are occurring in front of you, as objective as you try to be.

MH: Right.

MM: When you see some terrible thing going on, some tragedy, you can't help but get affected by it. Now, as you study totalitarianism, especially Nazism, how do you stay emotionally detached from a subject that would have murdered you? How do you stay objective while you're doing this research?

MH: That's a good question. I think one answer is that one shouldn't stay detached when one thinks about these questions. At the same time, you do want to be reflective, and you want to understand. I think that, having grown up in Germany as someone who is Jewish, and having dealt with these issues for a long time, I no longer have the same immediate responses, and I want to understand from the *inside*. I understand what happened, and I understand the history, or at least some of the history and politics of what went on. But what interests me most is the question that you referred to earlier: How someone like Heidegger, for example, could have participated. How could intellectuals, how could a whole culture, have become caught up in a movement that was so destructive to others and to themselves, and do so on the grounds of very deeply held theoretical beliefs?

MM: Do you feel a huge responsibility, in the sense that if you could understand what caused these things, you can make sure it never happens again?

MH: Well, history doesn't work that way.

MM: It comes back a different way every time.

MH: Things don't happen again in the same way. But perhaps it's also more of a personal thing. I think what's important is to see our own implication and to see what kinds of ways of thinking are ideological, are amenable to distortions and so forth.

267

MM: There's a term that really intrigues me that you use. *Totalitarian sublime.* What does that mean?

MH: Well, we spoke earlier about a certain kind of spiritual element to totalitarian movements. And the connection that I make in my work, following the political thinker Hannah Arendt, is between a certain kind of sensibility and structure of experience that is connected with the modern experience of freedom on the one hand and the aspiration of totalitarian movements on the other hand. The question I've asked is: How is the spiritual sensibility that drives totalitarian movements related to the ideals of the modern project of emancipation—the desire to set ourselves free from the burdens of the everyday, from the burdens of our history?

MM: I would think that would be almost antithetical . . . freedom and the desire to be a cog in this giant, totalitarian machine . . . to lose one's identity in this larger thing as opposed to gaining one's identity by becoming free.

MH: It's here that we would have to talk about different senses of freedom. The idea of freedom is not just an abstract idea, of course, but has to be connected in some fashion to our own experience, to our own experience of the world, and to our own self-experience. There's a strong element of transcendence inherent in the idea of freedom. So, for example, the idea of the sublime is actually an aesthetic category. It's a category that's taken from the arts: We call a landscape sublime; the raging ocean is called sublime. Thinkers like Edmund Burke, who wrote a very famous conservative commentary on the French Revolution, already connected the notion of the sublime with a certain type of experience that had political implications.

MM: That's right, and in that essay the excitement he saw in England among intellectuals, the excitement of being caught up in something vast that gave you a sublime feeling of being involved in a great move, a great force of nature. Is that the freedom, then? You lose all the daily burdens that wear you down, and you're caught up in the sweep of history?

MH: Yes. The philosopher Immanuel Kant talks about the experience and the movement of the sublime as an unburdening of the self from the cares and concerns of the everyday. And this kind of comprehensive unburdening is, I believe, part and parcel of the spiritual element in totalitarian movements. They had a very strong draw. It's easy to take a standpoint that is removed and fail to understand the great draw, the great pull, of these movements that involved millions of people. This is what I'm interested in understanding.

Michael Halberstam

MM: The satisfaction of being involved in something greater than yourself. I would think that intellectuals would like it and artists would like it—like Malevich, for example, and people like that in the Soviet Union—because it's essentially a new aesthetic that you can be part of. What about the average person?

MH: Well, let me talk a little bit more about this feeling or this sensibility. In the United States these kinds of reflections are not often made part of discussions about politics for some of the very reasons that we're talking about. So it's very hard even to bring into the public sphere or into conversation matters that are thought of as spiritual and religious and private. But these sensibilities were very important in Europe during the '20s. Sigmund Freud, for example, spoke of a religious feeling without religion, which he criticized, and was very persistent in criticizing, in his 1929 essay, *Civilization and Its Discontents*. And this experience of the sublime has a very long history that is intimately tied up with the modern experience of freedom and the modern attempt at self-fashioning, of completely breaking with the past, of creating a new self, of fashioning a new society and an entirely new way of life.

MM: Is there an element of escape from one's self, too? In the modern world you have to carry the burden of selfhood. You see in Italian cinema, when we look back at the Fascist era, people just seem relieved to put on the black shirt and be part of this. You don't have to think as much. There's a plan, there's a role, and there's this momentum. And you don't have to care about all that messy little stuff in your own life anymore.

MH: Yes. What I'm trying to do is precisely to create a relationship between these ideas that sound very abstract and the very specific aesthetic, felt experiences you're mentioning. So, for example, the great cathedral of light at the National Socialist Party congress in Nuremburg, which had these air field spotlights pointing up into the sky . . .

MM: Infinite pillars, yes.

MH: Infinite pillars. This is all part of a certain aesthetic that's bound up with these totalitarian spiritual sensibilities.

MM: Tell me something. When you study all these things, do you think you have a more acute sense of totalitarianism? Can you look around and say that this is a totalitarian urge here? Can you look at a building and see a sort of totalitarianism hiding in its architecture? Does philosophy help you to be like a canary in a coal mine, to warn us of things before they arrive?

MH: I can't really say that the philosophy that I do has any concrete application. I don't see these kinds of events taking place today in U.S. society. My motivation is mostly trying to understand . . .

MM: But from understanding comes wisdom and maybe with wisdom comes the ability to predict, to anticipate, to prepare?

MH: Yes, but not in such straightforward ways. I think philosophy never quite applies without elaborate transitions to practical affairs.

MM: Well, let's talk about three of those transitions: politics, teaching, journalism. You're involved, to some degree, with all three of them. Is that your way of getting your ideas translated into the world?

MH: Yes, surely. I do think the impulse to do philosophy is very different from the impulse to do something practical in the world. I think one of the things that might be said about philosophy is that it doesn't have any concrete application or use. Philosophy is precisely that which is *not* practical. But it's a reflection on our practical activities, and it's a reflection on politics which has us deepen our views and our understanding.

MM: But—knowing what you know, what you've learned—there must be some sort of personal impetus to tell the world: Look, this is what it was really all about. You've got to understand this so we don't make this mistake again or have it come out in another form. What do you tell your students when you're teaching them this stuff?

MH: Well, where I think this is relevant is actually very deeply with regard to American liberal democracy. I think, as a consequence of the totalitarian experience, American liberal democracy has taken a very hands-off approach to social and cultural issues. And the experience of totalitarianism is often referred to and called in to limit state action, to take the government completely out of educating its citizenry, except in very minimal ways. It is frequently appealed to in order to justify a very minimal state. You have to understand the experience of totalitarianism as having a very strong impact on American liberal politics. So what I believe is important is to rethink the relationship between politics and culture and to try not to give over too much to that particular experience.

MM: Let's go back to totalitarianism just for a moment. Is it implicit in the modernist project?

MH: Well, that's a good question. I think there are two ways of looking at it.

One way is that totalitarianism is a kind of resurgence of religious theological passions, a throwback to medieval times, and that all we have to do is to reassert the liberal project, the Enlightenment project of reason establishing a society based on freedom.

MM: This is the "barbarian's argument"?

MH: Yes, this is the "barbarian's argument," exactly.

MM: Do you buy it?

MH: No. I tend to believe that totalitarianism is intimately related to the modern project, and that it arises out of some of the same experiences, structures, and ideas that have informed modernity.

MM: Well, that makes it even scarier, then, doesn't it? That's the worst of the two scenarios: If it's part of our way of viewing the world, then we have a real problem.

MH: Well, it's part of the modern attempt to refashion man, to create the New Man, and it is related to some of the same impulses. I think it would be wrong to bring the two too close together—that is, liberal democratic society and totalitarian movements—but totalitarianism can be seen as a kind of reaction to liberal democratic society. And it shares with the latter the idea of remaking society. The attempt to remake society, according to a plan, is something that also functions within our own society. For example, the World Congress is held in this mall.

MM: Right.

MH: We have a completely artificial environment. We can't leave. The whole architecture completely encloses us, and it was built according to a plan . . .

MM: Crowd control.

MH: Yes, and for economic purposes and other very specific purposes.

MM: So totalitarianism isn't—if I have this right from what you're saying—it isn't the *other*. It's more the evil twin of liberal democracy.

MH: Well, I would want to be very careful about those kinds of statements. I think it's right to say that if we make totalitarianism the other, then we fail to understand how totalitarianism is related to some of the same aspirations that also inform our own society—namely, the idea of setting ourselves free entirely from traditional structures, from the way in which our own culture and our own history inform society. Karl Marx once said (in the introduction to his analysis of the eighteenth Brumaire of Louis Bonaparte) that men make history, but they do not make it as they please. They don't make it under circumstances chosen by themselves, but given and found and transmitted from the past. The totalitarian attempt can be seen as an attempt to break completely with the past and to create an entirely new culture, an entirely new poetry, a new mode of dress, a new way of relating to one another socially . . .

MM: Is that why it oftentimes rises during periods of social and economic crisis?

MH: Very much so, yes.

MM: The desire is increased to try something altogether new.

MH: Yes. And I think that the aspiration to liberate ourselves completely from history, from the past, and from tradition is also very much part of our contemporary political culture.

MM: Let's talk about tradition, let's talk a little bit about you. I understand you come from a long line of Hasidic rabbis. Do you see yourself, the work you do in philosophy, as part of that tradition?

MH: I can't say that it's part of that tradition. It's a very different tradition. I do think that the activity is very much the same. You pore over books, you read, you think about things, and so the activity is very much the same, trying to understand the world.

MM: Do you feel that ancestry stretching back behind you? Do you feel part of a continuous line with them? Or have you broken with the past like all the rest of us?

MH: Yes. I, like many of us, am in the same kind of predicament that, on the one hand, I'm only very tenuously connected to tradition and, on the other hand, I recognize the loss of this kind of a connection. So from that vantage point, the problem of modernity—or postmodernity as it's now referred to—it is very much also a *personal* problem.

MM: One last question that I need to ask you. Here we stagger out of one of the bloodiest centuries in human history, heading into the new millennium.

Michael Halberstam

Are you optimistic about the new century and the new millennium? Have we grown past these monsters of totalitarianism—have we learned how to deal with them?

MH: I feel that the role of philosophy—what philosophy can do—is not to solve problems or to answer questions, but to show us the real tensions that exist in our own way of thinking about things. I think we're often too impatient with those tensions. I think the role of philosophy is to reveal these tensions.

MM: Thank you, Michael.

LEWIS HAHN
Ambassador of Dialogue

Lewis Hahn, University Professor of Philosophy Emeritus, Southern Illinois University at Carbondale, is Editor of the Library of Living Philosophers. An ambassador for philosophy around the world, Lewis Hahn provides a concise summary of the major developments of philosophy throughout the twentieth century. He suggests that philosophic dialogue is the key to understanding other cultures. He talks in some detail as to how the Library of Living Philosophers is an example of this process.

MM: Michael Malone   **LH:** Lewis Hahn

MM: Tell me something, Professor Hahn. You're ninety years old.

LH: That's right.

MM: You've seen most of this century. How has philosophy changed in the twentieth century? From the philosophy you began with until now?

LH: In the early years of the century Hegel and absolute idealism were prominent, with people like Cunningham and Creighton being leaders among them. Among our Library of Living Philosophers, Brand Blanshard is one who falls into that tradition. The pragmatists replaced the absolute idealists a little later.

MM: Tell me what absolute idealism is, before we get into pragmatism. I'd like your definition of each of these.

LH: Hegel thought that there was only one individual and that was the absolute. The religiously inclined thought of the absolute in terms of God, but Hegel put it in metaphysical terms. And, according to the absolute idealists, there is a reason or cause for everything that happens, every event is connected with every other. Professor Blanshard used to throw something over his shoulder and say, "I have just changed the coastline of Australia." This emphasis upon necessary connections between events in the world is one of the things that the pragmatists question. They tended to emphasize the notion of novelty and the importance of being prepared for new and unusual circumstances. Accordingly, great pragmatists like John Dewey didn't call this view pragmatism, he called it instrumentalism because, if you're going to survive in a world in which each day brings you something new, you need to have some instruments to help control so far as possible what's going to happen to you or find ways of dealing with the changing world. Pragmatism was the rage up through the 1930s or so. And about that time we got a host of logical positivists, mainly stemming from Vienna: Moritz Schlick and the Viennese positivists said that everything depends on sensory observations. You start with what somebody has observed, you follow through on this logically to make sure you have a consistent pattern, and that is the way that philosophy should go. The positivists thought that too many of the philosophers teaching at that time had too much of idealism, of the Hegelian type, or of pragmatism, which they thought was a little too loose for their purposes. Idealism, they felt, claims necessary connection between the wrong things. The logical positivists thought that you could classify any statement as something dependent upon sensory observation or upon what you can reason out logically. If you can't reason it out logically or if it's not something that you directly observed, the odds are—in one of their favorite expressions—you may be talking nonsense. And among our subjects of Library of Living Philosophers' volumes, A. J. Ayer—Freddie Ayer we call him because he didn't like the name Alfred—just after graduating at Oxford, was advised to go to Vienna because they had some interesting things happening there. His volume, *Language, Truth and Logic* [1936] was a kind of primer of logical positivism and, arguably, if not the most popular book of the century, one that would have ranked very high. Freddie Ayer, in addition to being able to state clearly his views, was a regular participant in the British Broadcasting Symposium.

MM: This was in the '30s and '40s?

LH: Yes. And as late as the '50s. Ayer also traveled extensively, usually representing Great Britain, so that he was one of the first people from the Western part of the world to visit the Soviet Union. And he did a similar tour of duty in China. He was a felicitous speaker and he enjoyed meeting people with other views. He always thought that if he could talk to them long enough, they would see the truth of his way of putting things and he enjoyed that. But, at any rate, by the '40s, well, from logical positivism, we moved into so-called analytic philosophy, which embraced two main starting points. One of these was from ordinary language. Hence, we had and still have some people who claim to do philosophy in terms of ordinary language which most of the rest of us find extraordinary enough. G. E. Moore, who's in our Library of Living Philosophers, was one of the great advocates of the ordinary language approach. The other point was the emphasis on logic, set forth by Bertrand Russell and, to some extent, Rudolf Carnap, who had escaped from Germany and later came to this country.

MM: Did you know all these gentlemen?

LH: Yes. As it happens, Van Quine also went to Vienna on a postdoctoral fellowship at the same time that Freddie Ayer was there. Quine had a bit more junior status, although not in terms of age. Ayer somehow was invited to participate with the Vienna Circle directly and Quine was an observer. But during Quine's time there he became acquainted with Carnap and the Polish logicians. Apparently, in those days, Alfred Tarski and other Poles were doing very new things in logic. So it was a rather interesting time having both of these men, as well as numerous other well-known philosophers in, or just out of, Vienna. Since that time, we've had a kind of mainline analytic philosophy, which refers to this group of philosophers who believe that they have found improvements over what the ordinary language people or the logical positivists did—improvements in the sense of stating more precisely what they had and arguing more consistently. That group is still the mainline analytical tradition in our time. This has affected the course of philosophy in this country and, for that matter, in various other parts of the world. Most of the major universities have settled on some one philosophical outlook. Cornell University was a center for the Hegelian idealism and later for Wittgenstein's view. Although this is something that you sharpen tools with very effectively, it perhaps discourages part of what I like to see in philosophy—namely, dialogue between various contrasting views.

MM: And so you have these camps sitting in these different universities? They don't talk to each other?

LH: As a matter of fact, they talk mainly to people of the same outlook .

MM: So logical positivists talk to logical positivists—they don't talk to anybody else?

LH: The logical positivists have always been willing to tell the others where they were wrong, but when they got down to business of talking serious philosophy, rather than trying to persuade somebody, they thought it saved a great deal of time to talk to others of like belief. This is also contrary to the basic spirit of our Library of Living Philosophers where we want to see not just one or a few outlooks, but sample representatives of a number of different traditions. And, at this Congress, as you may have noted, some of the more popular sessions have been ones devoted to Chinese or Indian philosophical traditions. It's been interesting to find that there are striking parallels between, say, pragmatist John Dewey and Confucius, or the Taoists, and so on. What Professor Nasr was emphasizing in last night's discussion was that there had been a neglect of various major traditions, especially among some of the Eastern traditions, of what he calls "perennial philosophy," which he thinks one would find in the Taoist, the Confucian, and various Buddhist traditions. I think, in principle, Nasr is right about this. We live in a world that is smaller in ever so many ways, so that we ought to be able to talk with people who don't share our particular outlook so that we can understand what they have to offer and, in turn, improve on what we have in the light of what we can get from them. That's what I see as one of the virtues of pluralism, and I think of this also as being very much in line with the spirit of the Library of Living Philosophers.

MM: Does this new pluralism bring together these opposing camps in the Western tradition?

LH: I don't think that it will necessarily mean that they will come together in the sense of agreeing on things. But they will have a better understanding of where each of these stands and, accordingly, will be in better shape to make use of whatever they may find in these traditions that might go with their particular outlook. I'm convinced that no matter how good a view we may have, there is something lost if we limit it to that one view. As you know, I think that each of us sooner or later turns into a philosopher. We may lack the professional terminology used by the philosophers, but each of us views the world from a unique position. For example, one of my uncles who never went to college is one who I learned a great deal from about philosophy, although that's not what he called it. But he had a sense of what was important, a sense of what was basically real, and he loved to discuss it with me. When I went back home from college, I always had some sessions with him and though he didn't have the terminology, he picked up on the ideas very readily; moreover, in light of his experience, he brought something to the discussion that I'd not picked up from any of my professional tutors.

MM: After seventy years as a practicing philosopher, what have you learned from philosophy for your own life?

LH: Well, one of the things that I have learned is that dialogue is essential if we're going to make the best use of the resources available. We live in a changing world. So that, when you talk about getting a worldview or a world hypothesis, it has to be a worldview that has a way of dealing with change. If we take some of the ancient Greeks—Plato, for example, thought that if something changed, it was a lower or inferior form of reality. He had a scale of being ranging from the changing on up to the unchanging or eternal ideas. But, it seems to me, the evidence pretty clearly indicates that William James was right when he said even God doesn't know what will happen tomorrow. Change is present wherever we are, so that what we need is a way of dealing with that and one of the things we need, because of change, is to have a somewhat different view of the nature of explanation or interpretation. Plato and Aristotle thought in terms of analysis as a way of breaking combinations down into atomic or eternal particles of some sort. If I'm right in saying that we have a changing world, you have a better form of explanation or a better form of analysis if you think in terms of changes in a career. For that matter, for any who may share my fondness for detective stories, anyone who is acquainted with a detective story knows that, when homicide is suspected, this leads the investigators to try to check something out and in checking it out, they can't stop just with the scene of the crime because conditions spread out into a much wider environment. If the person died from poison, you have a different set of circumstances to run down from what you would have if he died from a blow on the head with a blunt object or if he was shot.

MM: Seventy years as a philosopher. Can you tell me if philosophy has given you a satisfying life? Did you make the right choice of choosing this career, looking back over, literally, the twentieth century?

LH: I think for me it was the right choice. I have found this an exciting field to be in. It's not limited to professional philosophers. After speaking with nearly anyone after a while, I can show them that they too have a philosophy. It has put me in touch with some of the leading minds in the world, but—equally important—has enabled me to talk with people in other fields, and in different countries.

ASHOK GANGADEAN   KARAN SINGH
EWERT COUSINS   ROBERT MULLER

A Dialogue on
Global Thought and Spirituality

Ashok Gangadean, Co-founder of the Global Dialogue Institute, organized and coordinated the Commission and serves as a guiding force behind the scenes. He leads off the discussion with an enthusiastic explanation of the scope and purpose of the commission and the reason for bringing these great minds together.

Karan Singh is the only former ruler of a princely state in India to voluntarily surrender his privy purse to charity. A prominent member of the Indian parliament, he is considered a likely candidate to assume the presidency. A humanitarian, scholar, and leader, he brings to this group discussion an opinion of great stature.

Ewert Cousins, Professor of Philosophy at Fordham University, has long been associated with efforts to foster global unity of thought and purpose. He adds to this discussion a sense of balance and reason as Chairman of the Commission.

Robert Muller, for many years Assistant Secretary General of the United Nations, has been called the "Philosopher" and the "Prophet of Hope" of the United Nations. Dr. Muller is known throughout the world as the "father of global education" and he received the UNESCO Peace Education Prize. He is the Chancellor of the University of Peace in demilitarized Costa Rica.

MM: Michael Malone   **AG:** Ashok Gangadean
 KS: Karan Singh   **EC:** Ewert Cousins
 RM: Robert Muller

MM: I have a question for all of you. Here we are at the end of one of the most violent centuries of human history. There's a hundred plus conflicts taking place in the world right now, sectarian violence. It would seem that there is no dialogue anywhere in the world right now. Dialogue seems impossible. How can we even use a term like that at this moment in time?

AG: I think that's a great question. It sounds like conversation, but we're thinking out loud in our group here. That's why we use the word 'global dialogue' and it means something very profound to us because you're exactly right, there's deep violence across the world and there's inner violence, too, within us and it really has to do with the boundaries between worldviews. I think that's the key to the whole thing. We haven't understood deeply enough that human beings live in different worldviews, different cultures, different ethnologies, religions. And when those boundaries are there, violence breaks out because each person thinks that his or her worldview is reality. And it's very hard to see the other worldview. And that's why communication breaks down. So the challenge for a deeper dialogue or global dialogue is to somehow move out of your own worldview and open your being to enter other worldviews. And that's a profound challenge.

KS: I wouldn't think it correct to say that there is *no* dialogue. I think that, in fact, dialogue is going on in a thousand different ways at many levels. Conflict has been with the human race ever since the dawn of history and the twentieth century has probably been the most conflictual, the most violent, of all the centuries of human history. But that is all the more reason that the processes of dialogue or multi-logue, if you like—the multiple dialogue on a global level—needs to be encouraged, and that I think is what we are all about. The greater the conflict, the more the necessity for dialogue. The more ill the patient, the more necessary the medicine.

EC: Of course, I think it would be a good idea to look over this century and to see if there hasn't been a change right in the middle of the century, that we're not where we were in the beginning, and this may be the most transition-ridden century in the whole of human history. Over violence itself. I'd like to ask Robert about that because he has some very dramatic stories.

MM: After forty years at an institution created for dialogue, the United Nations.

EC: Before that, before that. . . .

RM: Well, I was a very pessimistic young man in the Second World War, coming from Alsace-Lorraine, having seen the most incredible horrors between two countries, France and Germany, highly civilized, yet treating each other in ways which I've written a whole book about. When I came out from under, into life, practically all my friends from my class were dead, in German or French uniforms. I was the only one left, in fact. I swore to them that I was going to devote my life to peace. And my father said it would never work. I was a very pessimistic young man because he said, look, if the Germans and the French who are white and civilized had three wars in my grandfather's time, how can I expect that a world containing 5,000 religions, with blacks and white, communists and capitalists, will ever work? But today, I can tell you that after fifty years I have become an optimist because when the human species really looks into a problem and decides to cope with it, it is able to do so. For example, we no longer have international wars. Now what is left is internal ethnic conflict, as in Yugoslavia, Chechnya, and so on, and religious conflicts. And there's this feeling that has emerged that believes the UN has no competence in religious affairs. Can we find ways where the religions themselves are going to try to do what the United Nations has done between nations and find peaceful solutions to conflict? I asked myself: what was the biggest conflict at the beginning of the century? It was labor conflict. And labor conflicts gave birth to communism. Today labor conflict, from being number one is the *last* arena of conflict. Why? Because even before the League of Nations, they created the International Labor Organization with governors, labor, and unions and there are so many agreements and understandings between employers and laborers that today the worst labor can do anywhere in the world is to go on strike. So, you see, humans can really do it and this is why it is important now to deal also with ethnic conflicts and with religious conflicts because those are solely the remaining spheres of conflict.

MM: Aren't those the most intractable of the conflicts, as opposed to economic ones? You talk about a division, about opposing worldviews. I mean, different worldviews that are truly diametrically opposite worldviews in many cases. How do you bridge that gap between those when there's absolutely no common ground? They can even be antithetical.

AG: That is a challenge of our time and that's why your question is a good one. That's why we use the word dialogue, but is there dialogue in the face of all this? Yes. One often gets a sense of that moment in life, where you literally break through to another viewpoint, and I find that such moments suggest great possibilities for effectively dealing with these intractable barriers.

EC: I feel that we're in a period where the human race is going through an evolution or transformation of consciousness. If our consciousness as a human community were not transformed, then I would believe what you said that—these are intractable obstacles. But I think consciousness itself can be transformed. I'll give you my own example. I found myself on the Sioux Reservation in South Dakota working there during the summer just painting and branding cattle and after two or three weeks I was talking one day to my friends among the Lakota Sioux and I felt as if my consciousness went out of my head and went into their consciousness. And I looked back at myself from their point of view. First of all, in going into their consciousness, I felt enormously enriched. In other words, they were very different from me. At first I didn't think they were so different, but then I found out how different they really were because by getting into their mindset, it was not like the movies at all, the cowboy movies. And at the same time, in looking back at myself, I felt culturally deprived. I thought my culture didn't give me the values that their culture did—namely, their bondedness to the tribe, their harmony with nature, their lack of any alienation from mythical thinking, and their natural spontaneity in ritual. And, I thought, my modern civilization had wiped almost all of that out, you see. So I did feel that way, and it took me years, in a way, to get over that. I felt this kind of alienation. Ah, what it did was open up a whole new world for me and I thought, now I'll go on a journey and explore the world as I did later with Islam in a similar fashion and then the world of Hinduism, the world of Buddhism, etc. So I think that it's possible for human beings, and I think that this is an era when a lot of people are going through such things. Human beings can have a new mode of relationship to the Other.

KS: The Eastern philosophies, particularly, stress consciousness as the essential actor, and, therefore, the texture of one's inner consciousness is very important. Hence, the importance of getting in touch with your own sense of the light within, whether you do it through yoga or through Zen or through meditation or through prayer or whatever. Now that is one methodology of bridging what you call 'irreconcilable differences.' If each one of us goes within and is able to contact the deepest parts of ourselves, then in some miraculous way, that, perhaps, will help us contact others and build bridges. The second point I'd like to make is that what has happened is that science and technology have transformed the texture of consciousness on this planet. A global society has emerged, whether we realize it or not, with instant communications and satellite technology and everything becoming global. Now, collective consciousness is still stuck in pre-global attitudes. We have a global society, but we don't have a global consciousness. And that can be bridged in two ways. One way is by each individual going within, as Ewert and Robert have just said. The other way is by trying to set up some kind of a structure whereby these bridges can be built. And that, I think, is the basis for the World Commission on Spirituality.

RM: Well, you see, in the United Nations when a new global problem comes to the fore, and we always have to look ahead of time in order to avoid another explosion like the world population explosion or the climate and so on, we convene world conferences. We've already had one on the climate, twenty years ago. The climatologists of the world told us what was going to happen. We had the first world water conference and now water is an important problem. We had the women's conferences, we had the population conferences. When we see that there is another problem that has to be solved, and at the same time the governments are totally closed to it, then we come up with the idea of having an outside person, and it's usually a head of state, and we say, why don't you convene a world commission of eminent personalities on—let us say—the environment and we took Mrs. Brundtland from Norway who did it. And then governments suddenly become accustomed to the notion, yes, there is something that's happening to the environment. And one of the last subjects to which governments are open to in the United Nations is spirituality. I remember Secretary General U Thant, who was a deeply spiritual Buddhist, he always said to me, "Robert, I'm a spiritual person from the moment I wake up in the morning until I go to bed. How can you Catholics limit your spirituality to an hour on Sunday? And I go to all the meetings of the general assembly, I hear politicians, I hear economists, I never hear a spiritual voice." And then I said to him, "We'll have to do something about it." So then we invited the Pope because he's the head of a state, so he came twice. He even gave me this golden cross for having invited him to speak to the world on spirituality. But still, spirituality is not in the Charter, it's not in the discourses of the UN and this is why I felt, with Ewert, and with other friends, that maybe to get governments accustomed to the fact that we must have a global spirituality between all the religions which is common to them, we could create a world commission that opens the door. And I will make a prediction with this world commission which we have inaugurated today, in five to ten years, you will see the door to spirituality wide open in the UN and in the thirty-two specialized agencies within it. The same way as we did with indigenous people.

MM: What's the charter of the commission? Is there an established charter yet, or are you still developing it?

RM: We're articulating that now. I think in terms of the charter, the vision, the key innovation is that we've reached a point in our evolution with different worlds and different worldviews, different cultures and perspectives. So how do you find any common global truth? Is there any global truth? Universal human rights, for example, for, say, the Chinese people as well as for Europeans. That has never been established in history and I think that as the world has become more globalized, the vacuum that's there now in terms of common truths and rights has become an urgent situation. Do we have any global ethics at all? So the idea of the commission, the charter, is to bring eminent, recognized leaders, on the global scale, together in deep dialogue across perspectives to model the possibility of genuine global truth.

MM: How much does technology—for example, the Internet—force this situation? We now have an emerging situation in which one billion people on the Internet will be communicating with one another daily across national boundaries within the next ten years. We have people who feel as much citizens of the world as they do citizens of their own country. How much is this driving, I mean, the necessity of doing this?

KS: I think that's a point I made. That it's technology really that has virtually forced the human race now to come to grips with this problem. Because you can communicate across barriers. You no longer need a passport to communicate with somebody else. So we're being knit into a world community, the old concept of the world as family is becoming a reality through the Internet. And that makes it all the more exciting.

MM: And, ironically, it's happening without any planning whatsoever.

KS: Yes, thank goodness.

MM: We're backing our way into globalism.

KS: In spirituality, also, we want the world to be covered with a lattice of small points of light rather than one strong searchlight. We want a billion points of light so that ultimately this whole planet is covered by a lattice of understanding.

AG: I'd like to develop that because one of the fears that people have when they hear the word global dialogue is that there's one monolithic global unified reality or vision or government. That's a deep misunderstanding because I think what we find in our experience of genuine global dialogue is that different worldviews meet in a genuine way, and I open up to your worldview and experience it the way Ewert expressed a while ago with the Lakota Sioux—profound changes which effect the way you are as a human being. You can't go back to the old boundaries that you had before. You open up. That's the deep transformation possible with global dialogue.

MM: Now what about worldviews that are constructed to defend themselves against other worldviews where you have people whose points of view are so antithetical that they actually construct into a belief that to dialogue with the other side is to commit a sin, is to commit a crime, that the other side is evil? I can see bridging a gap between two different worldviews that sort of complement each other, but what about when they hit dead on like that? Now how do you bridge that one? It seems to me that's where the real violence occurs, during those collisions.

AG: Exactly right, and I think that's where global dialogue goes to work and that's what the commission will be unique in bringing out. I think the key—given a picture of different worlds cut off from each other, that may be their own self-vision—is in fact a deeper groundswell of commonality that pulls different worlds together through dialogue. The parties may not recognize or maybe even defended against it, but we might take for example the pro-choice and the pro-life ideologies. There seems to be no compromise. One side says that abortion is murder—it's wrong, period. The other side says human choice and freedom is an ultimate value. How do you negotiate that? Well, when you get into the question of dialogue, this deep level of global dialogue, you have systematic ways and that's what rationality is about—remember rationality, as in Socrates? There are ways to press the inner logic of one's own position to see how it touches your so-called opponent. Dialogue can be very powerful.

MM: So ultimately the process of dialogue begins with stripping everything away to find what it means to be a human being?

KS: I think there's one other aspect here which we should bring in and that is the interfaith dialogue. There are half a dozen organizations in the world which are specifically designed to encourage dialogue between spiritual leaders. And for the last twenty-five, thirty years, we've all attended some of the meetings. That is an important point. Our global spirituality transcends the religions, but the religions are a very important point. Much of the conflict we see today is based on religious beliefs, too. Therefore, that element has to be addressed. You cannot ignore religion. The idea that religion was something that was a hangover from the feudal era and it would disappear and as people got educated, they'd forget about it has been disproved in our own lifetimes.

MM: So it is one of the things that's fundamental to what we are?

EC: Yes.

MM: And you start the dialogue by saying, as human beings, we are spiritual creatures.

KS: Spiritual creatures.

MM: That's our common ground—that's where we start the dialogue, right there?

KS: Start the dialogue right there and then try and decipher where in the great religious traditions of the world are the meeting points. For example, this question of the inner light. Every religion in the world postulates an inner light.

AG: As a philosopher, I would put it slightly differently. I like the language of reason. Reason, you know, this idea that we are rational beings. When we use the word 'spiritual,' many think of the connotation of religions, right? Automatically, but to me, spiritual has to do with our rational awakening. What I learned from my studies of very different traditions of spirituality and philosophies across the cultures and through the ages is that the great teachers of all times have noticed that when human beings are in an egocentric way of being a human, that leads to disaster. All the great teachers, it seems to me, have been teaching this. Spirituality is a philosophical point of view concerning the rational awakening that enables you to break free of your ego perspective, your closed view, the egocentric point of view, and become, instead, dialogical, open to multiple views. And it helps you to negotiate them. You become a more mature, awakened rational being.

KS: There is a semantic problem here.

EC: Yes, I think so.

KS: This enthronement and worship of reason and of rationality has also brought about havoc because rationality is limited. Human reason is limited. And when you think that you have the monopoly of wisdom because you are so-called rational, what is rational today may appear to be wildly irrational tomorrow. I think that we are dealing here with something even deeper than the mind. The mind is not the highest faculty of the human being. There's something deeper than the mind. That is the spirit. And that transcends rationality, it doesn't negate rationality; but it transcends it.

MM: Well, I'm struck, when we get down to that core query of what it is to be a person, to begin that dialogue, we get to the very basic questions of philosophy, don't we?

EC: Well, yes, but it depends on which philosophy you're using and if it's the enlightenment philosophy as we've known it in the West, then it would be very limited, but if it were the philosophy of the Vedas, the Upanishads, the Vedanta, in India, I think that the West really is privileged to have that great tradition now at its disposal in a new way, not through colonialism, etc. because the wisdom that you represent and that you're drawing from right now I think is dealing with that deeper level. As you said, something deeper than what I would say the West means by reason. And it is deeper. I want to say that it's been my privilege to work not only in interreligious dialogue, but also in the history of spirituality. I've worked on a project called World Spirituality, an encyclopedic history of the religious quest, a twenty-five-volume, multinational—you might say transnational—collaborative endeavor, and it is fascinating to see the history of spirituality. Certainly India has the greatest technology of spirituality, I think, without doubt. But what is interesting to see is that, it's almost as if you enter into new territories and get a whole new view of the human person or the human community because you begin to see that in the spiritual quest there are more similarities between, let's say, my particular path, in the West and another path, I'd say the Bhakti path in India. The real deep, deep strands of unity appear. In fact, it's possible to see the whole configuration of spirituality in the major religions of the world. They all have the spiritual path of knowledge, of love, of action, and then the higher, mystical path.

Ashok Gangadean, Karan Singh, Ewert Cousins, and Robert Muller

MM: So the commonality is structure?

EC: Well, no not structure. It's the levels of the psyche that we already have, these multiple strands, these rivers that flow within us. They actually transcend the belief systems of the religions.

MM: Is that enough to structure a dialogue?

RM: Well, let me just tell you what I observed in the United Nations. The first one is that humans, from a physical point of view, have globalized themselves to an incredible degree. Our eyesight has become television to see from. We have telescopes to look into the universe. We have microscopes to look into the infinitesimally small. We have a global vision which has never existed before. Our ears have been multiplied by radio, by automatic communications. We have a hand, which has become an enormous machine. Our legs have been extended by automobiles and all kinds of means for communications—airplanes and so on. So the physical abilities of the human person have been multiplied in an incredible way and that created a new physical global species. The same has happened in the mental field. We have today a global brain. Through the media, through all the universities, through the United Nations, itself which is the biggest global brain with thirty-two specialized agencies among every subject on earth. Then comes the heart. Now that! We do not have a global heart. In the United Nations, I never hear the word love in a speech. Love is outer, something strange. Why not look into this, although we're beginning to see the birth also of love—for example, the love of nature, the love of peace, you have all this philanthropy which is coming to the fore of rich people wanting to give money. Philanthropy means love for humans. And the love for the planet. This is beginning. And then it comes to the soul, which is the highest love of all. We have a soul where we can each obtain an inner answer by saying, "I'm part of a mysterious universe. I'm very glad to be alive. My life is a miracle and I have to be a good person as a human being." And this, in international affairs, is almost totally absent. So we need a global soul.

MM: Is the soul of this new species that new?

RM: Sure.

MM: Or is it merely an amplified version of the soul we have now?

RM: What will come out of it is that when the religions will sit together, they will see that they have this all in common. You see, Jesus said it, all the great

---

289

leaders said it. Sometimes it is with a god or sometimes without a god. In other words, they were able to say what is good and what is evil in very enormous terms. There's a joke: God said to humans, I give you spirituality as an answer to your queries and the devil came behind and said, okay, now we'll organize the religions. You see, around this commonality, the religions say I am the truth and they are ready to kill each other for the truth which, in the end, is practically the same in all the religions.

MM: Which takes us back to where we began because at a time when fundamentalism is on the rise. By definition, fundamentalists believe they have the truth. They're not interested in dialogue.

AG: That's right, and the question about the reason and rationality . . . I believe we have a real difference of opinion because I spent my whole life as a philosopher, and I think that what I begin to see the great teachers showing us by holding up a mirror to the human being, saying that if you practice being a human being or the egocentric way of thinking, that it's going to lead to all sorts of alienations and divisions and dualisms and splits and fragmentation. And the great teachers have been teaching this for centuries and millennia. There's another way—the paradigm shift is a way of thinking about that. That's the core of this whole conversation, a shift to global consciousness. It's a shift in which the faulty view of thinking ourselves as human beings is to be individual egos, living in isolation. And what's the alternative? It's waking up to the realization that we are global in a profoundly interactive way. We are dialogical beings.

MM: Is this new creature, this new species, created by dialogue?

AG: I wouldn't call it a new species.

MM: It's a manifestation of the dialogue.

AG: I would . . . yes, I would say, two ways. It both produces the dialogue and comes out of the dialogue. The dialogical being is one that's interrelational. Martin Buber said it nicely: between an "I" where something is an object and "thou" where it's an other, and you can't reduce it. That's the key to moving into the dialogical way of thinking. And so it's not that it's a new species; it's a return to our natural, dialogical heritage.

MM: But we live in an era when we have these means of technology to convert living entities into things, into stereotypes; we've mastered propaganda. We're very skillful at stripping the Thou away.

Ashok Gangadean, Karan Singh, Ewert Cousins, and Robert Muller

AG: That's right.

MM: From anybody we don't agree with. Now how do you compete with that?

RM: Let me give you an example from my own life and, as a matter of fact, you're part of this dialogue and this television show is a tremendous way of dialoguing different religions and human beings. I come from Europe. I was educated by the French, and when the Germans invaded, they said everything the French told you were lies. We're going to teach you the right thing. And then Germany was the greatest, the German heroes, the German victories, the German celebrations, etc. And each time they gave you a rifle to shoot on the other side of the border in my hometown. And then the Americans came and said, all this is wrong, you have to do economics. Economics is the big thing of the future. So I have to go to a university, Columbia, to learn economics. And all this now is disappearing because in Europe we had the dialogue between the French and the Germans, we created the parliament, the consultative parliament without any power. But at least the representatives of Germany and of France could sit together and say can't we once and for all finish these wars between France and Germany? My grandparents changed nationalities five times without leaving the village. French, German, French, German, and French. Now what is this? And you kill each other in different directions by getting a rifle. Today it's finished. It took forty years. It took forty years of dialogues in the Council of Europe for the French and the Germans to figure out that they could work together as people in communities, and today we have a united Europe where sixteen countries have abolished their frontiers and my passport now reads European Union and under it France. And I can go to a court of human rights in Europe, if my country, France, violates my rights. It took forty years. Now what has happened between these two countries, which seemed impossible, is also possible for the world.

KS: I think this is a very important point, you know. What has happened in Europe? France and Germany were at each other's throats for five hundred years. The amount of bloodshed, the amount of hatred—it appeared intractable, like you now feel a lot of the differences are intractable. And yet it was overcome by dialogue. I would like to see that happening between India and Pakistan.

MM: Sure.

KS: One day, I have said it in my speeches constantly that if France and Germany can get over five hundred years of animosity, we've only had fifty years of animosity.

MM: Well, you're a member of the Indian parliament. And the subcontinent is one of the great, crazy quilts of different ethnic groups, different religions. How do you practically deal with the dialogue on a day-to-day basis when you're trying to pass laws? Stabilize currency rates and inflation and all that?

KS: In talking about India, what we've tried to do is what you've done in the United States. Our constitution states specifically that every human being will be treated equally regardless of religion or caste or creed or sex. So constitutionally and legally, every Indian citizen is what you call number one. And number two, we have an interfaith movement that is functional there—a Temple of Understanding. Now we get people from different religions in India and we constantly discuss and talk. So India is very aware of its multiple religious heritage. Four of the world's great religions were born in India. Another four have come from afar and are flourishing there. So India is, in some ways, an object lesson of how one can bring about dialogue. With Pakistan we've had this problem for fifty years; I'm not going into the politics of it. But I have always felt that the new commission on global spirituality or the interfaith dialogue could spearhead a creative dialogue between India and Pakistan and maybe it would make a positive contribution toward peace.

MM: Your statement about the constitution—how important is it to establish some sort of law or some sort of statement to use as the ground to build all of this on?

AG: Well, that's one of the problems that we in global dialogue face now. Because of the very powerful forces of different worldviews on the planet, I think the crisis, the cultural crisis, is that there are no clear fundamental laws. It has no foundation. Whose law is it going to be?

MM: So you encounter the element of fear out there which imagines that such laws might well be a setup to strip me of my national identity or to force me into a common religion when I'm happy with my own.

KS: That is the universal statement of human rights.

AG: I really appreciate the question Michael is pressing. He's been referring to the rise of fundamentalism and of intractable barriers, and asking how does dialogue work. Can it work? And we've been saying, it does work. And this is where I tried to re-introduce the word reason, global reason, not ego reason. I think you're right, Karan. Reason has been very dangerous and disastrous. When any culture alleges that we have reason, European reason, for example, by definition, it's now been seen again in a multicultural world that no one culture has the inner track on reason. Reason is deeper than we thought, and I think what I observed is that the exciting changes in our consciousness, in our global consciousness, are that we're realizing that ego-centered reason has imploded—it has not worked. And the reason may be the common ground between our worlds, which is deeper than ego mind. I agree. So what we're calling spirituality, to me, I'd rather call deeper reason, rationality.

MM: Okay.

AG: And so that, to me, is the ground of the law.

MM: So . . . guarantee equal rights. You have a declaration of human rights and in a sense these are protective devices that say you can now act safely knowing that these things are protected. Is there something that says out there, like fundamentalists, we're going to start a common, global dialogue, but we recognize your unique beliefs, your unique spirituality and how it manifests itself. We're going to protect that. You don't have to worry that this is some, you know, giant effort to strip you of your religion, you get to keep that, but we go from there. Is that how you overcome the fear out there?

EC: Let me just mention something. I think it's not so wise to accept fundamentalism as the norm of the time or even to say that fundamentalism itself is the major problem of the time. There's another way of looking at it, at least theoretically, and that is if we really are in a period of global transformation of consciousness as we've been speaking, it's understandable and we have many examples of this in other species as well as humans, that there's a resistance on the part of people to risk the possible—what they seem to see as their own loss of power and life. And there's lot of reasons to think that that's the dominant thing that's happening in the world today; that fundamentalism itself is a manifestation of the emergence of the deeper fear that you speak about. And I think it's very important theoretically to look upon it that way.

MM: That suggests that the tensions will increase.

EC: But . . . but, you see, the whole point behind this, and this is something that I think one can discern in terms of the survival of the human race through millennia up to the present time, is that there is a remarkable ability on the part of the human community as a whole to survive. In face of all kinds of obstacles. We have capacities that have not yet been activated and I think we're just at that cusp right now. We already see the signs. Robert is the greatest discerner of these signs in our time, globally speaking; and Karan has been involved in that in India and in the larger scene, as well. We see them, and they are signs that give

293

us hope, but on the other hand, there's a big backlash. The world has not entirely accepted these values that we're speaking of today. And it may have something to do with problems in the media. Not that I'm accusing you of that (*speaking to the film crew*) but the fact is that the media has the ability to bring us in touch with destruction and devastation and so forth, and that has an enormous psychological impact on the individual and collective psyche.

MM: But the backlash is not a theoretical thing. It means millions of people in conflict. And Karan is sitting in the legislature, and Robert's in the middle of an organization whose task is to keep millions of people from killing each other as we go through a period of reflection in human history.

EC: I'm accepting everything that you say, but I'm just adding another dimension. Let's for a moment take as theoretically possible what I just said. I think we'd have a different view toward fundamentalism.

AG: I think that we still have not gotten to the core of your challenge, which is when somebody is into their own way of being and is rejecting dialogue, how can this work?

MM: I'm saying that what is inherently structural to the fundamentalist worldview is the rejection of dialogue.

AG: Exactly right. And I'd like to talk about that now; that's what I've been leading up to because for years I've studied different worldviews and tried to find a common ground as a philosopher. I use the word *logos*, from the Greek word, meaning the word or the fundamental principle, to show that the greatest philosophies have converged on a deep truth that all worldviews must come out of the fundamental principle. I call that the logos, the Chinese, the Hindus, the Judeo-Christian tradition, the Islamic tradition—they all have different names for it, whether it's dharma, or Allah, or Yahweh, or Christ consciousness, or primal energy. We are all trying to get to the fundamental principle. I think what you were trying to say is if we can shift our way of thinking from egocentric, "my worldview," and just start with that principle as the groundwork out of which many different worldviews would come, you've got a very powerful jumpstart in trying to correct this fundamentalist barrier. Let me give you an example. When I have deep, long, multiyear conversations with fundamentalist friends, one example: Jesus is the only truth. They say, Ashok, I don't want to hear about Buddha, I don't want to hear about Zen, or any of them; Jesus is the only way. I then try to show, get him to accept, that there's a grain of truth in that. There's a grain of truth in the fundamentalist position—they say my truth is a universal truth, a global truth. Well, if you were to answer that and say, oh, let's play that out and see in dialogue how that goes. What would it take to realize from all these different worldviews that Jesus is the universal global truth? I think you can get them to move that way and tap their fundamentalism. You've got to break through their ego way of understanding.

KS: I must say one point here. What about the Nazis? They were the most vicious, the most destructive, the most acerbic force of the century. They did untold havoc. Were they at all open to dialogue? I think that at some point we are trying to gloss over the fact that there are and could be ideologies which are simply not amenable. I don't think the Nazis were amenable and I think you could have talked until the end of time. They would have destroyed the world if they had not been stopped.

AG: That is absolutely right but . . .

KS: Sometimes in history you have to confront such forces.

AG: Absolutely.

KS: These acerbic forces and say, enough is enough.

AG: That's right. And my point is, how—who—what gives you the authority to judge amongst the many different worlds that is an unacceptable view.

KS: If FDR had not jumped into the war against the Nazis, we wouldn't be sitting here today. We would have been under a swastika flag. Do you realize that?

MM: That is true. There's the pragmatic answer. At some point, there are moments when dialogue ends and action has to begin. But when do you know that? I mean, that seems to work against the whole idea of having a dialogue.

KS: That's what I'm trying to say—that, you know, we may be giving an impression that every fundamentalism is ultimately susceptible to a dialogue. We hope so; we will try that, but it is possible and that's what you kept asking us all the time? What are you going to do with the ultimate fundamentalisms? Because such fundamentalism is so strong that they are destructive and they're not prepared to talk with anybody. Then, ultimately, perhaps a stage may have to come when they may have to be confronted, like the Nazis. I think this Nazi experience in this century has been one of the most soul-searching experiences in human history. How is it that a great nation like the Germans with the greatest music and literature suddenly produced these horrendous creatures who were . . . who reduced mass murder to a so-called fine art? Women and children into gas chambers? Where did they come from? Is there a streak somewhere in the human psyche, is there something built, is the human brain a machine, pre-programmed for destruction as Arthur Koestler would say?

EC: Yes, oh, yes, and I was not ignoring that when I gave the more positive view. But I want to say that the Nazis are not here now. And that's what I was pointing to before, when I came in from another side. The fact that they did not triumph.

KS: But they did not go through dialogue.

EC: No.

MM: I can agree with the idea that this rebirth is happening and new consciousness is being born, but birth is never an easy process.

EC: No.

MM: And you're in the business of trying to minimize the pain of changes like that. How do you deal with a sudden point of inflection, a global point of inflection and consciousness and all the pain and suffering that's going to have to come with it if you're in the business of conflict resolution?

RM: I once asked the Union of International Associations, of which I'm an advisory member, why don't you establish a list of world problems? Do you know how many world problems there were? Eleven thousand four hundred world problems. And I said to the students, you think there's nothing to do on this planet—go to the encyclopedia and take your pick. Try to solve one of these problems. We are at the moment of evolution on this planet where we are confronted with the most unprecedented, incredible complexity ever. And yet you have to have a basic faith that it can be done. You mentioned a moment ago about all the wars we had during this century. At one point, I was confronted: "Mr. Muller," someone said, "all this doesn't work, look at all this." You know what I did? I went through the statistics of automobile accidents and I discovered there were twice as many people killed in automobile accidents than in the global conflicts that we have today. Nobody worries about that because they're just accidents. But when you have a few people killed between two religions, it's in the front pages of the newspaper. So here we have to have a rational view and we have to have the hope that it can be solved. So that there will remain fundamentalism, of course. And we have to deal with that. We have to sit down with them. I think that we have to dream, we have to use our capacities, our mind, our heart, and our soul and never give up that we will be able to have here a beautiful preserved environment. In the United Nations charter, you don't even have the word *extinction*. It is only since 1972 at the Stockholm world environmental conference that somebody pointed out that we were making a war on the earth. Every five hours a species disappears from this planet when it took millions of years to produce that species and each of these species—when you look in Costa Rica, at one butterfly as an insect—each of them is a miracle. So that's completely new, the destruction of the earth in which we are involved to make money, to produce more, to consume more. Look at the consumers of the United States. It's a disaster. When I go to a shop, each time I ask myself before buying something: Do I really need it? And what did it cost in terms of nature to produce this? That's a concept which is not yet here, but which will have to come up. My wife, today, said, you know, one thing I'm going to propose is that every American household should instead of throwing the cans and the glasses and the packages away, should keep them and look at the end of the month the mountains of packaging and things they have. It would be a revelation to them. So this is a new problem. You have never had to deal with overpackaging and overconsumption of this planet. The human species goes through incredible things, but we are successes. For example, we have prolonged life from fifty to sixty years on the average in the poor countries and from sixty to seventy-two years in the rich countries. We have reduced the deaths of children at birth to one-third of what it was at the time. And when we did this, we went to the developing countries and when we said, you can't let these children die, so President Truman and the World Health Organization went there. The United Nations went there and we said we cannot let these children die almost a soon as they are born. And by not knowing what the world population figure was, and what the fertility of women and all this was, we created a world population explosion. We should have said to these mothers, "you don't need six children in order to have some left at the end of your life for your personal security or to till the lands." And then we discovered in 1952 for the first time that we were two and a half billion people. And since then we have exploded to 5.9 billion people today. So this is what the human species is going through in terms of looking out for the new global problems, like the climate and so on. It is incredible, and the tendency in such conditions is just to give up. They say, look, this is impossible; this planet is in trouble, the human species is half crazy—look at the atomic bombs they have, look at all the nonsense that they are doing. But you can't, I think we have to have faith in the future. And the strange thing is that from a pessimistic young man after the Second World War, all the horrors I saw between the French and the Germans, after fifty years in United Nations, I'm a seventy-five-year-old optimist. I've proposed now 2,000 ideas for the year 2000 where we can work on many, many subjects to get to a better world. And I'm absolutely sure that we can have a beautiful, preserved planet here with a harmonious population, limited with a certain harmony in numbers, in harmony with each other, in harmony with the planet, and in harmony with the past, the future, and the universe. We can do this. We have to dream it.

MM: I want to know if the man in the trenches over here is optimistic. Of all those thousands of problems, a lot of people would say, somewhere in the top ten, is the nuclear . . . the potential for a nuclear conflict.

KS: The population explosion, to my mind, is the biggest single problem we are facing in the developing world. Nuclear conflict—well there have been nuclear powers for the last fifty years and they have huge arsenals. The United States, for example, has more nuclear weapons than all the other countries of the world put together. One can only hope that there will never be a nuclear conflict.

MM: Well, at some point there was a dialogue between the United States and the then Soviet Union, SALT talks. What's the potential for a dialogue between India and Pakistan?

KS: There must be a dialogue between India and Pakistan.

MM: Well, it would seem a very interesting test of this approach to dialogue.

KS: It's a very important point. And I'm sure that the leaders of the two countries realize the horrendous risks that will emerge in any kind of conflict and, therefore, there is already talk of a dialogue. Many of us in India and I think some people in Pakistan also have been urging a dialogue.

MM: I'm curious. In the day-to-day give-and-take of politics, are you as much of an optimist as Robert is?

KS: Well, I'm a few years younger, but perhaps I have not quite as much optimism. But basically, yes. Basically I'm an optimist because I have immense faith in the power of the human spirit. I feel that there is something within the human spirit that will overcome and survive. The question is: How long it will take? And we can't wait indefinitely. There is a certain sense of urgency now which we must inject into the processes of dialogue and into the process of healing and harmony.

MM: And the world is speeding up, or some of it.

KS: And time is accelerating and we cannot carry on in the same old leisurely fashion.

MM: So the deadline isn't even approaching us at a continuous pace; it's actually moving faster toward us.

KS: Without panicking, without working from fear because that is the worst possible place to work from, without working in panic, we should, in a very calm, cool, compassionate and measured fashion, we should confront the problems that we face from the very deep recesses of our being. And if we do that, I am confident that we will ultimately survive.

MM: How about our two philosophers here? Any thoughts, are you optimistic?

AG: I'm deeply optimistic, and I don't think I'm a naive optimist. I think that I'm an optimist because the way I use the term is that there's a fundamental reality at the heart of all our worlds. That force—which a physicist might call the ultimate energy, the logos, the fundamental principle—is more powerful than anything else and I think that the source of optimism, objectively, for me, is that that force is a force of goodness and that the evils that come out, emerge from our own ignorance, and that that force is going to win. And that's a fundamental law of all the great religions: that truth and justice and goodness will predominate over falsehoods and ignorance.

MM: Ewert?

EC: Well, I agree with that evaluation. And I believe that this is a great adventure that we're privileged to be on and one that calls forth all of the creativity that has been wasted in warfare in the past. I think that, as Robert well knows, that the giving of human energy to collective warfare and destruction is no longer a viable way of life and that's changed only in our century. So with that kind of commitment that used to be given to destruction, if we can give it instead to the to creative transformation, then I think that there's much hope.

RM: Let me give a word of advice to the listener and reader, those who are viewing or reading this. My advice is that each of you try to think of some good you can do. Ask yourself if you have a dream. If you had a dream when you were young and you could never fulfill it and now, perhaps, at a certain age you can fulfill it and what will happen is that if you do good, you will be recompensed by untold happiness. This is the reward which the cosmos of God gives you. I remember once being with an African elder and he said, I cannot give advice for your life, but one advice I can give you: If you are of service, if you do good, you will be surprised at the amount of happiness with which you will be recompensed. So all of you out there, think of doing some good somewhere and you will be absolutely surprised how your life will be improved and how your dreams are likely to come true. It seems that there are invisible forces surrounding you. I always say that there must be many things floating around this planet and they cannot help you because you are not open. So if you open yourself, they help you. They create coincidences—you cannot imagine how many of my dreams have become true. And, as a matter of fact, the creation of this world commission on spirituality is another dream of mine which has finally come true.

MM: Thank you, gentlemen.

About the Editors

Michael Tobias is the author of nearly thirty books, and the writer, director, and producer of more than 100 films. A former professor of environmental affairs and the humanities at Dartmouth College, Tobias holds a Ph.D. in the History of Consciousness from the University of California–Santa Cruz. He is best known for his ten-hour, dramatic miniseries and novel, *Voice of the Planet,* and, among his most recent books, *A Parliament of Souls, World War III—Population and the Biosphere at the End of the Millennium, A Vision of Nature,* and *The Search for Reality—The Art of Documentary Filmmaking.*

J. Patrick Fitzgerald is honors professor of philosophy and television production at Seminole Community College, Sanford, Florida. He holds an M.A. and a Ph.D. in philosophy (aesthetics) from Southern Illinois University–Carbondale. Apart from teaching philosophy for twenty years, he is a co-founder of a television production program. This project represents his continuous effort to merge philosophy and television. He has received national recognition for some of his programs with previous work that has appeared on Time-Warner, MTV, HBO, and PBS.

David Rothenberg is associate professor of philosophy at the New Jersey Institute of Technology, and the editor of the award-winning journal *Terra Nova.* His books include *Hand's End: Technology and the Limits of Nature, Is It Painful to Think? Conversations with Arne Naess,* and several edited collections, the latest being *The New Earth Reader.* Rothenberg is also a composer and jazz clarinetist, and he lectures and performs all over the world, with an environmental concern central to all of his work.

Index

Index

Index

Index

Information, 224
Injustice, 216
Inner Light, 287
Innocent Eye, The, 237
Interactive Intelligence, 223
International Labor Organization, 283
Internet, 9, 172, 184, 199, 285
Iroquois Confederation, 68
Islamic, 5, 8, 91–107
Italian Cinema, 269
Ivory Tower, 221

James, William, 64, 65, 158, 181, 191, 194, 278
Japan, 58, 213–219
Japanese Philosophy, 213
Jargon, 189
Jaspers, Karl, 81, 158, 162
Jazz, 157, 175, 179
Jefferson, Thomas, 181, 208
Jews, 92
Judaism, 264
Judgment, 237
Jung, Carl, 48

Kant, Immanuel, 11, 59, 71, 73, 74, 81, 102, 159, 164, 206, 233, 235, 236, 239, 240, 268
Keats, John, 177
Kierkegaard, Soren, 162, 200
Koestler, Arthur, 296
Koran, 95, 96
Korea, 58
Kosovo, 26, 27

Language, 233, 259
Law, 191, 292
Leaves of Grass, 66
Lehman High School, 159
Leibniz, Gottried Wilhelm, 58
Lewis, George, 179
Liberal Democracy, 270
Liberal Society, 257
Library of Living Philosophers, 275–279
Limbaugh, Rush, 34

Locke, Alain, 160
Locke, John, 72, 77, 265
Logic, 125, 126, 193
Logical Positivists, 277
Logos, 129, 130, 135, 294
Lolitas, 154
Long Day's Journey, 66
Love, 43, 227, 231
Lucretius, 43
Lukacs, Georg, 264

Magic, 167
Magnificent Life, 226, 228
Malevich, 269
Malone, Michael, xi, xii, xiii
Mandela, Nelson, 18
Margolis, Joseph, xviii, 109–123
Marx, Karl, 68, 70, 93, 158, 272
Mathematics, 265
McCullers, Carson, 66
McDermott, John J., xvi, 61–75
Mead, Margaret, 68
Media, 222, 294
Meditation, 127, 176
Meditations, The, 67
Meliorism, 194
Merleau-Ponty, Maurice, 82
Metaphor, 230
Metaphysics, 100
Mills, John Stuart, 42
Modernist Philosophy, 6
Modernity, 266, 272
Money, 202
Montaigne, Michel de, 44
Moore, G.E., 276
Moral Dilemma, 206
Morality, 201
More, Thomas, 51
Motherhood, 85
Muller, Robert, xiii, xiv, 281–300
Multiculturalism, 247
Music, 169–179
Mystery Novels, 252
Mysticism, 288
Myth, 116

Index

Naess, Arne, 171
Nagarjuna, 127
Naivete, 224, 230, 299
Narrative, 252
Nasr, Seyyed Hossein, 91–107, 277
Native American, 161
Nature, 240
Nature, and Music, 175
Nazism, 264, 295
Neville, Robert, xvi, 3–13
Newton, Isaac, 101, 265
Nishida, Kitaro, 215
North Korea, 57
Nous, 98
Nussbaum, Martha, xvi, 31–45

O'Neill, Eugene, 66
Opium War, 58
Oprah, 226
Optimism, 298, 299
Optimistic, 123
Origins of Language, 142
Ottoman Empire, 92
Oxbridge Analysis, 61

Pacific Region, 57
Paideia, 35
Painting, 234
Pascalian Wager, 69
Passion, 43
Patriarchy, 144
Pedagogy, 74
Peirce, Charles, 72, 81, 181, 194, 210
People's Republic of China, 52
Performance, 223
Performance Art, 226
Pericles, 41, 42
Persia, 92
Phenomenology, 7
Philanthropy, 289
Philosophical Testament, A, 86
Philosophy, Applied, 251, 270
Philosophy Curriculum, 33
Philosophy of Language, 167
Philosophy of Science, 6, 200

Philosophy, Task of, 61
Physics, 100, 208
Plato, 8, 34, 39, 73, 81, 87, 95, 98, 128, 137, 148, 159, 165, 177, 186, 191, 211, 278
Plessner, Helmuth, 78
Pluralism, 182, 184, 278
Politics, 51
Popular Culture, 184
Popular Music, 188
Population, 297
Pragmatism, 8, 12, 65, 181–195, 275, 295
Primacy of Perception, The, 82
Primatology, 142
Privatization, 192
Process Philosophy, 6, 8, 11
Propaganda, 290
Protestant Reformation, 94
Proust, 238
Public Philosophy, 260
Puritanism, 194

Quine, Van, 276

Race, 247–261
Racial Solidarity, 257
Racism, 160
Radin, Robert, xiv
Rape, 150, 153
Rationalism, 265
Reality, 109
Reason, 287, 292
Reason, Worship of, 288
Reductionism, 189
Reflection, 265
Relationship, 241
Religion, 13, 93, 99, 201, 282
Religion and the Order of Nature, 104
Renaissance, 94, 104, 105
Republic, The, 200
Responsibility, 170, 244, 267
Revelation, 105
Revolution, 107
Role of Philosophy, 3–13, 87
Roman Catholics, 68
Romans, 41

Index

Index

Tu Wei-ming, xiv, xvii, 12, 47–59
Twentieth World Congress of Philosophy,
  xi, xiii, 3, 35

United Nations, 20, 24, 282, 284, 289
United States, 297
Universal Human Rights, 285
Universals, 214
University of Pittsburgh, 33
Upanishads, 288

Value, 228, 229
Value of Philosophy, xiv-xvii
Vermeer, 238
Vienna Circle, 61, 102
Vietnam War, 44, 57, 191
Violence, 133, 281
Virtue, 35, 256
Voltaire, 58, 77
VonBaader, Eckarthausen, 96

Warhol, Andy, 234
Weber, Max, 264
Whitehead, Alfred North, 6, 10, 12, 77, 209
Whitman, Walt, 66
Whitney, Eli, 187
Wilde, Oscar, 234
Wisdom, 270
Wittgenstein, Ludwig, 77, 125, 277
Women in Japan, 216
Work, 228
World Commission on Spirituality, 284
World Health Organization, 297
Worldview, 281, 286

Young, Neil, 184
Yugoslavia, 17
Yugoslavis, 26

Zen Buddhism, 12, 284, 294